EX LIBRIS

*Books of Merit*

# VICTORY AT VIMY

ALSO BY TED BARRIS

MILITARY HISTORY

*Days of Victory: Canadians Remember, 1939–1945*
   (with Alex Barris, 1st edition, 1995)

*Deadlock in Korea: Canadians at War, 1950–1953*

*Canada and Korea: Perspectives 2000* (contributor)

*Juno: Canadians at D-Day, June 6, 1944*

*Days of Victory: Canadians Remember, 1939–1945*
   (Sixtieth Anniversary edition, 2005)

*Behind the Glory: Canada's Role in the Allied Air War*

OTHER NON-FICTION

*Fire Canoe: Prairie Steamboat Days Revisited*

*Rodeo Cowboys: The Last Heroes*

*Positive Power: The Story of the Edmonton Oilers Hockey Club*

*Spirit of the West: The Beginnings, the Land, the Life*

*Playing Overtime: A Celebration of Oldtimers' Hockey*

*Carved in Granite: 125 Years of Granite Club History*

*Making Music: Profiles from a Century of Canadian Music*
   (with Alex Barris)

# VICTORY AT VIMY

## CANADA COMES OF AGE, APRIL 9-12, 1917

# TED BARRIS

Thomas Allen Publishers
Toronto

**Library and Archives Canada Cataloguing in Publication**

Barris, Ted
    Victory at Vimy : Canada comes of age, April 9-12, 1917 / Ted Barris.

Includes bibliographical references and index.
ISBN-13: 978-0-88762-253-3
ISBN-10: 0-88762-253-4

1. Vimy Ridge, Battle of, France, 1917.
2. Canada. Canadian Army. Canadian Corps—History.
3. World War, 1914-1918—Canada.
I. Title.

D545.V5B37 2007     940.4'31     C2006-906367-2

Editor: Patrick Crean
Cover image: Library and Archives Canada, PA-1267

Published by Thomas Allen Publishers,
a division of Thomas Allen & Son Limited,
145 Front Street East, Suite 209,
Toronto, Ontario M5A 1E3 Canada

www.thomas-allen.com

Canada Council
for the Arts

The publisher gratefully acknowledges the support of
the Ontario Arts Council for its publishing program.

We acknowledge the support of the Canada Council for the Arts, which
last year invested $20.0 million in writing and publishing throughout Canada.

We acknowledge the Government of Ontario through the
Ontario Media Development Corporation's Ontario Book Initiative.

We acknowledge the financial support of the Government of Canada through the Book
Publishing Industry Development Program (BPIDP) for our publishing activities.

11 10 09 08 07    2 3 4 5 6

Printed and bound in Canada

*For Kay Barris. . . Born after the Great War,*
*she has always lived by the peaceful principle*
*that family is everything.*

# CONTENTS

# Acknowledgments

I found Vimy right in my own backyard. On a spring day about twenty years ago, the then president of the regional historical society drove me to the outskirts of the town I had recently adopted as home— Uxbridge, in south-central Ontario. Doris Stewart stopped her van and pointed into a densely wooded area off the Brookdale Road.

"In there," she said. "That's where they trained for war."

We left the van and walked through the roadside bushes into an area reforested with evergreens. Hundreds of Scotch pines, planted two generations ago, stretched east and west and blocked out the sun sixty feet above us. As we stepped through the symmetrically lined trees, Doris explained that this area in 1915 had been open farm fields where the newly recruited members of the 116th Battalion had come for special training. Men from across central Ontario had travelled to Uxbridge to be processed and initiated as the Ontario County Battalion. Lt.-Col. Samuel S. Sharpe, formerly the founder of a legal firm still operating in Uxbridge today, had then led the 1,100 members of the regiment overseas for service in the Canadian Expeditionary Force during the First World War.

When Doris and I reached the centre of the reforested woods, she knelt down. I did the same. She pointed west to a bump in the terrain. A long earthen hump, about a foot high, stretched north and south through the woods. Beyond it—a hundred yards farther west—a second hump stretched out parallel to the first. In the opposite direction—maybe two hundred yards off to the east—I could see the lip of a bunker through the pines. In the bunker, still intact, stood steel frames that had once held cardboard targets. In the fall of 1915, members of Sam Sharpe's Ontario County Battalion had marched to this spot. Carrying their army-issue Ross rifles, the recruits had then flopped down onto those earthen humps, or butts, for target practice. As the wind rose through the pine needles over my head, I could almost hear the training officer barking out commands to "Aim" and "Fire."

From these modest firing ranges had come some of the young Canadians—farmers, lumberjacks, merchants, some university students and others unemployed—all eager to serve in the defence of "Mother England." Within a year and a half, their British commanders would thrust the men of the 116th into the fighting on the Western Front. Their baptism of fire was the Battle of Vimy Ridge, April 9 to 12, 1917. At Vimy their ranks would be blooded for the first time. They would suffer their first casualties, scores of enlisted men and officers. Their commander, Lt.-Col. Sharpe, would write home that "Old Ontario County is paying its toll in the great struggle."

The struggle of the war to end all war would drag on for another eighteen months, and the 116th Battalion would continue to pay its deadly toll. So dearly would it pay that fewer than 200 of its original volunteers would come home. But in that victory at Vimy, the troops of the 116th and thousands of other Canadians at the front would win something perhaps none of them expected. Fighting together for the first time, the four divisions of the Canadian Corps would earn a unique reputation as shock troops. They would gain new respect as a national army. They would enjoy recognition as a body of men and women serving Canada as well as the empire. And this was a story I would pursue partly because of that trek to the firing range in that pine forest in my own backyard.

Also in my literary neighbourhood and very definitely an inspiration for this project was the work of colleague and mentor Pierre Berton. Through many years' association—beginning when he recommended the publication of my first non-fiction manuscript, through our relationship as fellow broadcasters and certainly as friend and brother in the Writers' Union of Canada—Pierre and I have travelled many of the same paths in literary non-fiction as kindred spirits. It was in 2006—two years after he died and left unrestricted access to his literary papers—that Pierre and I met again figuratively. During visits to the William Ready Division of Archives and Research Collections at McMaster University, I discovered Pierre's original research and interview transcripts. As I pored over documents he had compiled for his 1986 book *Vimy*, I realized how much more could and should be written about those extraordinary days in April 1917. I owe a great debt to Pierre, who assembled much more of the human history of Vimy than one book could possibly portray, and to McMaster archivist Carl Spadoni and his colleagues, who helped direct me to the unpublished resources that Pierre's papers contained.

To my equal surprise, I unearthed an additional bonanza of first-hand Vimy material within the reach of my extended family. Some years ago, by way of my late mother-in-law, Sannie MacAulay, I met Ardith and Reginald Roy, the latter a long-time professor of history at the University of Victoria and military historian in his own right. Sensing the urgency to record the reminiscences of First World War veterans before they passed, in the 1970s and 80s, Prof. Roy encouraged some of his history undergraduates to tape-record conversations with the veterans. There in the care of the UVic archives, those tapes were catalogued for those such as I to discover a quarter-century later. I am also indebted to now retired Prof. Roy and the cooperative University of Victoria McPherson Library staff, in particular special collections assistant Terrence Tuey for preserving those wartime accounts, some of which have yielded first-hand accounts at Vimy.

Another unexpected source, extremely close and familiar to me, was the CBC. As a regular contributor to the Canadian Broadcasting Corporation's radio and television programming, I have long enjoyed access to the corporation's enormous archive of landmark programs and first-hand accounts. In the 1960s, producer J. Frank

Willis, originator A.E. Powley, and researcher Frank Lalor recorded interviews with some 600 veterans of the First World War. Ultimately, they produced seventeen episodes of the series "In Flanders Fields," broadcast between November 1964 and March 1965. Having prepared similar broadcasts on the Second World War and the Korean War for CBC Radio, I sensed there might be more to the raw tape than was heard in the seventeen episodes on air, including in the ninth episode on Vimy Ridge. The transcripts of the original interviews fill twenty-two boxes at Library and Archives Canada. Their contents revealed some extraordinary new material for this manuscript. I am therefore grateful to my CBC predecessors—Messieurs Willis, Powley, and Lalor—for their thoroughness, to LAC archivist Dan Somers, and to current CBC archivist Keith Hart for his assistance in tracing the original broadcasts.

In addition to my contacts at McMaster, UVic, and CBC Radio, others I wish to thank at military museums, universities, libraries, and other historical organizations include Fred Addis at the Stephen Leacock Museum at Orillia, Ontario; Barry Agnew at the Museum of the Regiments in Calgary, Alberta; Bruce Beveridge with the Masonic Order in Uxbridge, Ontario; Dan Black at the Royal Canadian Legion in Ottawa; Piet Chielens at the In Flanders Fields Museum, Ieper, Belgium; Tim Cook (historian), Carol Reid and Maggie Arbour-Doucette (collections managers), and Dennis Fletcher (image archivist) at the Canadian War Museum in Ottawa; Jeremy Diamond with the Memory Project at The Dominion Institute; Marnee Gamble and Barbara Edwards at the University of Toronto Archives; Stephen Harris at the Directorate of History, Department of National Defence in Ottawa; the Lucy Maud Montgomery Society of Ontario; Penny Lipman and Arthur Manville (librarians) and Gregory Loughton (curator) at the Royal Canadian Military Institute in Toronto; Margaret McBurney and archivist Scott James at the Arts and Letters Club in Toronto; Jill McFadden-Bartley (educational coordinator) and A.J. Bauer (veteran) of the Billy Bishop Heritage Museum in Owen Sound, Ontario; Allan McGillivray, curator of the Uxbridge Scott Museum; John O'Leary (president) and James

Morrison (archivist) of Frontier College in Toronto; Mary Olde (director of administration) and Ian Raven (curator) at the Elgin Military Museum in St. Thomas, Ontario; Megan Schlase, archivist at the City of Vancouver Archives; Donald Smith at the University of Calgary; Jill ten Cate, corporate archivist at the CIBC Archives in Toronto; Hélene Vallée and Janice Rosen at the Canadian Jewish Congress National Archives in Montreal and Ellen Scheinberg with the Ontario Jewish Archives.

Thanks to those principal resources, I gained access to first-hand accounts of such Vimy veterans as John Alvis, Will Antliff, F.C. Bagshaw, Royden Barbour, Harold Barker, Gordon Beatty, Billy Bishop, Arthur Bonner, Gerard Bradbrooke, Bill Breckenridge, Raymond Brutinel, Lewis Buck, Eedson Burns, Harold A. Carter, Harold G. Carter, Art Castle, Jim Church, Greg Clark, Fred Claydon, Robert Clements, Harry Clyne, Ray Crowe, Harvey Crowell, M.H. Curll, Wilfred Darknell, G. Dorman, William Douglas, Douglas Emery, Norman Evans, Art Farmer, Rubie Duffus, A. Fortescue Duiguid, L.R. Fennel, Eric Finley, Donald Fraser, Cecil Frost, Leslie Frost, Lester Giffin, L.D. Giffin, F.J. Godfrey, Edgar Goldstein, Clarence Goode, Tom Goodhall, Bill Green, Eric Grisdale, J.N. Gunn, George Hambley, George Hancox, Roy Henley, Fred Hodges, John Holderness, Harold Innis, Alex Jack, Fred James, James Robert Johnston, Cyril Jones, Reuben Jucksch, Charles Keeler, George Kilpatrick, Alvin Kines, Gordon King, Sam Kirk, Joe Labelle, Joe Lafontaine, Bill Laurie, Charles Lindsey, Harry Loosmore, H.W. Lovell, Thain MacDowell, Frank MacGregor, Duncan Macintyre, Grace MacPherson, John Mason, Andrew McCrindle, C.D. McDonald, Gavin McDonald, Jack McLaren, Andrew McNaughton, Gordon Mitchell, David Moir, Ernest Morison, Harold Morison, Byron Morrison, John Mould, Jay Moyer, George Murray, Gad Neal, Lyman Nicholls, Henry Norwest, Frank Ormiston, Arthur Pollard, Howard Pawley, Alfred Pearson, William Pecover, F.R. Phelan, Elmore Philpott, Jack Pinson, Lyle Pugsley, John Quinnell, J.L. Ralston, Dodge Rankine, R.S. Robertson, Wesley Runions, Ed Russenholt, Lewis Robertson, Evan Ryrie, Otto Schroeder,

Stewart Scott, Samuel Sharpe, Gordon Shrum, Ellis Sifton, Gus Sivertz, Sid Smith, William Smith, John Spears, Gordon Thomas, David Thompson, Alfred Thomson, Percy Twidale, J.C. Uhlman, Charlie Venning, Michael Volkheimer, George Walker, Hal Wallis, James Wherrett, Claude Williams, Frank Yates, and Leonard Youell.

From their personal libraries, Mary Lou Fallis loaned a copy of her father George Fallis's published memoirs *Padre's Pilgrimage*; Peter Gilbert supplied a copy of *The Royal Montreal Regiment, CEF, 1914–1925*; John Mullin provided a copy of *The Vimy Pilgrimage, July 1936*; Barbara Nelson offered the loan of *The History of the Fifty-Fifth Battery C.F.A*; Joyce and Howard Walker provided the regimental history of *The 4th Canadian Mounted Rifles 1914–1919*; and Robert Woodland member of the Uxbridge Senior Scribes offered a copy of *Uxbridge 200, Through the Years*. Meanwhile, generous collectors offered access to many books, photographs, and unpublished documents. They included Blair Ferguson in Wallacetown, Ontario, for the letters of Ellis Sifton; Dennis Fisher in Saskatoon for access to his files on native veterans; Fred Tripp (courtesy Linda Crabtree) in St. Catharines, Ontario, for access to the papers of Richard Hocken Joyce. I reserve special thanks to collectors Dave Zink and Gary Roncetti in Port Perry, Ontario, for their generous guidance, generosity, and support throughout.

Personal diaries, journals, photographs, and other unpublished papers came by way of the following individuals: brothers Glen and John Carter, in Ontario, allowed access to pictures of their uncles Harold G. Carter and Ernest Carter; Tom Clark, in Aurora, Ontario, provided photo material of father Joe and uncle Greg Clark; Jean Gordon and Judy Wood, in Saskatoon, provided the unpublished memoirs of their uncle Gavin McDonald; Stan and Steve Harwood offered information about their grandfather George W. Harwood; Dale Henley, in Sidney, B.C., found photo material of his father, Roy Henley; Fred MacKay (and Diana Bishop) in Toronto loaned the letters of airman Billy Bishop; John McLaren, in Toronto, provided letters, drawings, and photos of his father, Jack McLaren; Barry Matteson, in Toronto, offered data about her father, Frederick O. Loft;

Barbara Pratt, in Uxbridge, Ontario, loaned the diary of her father, William Hewlett; Paul Pugsley, in Amherst, N.S., for the photo of his grandfather Lyle Pugsley; Josephine Annett, in Toronto, gave me access to the memoirs of her father, James Wherrett; Scott Ramsay offered the military records of his grandfather Charles Ramsay; Dave Wallace provided pilots logs of his grandfather Malcolm P. MacLeod in the Royal Flying Corps; Wayne and Craig Venning and Linda McMillan offered the papers of Charlie Venning; Don Whitcombe (courtesy of John Beatty) gave me access to his father Harold Whitcombe's private photo collection (with thanks to Alan Pettit for the German-English translation).

Publishers and fellow writers have offered guidance and assistance in procuring first-hand accounts of Vimy veterans. They include author David Pierce Beatty, who provided first-hand research and interview material on Carlyle Pugsley; writers Michele and Ted Boniface; author Dr. R.B. Fleming for access to the wartime letters of Leslie Frost and Cecil Frost; authors Paul and Audrey Grescoe for access to their *The Book of War Letters*; Malcolm Kelly for his expertise on things military; author Bruce Meyer came up with a copy of *We Wasn't Pals: Canadian Poetry and Prose of the First World War*; my colleague at Centennial College, Prof. David McCarthy, who assisted in tracing Vimy sources; Barry Penhale, publisher of Natural Heritage Books; James Reaney, reporter with the *London Free Press*; R.H. Thompson, actor and author of the play *The Lost Boys*; Michael Valpy, for assistance in contacting author Alexander John Watson, author of *Marginal Man*, and consequently access to the papers of Harold Innis.

As usual, I depended on a stable of reliable transcribers—Braunda Bodger, Marlene Lumley, and Caitlin Bagg—to assist me at the research stage of this project.

My association with Thomas Allen Publishers continues to flourish. From the moment I presented this idea, everyone at T A has provided enthusiastic endorsement, including editors Janice Zawerbny and Wendy Thomas, designer Gordon Robertson, image specialist Beth Crane, publicity manager Lisa Zaritzky, marketing team Tom

Andrews and David Glover, editorial assistant Sharon Barclay, and president Jim Allen. Special thanks to publisher Patrick Crean for his guidance on this project; from the moment a family photographer captured his boyhood visit to the Vimy Ridge battleground on film in 1959, he too was smitten by its mythic power.

No work such as this sees completion without the obvious and not so obvious support of friends and family. I thank Rob Lambert in Cambridge; Carolyn and Bruce Waddell in Ottawa; Dave Robinson and Nancy Hamer-Strahl in Port Perry; Howard Welch in Edmonton; Wayne Skene, Sean Rossiter, and Valerie Grusin in Vancouver; my family members and especially my wife, Jayne MacAulay, who allowed me the time and space to write. And from weekends long ago, when boyhood friends and I explored historic battles on huge replica maps on recreation room floors, I thank fellow lifelong history buffs Colin Kaiser, Wesley Begg, Michael Clancy, and Ross Perigoe. They too inspired my quest to tell people stories that matter.

— Ted Barris, 2006

*List of Maps*

# SNIP A FEW EPAULETTES

R OY HENLEY LIED *about his age when he enlisted with a Toronto cavalry regiment in 1915. Born in 1901 at Kent, England, young Roy had travelled to Canada to seek his fortune in the care of relatives in Ontario. He was tall and husky for his age and worked outdoors with grown men and teams of horses. In 1914, when war was declared, he told the recruiting officer he was sixteen. That got him a job as trumpeter in the Royal Canadian Dragoons and then onto an overseas draft because "when they were looking for bodies, they looked in one ear and if they couldn't see right through, you were in." When he went over the top at Vimy Ridge with the 5th Royal Highlanders Battalion on April 9, 1917, he was barely sixteen.*

*Pte. Henley was a member of a Lewis machine-gun crew. In addition to ammunition or parts for the Lewis gun, each man in his platoon was weighed down by a box gas mask, a pick or shovel, four hand grenades, two unfilled sandbags, a mess tin, and a haversack with two days' rations. In spite of taking a bullet through his water bottle, two through his kilt, and another through his sock, bruising his foot, Henley survived the worst of the battle across No Man's Land that day. He shrugged off the danger. A non-mortal wound—a "Blighty"—would get him away from the front and back to England. If it were any worse, he figured he wouldn't be around to have to worry about it. More than being fatalistic about the attack, though, Henley felt a rising pride in what he and his comrades-in-arms accomplished during the four-day battle.*

*"We were good soldiers, very good," he said. "At Vimy, it was the first time that we did what the Brits couldn't do, what the French couldn't do. . . . If the officer was killed, the senior NCO took over. If he was killed, the private carried on. In most armies, if the officer is gone, well, what are we going to do now. We were a proud group. We were Canadians. . . . I think Canada was born at Vimy."*

In December 1916, as Europe approached its third Christmas embroiled in a world war, an Allied army commander, recently promoted to General-in-Chief of the French Armies, tabled a decisive plan to overcome the Germans "without chance of failure" no matter what the enemy might muster. Gen. Robert Nivelle's lightning manoeuvre called for three Allied armies, totalling twenty-seven divisions—more than half a million troops—to completely destroy the enemy's forces across the Western Front in France, between Reims in the south and Lens in the north. Along that one-hundred-mile front, in the British sector of the proposed attack line, lay a prominent geographical feature, nine miles long, known as Vimy Ridge. Because they occupied it, the Germans had held a commanding view of central France for nearly two years. On it, the enemy had established a virtually impregnable Gibraltar-like fortress the length of the ridge. In front of it, the defenders had caused their enemy—first the French Army and then the British Army—to have tens of thousands of casualties in futile attempts to capture it.

Just after the new year—January 1917—the commander of the British First Army informed Lt.-Gen. Julian Byng his Canadian Corps would be responsible for capturing the bulk of Vimy Ridge on or about April 1, 1917.

Byng had just over two months to organize the proposed attack. Neither the strength of the German Army nor the short time span before executing the plan appeared to be his greatest enemy. Losses in the Canadian ranks—the result of defending the Ypres salient in Belgium and the disastrous Somme offensive the previous summer and fall—had to be reinforced. Recruits were arriving from Canada for the French front, but most had little or no battle experience. In a war that had clearly illustrated that defensive action was more powerful than offensive action, a Canadian advance would have to dislodge German defenders who had been entrenched atop the ridge since 1915. A sophisticated counter-battery plan would have to be developed to neutralize the enemy's firepower as the attack began. An entire network of supply lines—trenches, subways, galleys, tramways, water mains, electrical trunks—would have to be constructed all underground and all under the very noses of the enemy. Just as secretly, a system of saps, or horizontal mine shafts, beneath No Man's Land would have to be excavated and then at Zero Hour be blown open to position some of the Canadian attackers on the doorstep of the German front trenches. Finally, an exacting plan to have infantry walk into battle behind advancing friendly fire—a creeping barrage—would have to be rehearsed again and again so that infantry, artillery, and air force worked in perfect synch to achieve the desired objectives. Meanwhile, four Canadian divisions—about 100,000 men—that had never before assembled as a single fighting force would suddenly have to. Almost overnight.

During the time it took to prepare the Canadian Corps for its role in this risk-filled spring offensive, many changes would occur on and off the main stage of the world war. American president Woodrow Wilson, after attempting to broker a "peace without victory," would himself sign a declaration of war against Germany. Czar Nicholas of Russia would abdicate, throwing the entire Eastern Front of the European war in limbo. In the skies above the Western Front, the one Allied advantage—air supremacy of the Royal Flying Corps—dissolved in the face of decisive attacks by German flying ace Manfred von Richtofen and his Flying Circus, and the Allies would suffer their worst air defeats of the war. Yet one of the factors that Byng wondered about in these Canadians—their lack of discipline or at least their suspicion of authority—turned out to be the plan's salvation. Even before the battle was engaged, the newly united four divisions of the Canadian Corps would begin to gel as a national army. The men would start calling themselves the Byng Boys. As one soldier observed, Canada's citizens "are being knit together into a new existence, because when men stand side by side and endure a soldier's life and face together a soldier's death, they are united in bonds almost as strong as the closest of blood ties." In other words, he contended that the Canadian Corps was experiencing not only a sudden esprit de corps in battle, but a greater sense of nationhood, or as he put it "the foundation of a national construction."

The story of the Battle at Vimy Ridge began and ended with politicians and generals. They determined the strategy and gave the orders. They claimed much of the responsibility and credit for the ultimate victory. In truth, as one of the Vimy veterans pointed out, the minute the battle began, at Zero Hour, the politicians and generals could do nothing but wait. In conditions of the First World War, with no radio, limited telephone contact, and vast stretches of No Man's Land lying between headquarters and the sharp end of the battle, the decision-makers were left to be spectators. Victory at Vimy depended on "blood brothers, friends who knew each other as more than brothers and who hardly knew anybody else in the whole bloody British army," the veteran wrote.

That the Battle at Vimy Ridge was won by Canadians is history. That Lt.-Gen. Julian Byng sensed it could be a victory on paper is also history. Byng's inner circle of officers recognized potential success in the strategy. Vimy would not become another example of "lions led by donkeys," brave soldiers sent to their deaths by incompetent and indifferent leaders. On the contrary, since Byng was determined that all members of his corps—officers and enlisted men—would have access to the plan, many of the rank and file Canadian troops sensed the unique opportunity too. What is lesser known through the ninety years since the Canadian Corps took its place in the history of the First World War and the mythology of Canada's coming of age as a nation are the moment-by-moment trials faced by those blood brothers in the trenches and in No Man's Land. Not so often told is what the riflemen, battery and machine gunners, tunnellers, engineers, airmen, padres, scouts, signallers, stretcher bearers, ambulance drivers, horse handlers, and quartermasters experienced up and down the front line as the Battle at Vimy Ridge progressed. Their individual hopes, fears, successes, and setbacks are the largely untold stories of the victory at Vimy.

As is the unexpected event, in the countdown to Easter Monday 1917, that suddenly jeopardized the entire operation.

Anybody with any front-line experience in France knew about trench rats.

They ate through canvas, burlap, and even wooden boxes, burrowed into food supplies, and some were daring enough to venture into the very bedrolls of soldiers who often woke at night to find themselves nose to nose with the vermin. Some troops tried to control the rats by shooting them; that stopped when men were told any rats they shot had to be buried.

Deadlier than the rodent menace, however, were the man-made "rats," canisters of poisonous gas used against the enemy. Since taking over front-line positions on the western edge of Vimy Ridge, in northern France, just before Christmas 1916, men of the Canadian Corps had faced repeated gas attacks launched by the Germans from the heights to the east. Not to be outdone, in mid-January 1917, the Canadians prepared to retaliate by transporting scores of gas canisters forward for use in support of a series of raids against German positions when conditions were right. To help keep the preparations secret and to enhance the element of surprise, British and Canadian gas specialists worked mostly at night.

Carrying parties, known as "the frightfulness squad," loaded the gas cylinders—the rats—containing poisonous chlorine and phosgene gas onto sleds (each holding three canisters) and hauled them from behind the front lines to the Canadian trenches closest to No Man's Land. Some of the sappers carried the heavy gas canisters one by one, each tank hanging from a steel bar that clanged noisily against the tank at every step. Each night, all night, carrying parties lugged the canisters the four miles from ammunition dump to front line. There, British engineers dug holes—rat traps—in the trench floors and parapets where the canisters were partially covered with earth and secured with earth-filled sandbags. As part of the excavation, the engineers finally connected rubber hoses to the canisters and trenched the hoses out into No Man's Land in the direction of the German lines.*

Few soldiers felt comfortable with live gas canisters buried in their midst, but at least Eric Grisdale could relate to the hauling, digging, and construction going on around him that winter in France. Born in Britain but raised near Kamloops, British Columbia, the teenaged carpenter had worked alongside fellow English and Scottish immigrants who'd become loggers and miners working for $1 a week in the B.C. interior region of western Canada. At the outbreak of the First World War, he and his friends had all rushed to join the Rocky Mountain Rangers. Initially, an army doctor refused Grisdale entry because at seventeen he was underage, but by the following August of 1915 he had turned eighteen and was allowed to enlist. He caught up with the 54th (Kootenay) Battalion in France in time for the Battle of the Somme in 1916. There, Private Grisdale received a head wound, but within six weeks was discharged from hospital and going back to the front lines.

En route to the Vimy Ridge sector, where the 54th Battalion and the rest of the 20,000-man 4th Canadian Infantry Division had recently been posted, Grisdale picked up something he thought he'd share with his deprived buddies at the front. Wine was cheap, so he purchased a bottle, put it in his pack, and carried it all the way to the forward trenches occupied by his Kootenay comrades.

Even to a private in the scout section of the battalion, however, the activity Grisdale witnessed on his way back up to Vimy suggested something big was coming, probably a major offensive. The young private noted movement on every transportation artery. From the

---

*Despite having signed the Hague Convention in 1909 against the use of asphyxiating gases, in late April of 1915, during the Battle of Second Ypres, the Germans fired chlorine-filled gas shells into Allied lines. To defend themselves, Canadian troops covered their faces with cotton bandanas (some soaked in urine). Of the 6,000 Canadian casualties at Second Ypres, a quarter to a third resulted from the gas attack.

roadways and railways through rear echelon depots to the wooden duck boards in trench passageways, everything behind the lines was alive with traffic. Artillery shells, digging equipment, wire, portable cook kitchens, and food stuffs were on the move everywhere. He could even smell the increased activity. Horse and mule trains loaded with ammunition and rations seemed to be everywhere. Supplies were so plentiful, Grisdale discovered, that when he presented his prized bottle of wine to his pals at the front, "they just threw it over the bank. . . . There was lots of rum (in the trenches) and . . . very few men to drink it. They were feeling pretty good, so they didn't want this bottle of white wine. It wasn't good enough.

"The friends you made, they lasted forever," Grisdale said. "We were one company from Nelson, one from Cranbrook and one from Kamloops. . . . They were a good bunch of guys. They got the job done. . . . [Arriving] at Vimy we still didn't need reinforcements. . . ."

Eric Grisdale's sense of confidence and invincibility changed suddenly in late February of 1917. Canadian Corps commanders scheduled a hit-and-run raid against a 2,000-yard-long stretch of German trenches atop Hill 145, one of Vimy Ridge's most prominent vantage points. The "reconnaissance in force" raid called for 1,700 men of the 4th Division—the 54th (Kootenay) and the 75th (Mississauga Horse) battalions from the 11th Brigade on the right and two battalions from 12th Brigade on the left—to surprise the Germans during a pre-dawn assault. The Canadian raiders would inflict some damage on the Germans' commanding positions on the ridge and perhaps capture prisoners with valuable information. Similar smaller raids by the 4th Brigade on January 17 and the 10th Brigade on February 13 had succeeded, why shouldn't a larger operation? The combined 11th and 12th Brigade raid would take place the night of February 25/26. Since an artillery barrage or a wire-cutting patrol across No Man's Land might alert the German defenders of an imminent attack, Canadian planners decided instead to use poison gas as a disabling weapon to assist the hit-and-run.

The *bête noire* of any combined infantry and gas attack was the wind. Success depended entirely on prevailing breezes carrying the colourless, noiseless, and heavier-than-air weapon in unbroken clouds from the western Canadian side of No Man's Land to the eastern German side. A few days before the planned assault, Canadian officers and platoon commanders received photographs and maps to study the terrain the troops would traverse to enemy lines. In theory, the Kootenays and Mississaugas were told, the wind-borne gas would roll silently into German trenches. It would instantly corrode every piece of artillery, machine gun, and rifle it touched and simultaneously incapacitate or kill most of the enemy troops. All the Canadians would have to do was leisurely walk across No Man's Land, leap into enemy trenches, "snip a few epaulettes off uniforms for identification," and return unscathed to the Canadian lines. That was the theory anyway.

At least one member of the 75th Battalion thought commanding officers were selling the men a bill of goods. As a scout, a sniper, and a runner with the battalion, John Quinnell had spent several nights prior to the planned February raid as a sapper hauling the 160-pound gas-filled cylinders from the rear to the battalion's forward positions. The eighteen-year-old from Toronto had watched the engineers bury the canisters there. He wasn't impressed. Quinnell knew the Canadian trenches lay at the western base of a gentle slope that rose continuously eastward through No Man's Land to the German positions located at the highest point of the ridge with a steep reverse slope situated behind enemy lines. Even rank and file men, inexperienced in the mechanics of poisoned gas attacks, recognized it would be difficult, if not impossible, for any heavier-than-air gas to roll uphill. Worse still, the gas would tend to settle into depressions—shell holes and bomb craters—in which advancing Canadian troops might well seek cover during the assault. A few nights prior to the hit-and-run, Quinnell said that a German shell struck one of the rat traps, releasing phosgene gas in a forward Canadian trench. Nobody was killed or injured, but the whole mishap was hushed up so as not to demoralize the men.

Nor was Pte. Quinnell impressed with brigade secrecy around the approaching operation. The code words for the mission—"game" and the attack was on, "fish" and it was off—seemed to be flying around the forward trenches far too liberally. And more than once behind the lines, Pte. Quinnell encountered total strangers with a curious question on their minds.

"When's the gas attack?" they would ask.

So, Quinnell deduced, if troops outside his battalion and unknown villagers all knew a gas attack was in the wind, "then the Germans knew all about it too."

Even those at brigade headquarters had misgivings about the planned February 25 operation. Eedson Burns, a young staff officer from Montreal, had packed a lot of military experience into his nineteen years. Initially indoctrinated by his militia-serving father, Burns rose through the ranks of the 17th Duke of York's Royal Canadian Hussars to become a signals sergeant in 1913. Because his acceptance at Royal Military College in Kingston, Ontario, coincided with the outbreak of war, his courses were shortened; he was commissioned and immediately posted to France to join the signal section of the 4th Division in March of 1916. That autumn, during the Allied operations to capture the Regina Trench and Desire Trench at the Somme, Burns was awarded the Military Cross.

"It was our job to mend the wires when enemy shelling broke them," Burns said. "Linesmen went out in pairs to find breaks and repair them. We had advanced six or seven miles, fighting through trenches and over shell holes and . . . we were fortunate enough to maintain communication [lines] during both operations and Brig. Gen. [Victor] Odlum apparently thought that this was something worthy of recognition."

With the trust earned at the Somme, Burns remained in close contact with the brigadier during the days before the planned hit-and-run at Vimy in February 1917. Burns recalled that while Gen. Odlum strongly supported the tactic of trench raiding, he apparently opposed the planned use of gas and "tried to get the operation cancelled, but Division [commanders] insisted on its going ahead. He thought it was bound to be a failure. Preparations had been going on for so long, that the Germans would be well aware of it."

In notes written during training, Alvin Kines, with the 72nd (Seaforth Highlanders) Battalion from Vancouver, took great pains to know the history, tactics, weaponry, and protocol of the battlefield. Each wartime subject occupied a neatly organized section of his study notebook. Included were copious notes on gas warfare that Kines sensed he would need in the classroom or at the front. He had organized his gas notes, charts, and diagrams into sections covering the history of gas usage, methods of attack, guns used to fire gas shells, how to clear gas from trenches and dugouts, how wind affects gas distribution, the care and construction of protective dugouts, gas alarms, and, finally, anti-gas procedures, including the proper use of the small box respirator (SBR).

"On the command 'Gas' or on the alarm sounding, the breath is to be held as soon as warning is given," Kines wrote in his training notebook. "On word 'One' if rifle is not slung, place it between knees. Place closed fist of left hand on nose and knock steel helmet off from behind, so that it falls and is caught on left arm by chin straps. . . .

"On word 'Two' bring mask smartly out of the H[aver]sack, hold it in both hands with the fingers 'round the binding of mask, thumbs inside and pointing upwards under the elastic bands. Throw chin well forward, ready to enter mask. . . .

"On word 'Three' bring mask toward the face, dig chin well into it and bring elastics back with thumbs over the crown of the head to the full extent of the retaining tape.

"On word 'Four' seize metal elbow tube outside the mask. . . . Push rubber mouthpiece well into the mouth and pull it forward until the rim of the mouthpiece is between the teeth and lips. . . .

"On word 'Five' adjust nose clip. . . . Place it on soft part of nose.

"On word 'Six' run fingers round mask to make sure edges are not folded. . . . Replace steel helmet. . . . Spring smartly to attention. Pace forward. Inspection, then one pace step back. Stand at ease. Stand easy."

No doubt Alvin Kines passed his gas training course with flying colours. Indeed, following the Canadians' experiences during gas attacks at Ypres and the Somme, men like him were recruited by the

Canadian Gas Service to train others in gas-attack discipline. By late 1916, the service had posted gas officers to every battalion to ensure that under real conditions the respirator did the job intended. If used properly, the SBR was completely effective. Air entering through a valve at the base of a satchel (worn around the soldier's neck) passed through a metal box containing chemical granules that neutralized the poisonous gas. The purified air moved up a rubber tube into a mouthpiece inside the mask (a nose clip kept the nostrils closed) allowing the wearer to breathe safely through his mouth. This technology, together with the procedure Kines so meticulously spelled out, was almost perfectly effective against gas attack—effective under ideal conditions.

Conditions on the night of February 25, however, were not ideal. The British Army gas experts, in charge of releasing the gas in front of the 11th and 12th Canadian Brigade positions, recognized that the wind velocity and direction were not conducive to a successful gas attack up Hill 145. They decided against it that night.

The postponement allowed several of Brig. Gen. Odlum's subordinates to register their concerns. Lt.-Col. Sam Beckett was worried that members of his 75th Battalion had not been adequately trained to fight during a gas release. Meanwhile, Lt.-Col. A.H.G. Kemball complained that lack of substantial artillery support could jeopardize any advance attempted by men of his 54th Battalion. Odlum first communicated his battalion commanders' misgivings on paper up the line, then visited Lt.-Col. Edmund Ironside personally to argue for postponement or cancellation of the raid. Odlum's superiors apparently turned a deaf ear to all their concerns: poor weather conditions, insufficient gas training, inadequate artillery backup, and, perhaps most important of all, if the gas attack failed, how the Kootenays and Mississaugas were expected to advance up Hill 145 against positions the enemy had been fortifying for two years—since 1915. Despite their eyewitness sense of insurmountable battlefield realities, battalion commanders Beckett and Kemball were ignored. The raid would not take place on February 25/26, but it *would* take place.

Three nights later, in the early hours of March 1, the operation got the go-ahead from British gas experts. In their view the wind direction and velocity would deliver the poisonous gas on target to the enemy positions 200 to 300 yards in front of the Canadian lines. Identified by specially coloured armbands, the gas sergeants took their positions in the forward trenches of the 11th and 12th Brigades. At 3 a.m. they began releasing the phosgene gas from hundreds of canisters. A stiff breeze—blowing at about ten miles per hour—appeared to catch the first clouds of phosgene and send them quickly in the intended direction. At 5 a.m. the 1,700 raiding troops were to expect a second gas release, this time chlorine gas, and forty minutes later they were scheduled to go over the top against the enemy.

Some of the raiders never saw 5 a.m.

As soon as the Germans in the forward trenches realized a gas attack had begun, they sounded gas alarms. As a further response, they fired off coloured flares over the ridge; that action triggered German artillery to fire at pre-arranged Canadian targets across No Man's Land. They accompanied the artillery barrage with a steady enfilade of rifle and machine-gun fire until the gas clouds had passed over their trenches. Some of the first German artillery shells fell into the 12th Brigade assault line, where Captain Harvey Crowell, serving with the 85th Battalion, witnessed their impact on the 72nd (Seaforths) Battalion trenches.

"The Germans put on their artillery and lots of it. They had every [Canadian] trench registered," Crowell reported. "It was a terrific bombardment. International Avenue was the best-built communication trench I ever saw. It ran diagonally uphill for 200 yards and in minutes it was levelled."

The shells also landed among rat traps and ruptured the buried gas cylinders amid the Seaforths. There was little time to react in the manner of Alvin Kines's training notes; it was mask up instantly or die. Half of one company was overcome by the gas, while a second backup company was forced to hunker down, unable to assist the forward troops. Tougher still was the German barrage to the right of the 72nd Battalion, in the 11th Brigade's jumping-off trenches where the 75th Battalion troops, including John Quinnell, had gathered in large numbers waiting for the second Canadian gas attack and the signal to advance against the German trenches.

"All of a sudden I heard this tremendous roar," Quinnell said, "and I saw this wave of yellow gas going across," as cylinders strategically buried in the 75th Battalion's trench floors and parapets began erupting and releasing their contents within the Canadian trenches. "I thought: 'Where's all this quiet gas? This is a failure.'"

Making matters worse, the wind had changed direction. The release of the second wave of gas to supposedly finish off the German defenders began blowing back in the faces of the Canadian brigades. It also began to settle into every natural and man-made depression in No Man's Land where unsuspecting Canadian raiders would soon seek shelter from enemy fire.

At the signal to attack, members of the 11th Brigade climbed over the parapets to begin the infantry assault. The war diarist for the 54th (Kootenay) Battalion reported that the commanding officer, Lt.-Col. Kemball, "foreseeing the failure of the gas cloud, personally led the battalion over the top in an endeavour to carry out the orders as laid down," but any gallantry under these conditions was short-lived. The first ones out of the trenches, including Kemball, dashed toward white markers that had been positioned near gaps in the razor wire to show the men the way through to the German front lines. But the markers simply made a bad situation worse. German gunners merely trained their weapons on the very same markers to bring down anyone moving through the gaps. Kootenay scout Eric Grisdale went over the top virtually unarmed. He wore his SBR gas mask and around his neck he'd slung a clipboard that indicated the locations of German trenches ahead. Somehow he survived his first steps up Hill 145.

"We didn't get more than across the street," he said. "They knew we were coming over and they shot us down. . . . The idea was for us to walk over there—the gas of course was supposed to have killed the Germans—and we were supposed to mark down where the machine-gun nests were. But we never got there."

A sergeant major also in the 54th Battalion, Alex Jack, recorded the carnage of the early morning in his sector.

"We were badly smashed up," Jack said. "Col. Kemball was killed in the German wire. We lost two company commanders killed and two badly wounded and about 190 men all in five minutes. It was an absolute nightmare of a raid," since only five men actually reached the German trenches. Three tried to mount the enemy parapet and died in the attempt. The other two retreated by creeping back across No Man's Land from crater to crater through clouds of remnant phosgene and chlorine gas.

Troops in front of the neighbouring 75th Battalion trenches witnessed similar scenes of chaos and death. Pte. Quinnell climbed over the Canadian parapet, he thought, fully prepared for the challenge ahead. Though his box respirator and mouthpiece were correctly in place, his vision was suddenly obscured. He saw men falling around him, but not much else. The mask was fogging up. What training hadn't taught them, but experience soon would, was that smoke and fire could easily fog up the goggles of the gas mask. Further, any heavy breathing, such as the human response to stress or running across a battlefield, pushed the ventilating equipment to the limit; it couldn't deliver enough clean oxygen to keep a man from nearly strangulating. Very quickly that morning, John Quinnell sensed the only way to survive was to see his way to cover, so he pulled off the SBR and dashed to the nearest crater. One of his battalion officers had found the same shell hole, but he didn't stay put long. The man announced he would make a run for it, and as he did, immediately Quinnell saw the man's helmet go flying. He'd been shot.

"Being a scout, my training was always to have a low profile, to go under rather than over," Quinnell said. "So I took my helmet off—it made a very fine silhouette that helmet of ours. I crawled and I kept on crawling. I finally saw the sign [at the gap in the wire] for the 75th Battalion. The closer I got to it, the more bodies I saw. There was one of my good friends, George Meade, and my colonel," Sam Beckett, shot through the heart by a sniper. In the dim light he saw a battalion mate with wire cutters making his way to retrieve Beckett's body. But Quinnell was too weak to help. He was coughing and puking from what gas remained in the depressions through which he crawled. Even the brass on his coat buttons and his regimental badge had turned green from the corrosive gas.

Worse still were the symptoms of those struggling and dying around him. Chlorine and tear gas, such as the Canadians had first endured along the Ypres Salient in April of 1915, had left any survivors vomiting or gasping, their lungs scarred for life. Phosgene proved many times worse. Victims first found it impossible to breathe. Their hearts raced abnormally, but their skin features remained pale, their lips blue. Inside their lungs, the lethal agents of the gas caused a liquid discharge and within a few hours victims either coughed their insides out or asphyxiated from the fluid buildup in their lungs. Quinnell had somehow managed to dodge the worst concentrations of gas, and by daybreak the young private had reached the Tottenham Trench, where the raid had begun, and tumbled into the arms of his comrades. They poured mug after mug of tea into him, but he couldn't keep any of it down.

"I kept vomiting, and that saved my life," Quinnell said.

Out in No Man's Land, the dawn began to reveal the carnage of this "reconnaissance in force" raid. Among the hundreds of dead and wounded Canadian troops in the 75th Battalion sector, a young private from central Ontario, Charlie Venning, struggled to get his section back to the safety of the 4th Division trenches. Not all the men could move, however, including a fellow rifleman in his section. So Pte. Venning, who had also taken a bullet in the right leg, stayed with his wounded comrade. He hoped Canadian stretcher bearers might find them before the enemy did. It wasn't to be. Before long, Venning heard German troops approaching and the two Canadians decided to play dead.

"The Germans poked them and realized they weren't dead," explained Venning's son Wayne. "There was some discussion. Three of the Germans wanted to shoot them on the spot. The fourth argued not to. That's how he was captured."

Pte. Charlie Venning proved to be among the fortunate casualties of this day. He survived the March 1 fiasco, but spent the next twenty-one months in German prison camps.

For two days afterward, the battlefield in front of Hill 145 fell virtually silent. As best they could, the four battalions of the 11th and 12th Brigades that had spearheaded the March 1 raid counted their dead, wounded, and missing. It had been a debacle. Of 1,700 attackers, it appeared that more than one-third had become casualties. Exact counts could not immediately be made since most of the casualties remained on the battlefield in No Man's Land.

Then, on March 3, an odd event took place. Junior communications officer Eedson Burns, still posted behind the lines at 11th Brigade headquarters, got wind of an extraordinary message from the other side.

"The Germans declared an unofficial armistice," Burns said. "A German staff officer wanted a suspension of hostilities so that we could remove the [Canadian] dead and wounded from the battlefield. The Germans, I guess, didn't want dead men in front of their lines."

Shortly thereafter, an unarmed German officer carrying a Red Cross flag walked out into No Man's Land in front of Hill 145. He called for and was met by a Canadian officer to discuss a two-hour truce—from 10 a.m. until noon that day—during which time Canadian stretcher bearers and medical staff could carry back the casualties and remains. What seemed even more remarkable to Alex Jack, with the 54th Battalion, was that the Germans said they would assist by bringing Canadian casualties halfway.

"A party of Germans brought Col. Kemball's body over," Sgt. Maj. Jack said. "They treated it with the very greatest of respect and one of them who spoke English identified Kemball by name. . . . In all our time in France, I never saw anything like it."

Nor had Lt. David Thompson witnessed any such event before. The former Bank of Commerce clerk from Niagara Falls, Ontario, now serving at Vimy with the 26th (New Brunswick) Battalion, couldn't believe what was happening. Out in No Man's Land himself to assist in the casualty clearing operation, Thompson had a chance to speak to the German brigadier. Thompson learned he came from Bavaria, spoke perfect English (having attended St. Paul's School in London), and had great praise for another of the deceased Canadian officers, Maj. Travers Lucas.

"Not a bad sort," Thompson wrote to his family at home. "[The German brigadier] didn't like the war, he said, and hoped it would soon be over, and mentioned how queer it would seem to go back to our different lines after the truce and 'pot at one another again.' Indeed, the whole affair seemed so queer, standing upright out there in broad daylight, without a shot being fired, that it seemed to most of us like a dream."

Consistent with such remarkable midday proceedings, not a shot was fired the rest of the day.

The final Canadian casualty total was 687. In the days before March 1, infantry scout Eric Grisdale had praised, even bragged about, his regiment's fighting fitness. After a year fighting in France, he noted, the 54th Battalion had not once needed reinforcements. The failed hit-and-run raid on Hill 145, however, had reduced the Kootenays to little better than a half-strength unit. Of 420 original fighting members in the battalion, 200 were now casualties. The rest of the 11th and 12th Brigades had suffered similar maulings. Recalled signaller Eedson Burns, "We now desperately needed replacements, but none had experience and morale was at an all-time low."

Poor morale in the trenches was just the beginning of the Canadian Corps commanders' problems. At least four of the forty-nine battalions strung out in the Canadian sector in front of Vimy Ridge were now at less than battle strength. The March 1 operation had left forward trenches, observation posts, communication lines, and defensive barbed wire and ramparts in the 4th Division sector either destroyed or badly damaged. It had also left a black mark on the 4th Division leadership, the ones who had organized and carried out the aborted raid. Battle tactics such as using reduced artillery and very little machine-gun support as an element of surprise had to be reviewed.

Strategists could not expect gas attacks alone to deliver the *coup de grâce* against the enemy; indeed, no further combined infantry-gas attack assaults were attempted during the Great War. And even though trench raids continued through the month of March (resulting in 1,653 casualties, the equivalent of nearly two infantry battalions), the entire notion of small-scale attacks needed reconsideration. What's more, any so-called innovations or exotic strategies needed testing before implementing.

Warfare on the Western Front was nearing thirty months of numbing stalemate. Since the Germans had convincingly pushed the last opposition off Vimy Ridge in the winter of 1916, no Allied troops had successfully mounted that nine-mile stretch of elevated land. No Allied infantrymen had set eyes on the Douai Plain east of the ridge in more than a year. Having been assigned the job of seizing Hill 145 and the rest of the strategic Vimy heights from the Germans, the Canadians appeared to have stumbled in their preliminary attempts. Chuffed with pride at being a united national army for the first time in the war, the Canadian Corps had initially come up short. If they were going to gain victory in the coming spring offensive, the Canadians would have to change tactics on the double.

Perhaps the greatest challenge facing those at 4th Divisional and even Canadian Corps planning tables was the need to develop a more credible and effective way of disseminating battle tactics. Despite claims to the contrary, Canadian leadership had come off looking like donkeys leading lions. If for no other reason than out of respect for the dead at Hill 145, the hierarchy that had ignored the experience of two front-line battalion commanders had to be reviewed. No longer could ward-room strategy always overrule front-line wisdom. No more could those at the front be left in the dark if corps commanders wanted the front line to deliver the victory. If the rank and file were expected to operate in secrecy, they should at least be in on the secret. And the about-face would have to be credible from top to bottom.

The brass would have to convince the likes of Pte. John Quinnell, who had complained following his nightmare on March 1: "All they said in a communiqué . . . after all those men were killed was, 'We released gas south of Lens.' Nothing else. Men lying on their backs gasping from the gas, dying, and all they could say [were] those six words, 'We released gas south of Lens.' We were taken down the garden path with no regrets or excuses offered."

The disastrous late-winter gas raid had revealed vulnerability in the Canadian line. The German defenders of occupied Vimy Ridge had turned back the French and then the British in 1915 and 1916. They had then repulsed the Canadian newcomers' gas attack early in 1917, feeling perhaps emboldened enough by their March 1 victory to offer a truce for the return of Canadian casualties. In part the setback could be blamed on the relative inexperience of 4th Division, the most recent arrival at Vimy Ridge in November 1916. Still, it would be this same late-arriving division—now united with its sister 1st, 2nd, and 3rd Divisions of the Canadian Corps for the first time in the war—that would survive the greater test and savour the greater victory just five weeks later. Their setback on March 1 would make the coming crucible of April 9 to 12 even more profound.

The Canadians were thirty-nine days from the greatest Allied military achievement of the war to date—the taking of Vimy Ridge.

# THE SIX-FOOT BURY

### February 12, 1917 — Haillicourt, France

IT MIGHT HAVE BEEN his lack of attention in high school. Possibly the declaration of war in the summer of 1914. But it was quite likely the words of encouragement from two recruiting sergeants who came to Lyman Nicholls's home in Uxbridge, Ontario, that autumn. They'd heard the fifteen-year-old had served as a bugler with the Boy Scouts and they needed one for their Mississauga Horse regiment in Toronto. However it was that Lyman got the bug to enlist, the spark happened on a June day in 1915.

"We were having a French lesson," Nicholls said. "Our teacher . . . Miss Topin went out of the classroom for a few minutes and I stood up and started for the window. I said, 'This is our chance, fellows,' and climbed out the window. Seven others followed me."

The eight teenagers walked quickly—they actually walked in step as if marching—to the Uxbridge post office, which had been turned into a military recruiting office. All the boys took their medical exams, signed the enlistment papers, and then went to the quartermaster's office to pick up their uniforms. They were told to report back to the recruiter the next morning at six o'clock, when they would officially become members of the Canadian Expeditionary Force en route to fight overseas. By that time, however, most of the boys' parents had intervened since they were all underage. Nevertheless, by his next birthday, his eighteenth, Lyman Nicholls had signed his legitimate attestation papers and joined the brand-new 116th Battalion.

It was difficult to avoid the recruitment euphoria sweeping that southern Ontario township. It had begun in 1915, when Ottawa contacted local professional and high-profile personality Samuel S. Sharpe. Born on a farm north of Uxbridge in 1873, Sam and his family had moved into town a few years later, when his father took a job operating the Joseph Gould Mansion House Hotel. Once the Sharpe son had received his education locally, he attended law school in Toronto and then returned home to establish the Uxbridge law firm of Patterson and Sharpe. He'd then served as town solicitor for ten years, married Gould's granddaughter, Mabel Crosby, and by 1908 had become the elected Conservative Member of Parliament representing the county. In the autumn of 1915, the Canadian Army searched for the right individual to raise a volunteer military unit in south-central Ontario for overseas service. On November 9, Sharpe became the first lieutenant-colonel of the 116th Ontario County Battalion with headquarters in Uxbridge.

Overnight, the recruiting and training of a full battalion, about 1,000 men, transformed the sleepy valley village of Uxbridge, northeast of Toronto, into a thriving military centre. Sharpe's recruiting speeches, posters, and published editorials attracted men from all professions and trades in town and from surrounding communities, including Argyle, Atherley, Beaverton, Cannington, Sebright, Sunderland, and Woodville. Uxbridge town fathers faced a sudden population explosion and responded by providing impromptu sleeping quarters and billeting in private homes. Each day that fall a sandy farm field just south of town became the focal point of the battalion, as recruits sprawled on butts—long lines of mounded earth—and fired round after round from their Ross rifles into steel-framed targets several hundred yards away. Young Gordon King and his chums—en route to poaching trout at the local Fish and Game Club's pond—stopped to take in the art and science of army marksmanship. During the following spring of 1916 the 116th even conducted drill demonstrations at Elgin Park, in downtown Uxbridge.

"Then a company was formed up on a field east of the post office," King wrote. Only five or six at the time, Gordon became swept up in the military fervor too; he wore a khaki uniform, complete with corporal's stripes and unit cap badge that his mother had made for him. "The men fired a salute . . . as they marched to the train en route to war."

As part of their formal send-off, Uxbridge residents erected arches and banners over downtown streets with religious and patriotic slogans, including "God bless our splendid men. Send them safe home again." The Junior Relief Club participated by presenting the battalion's standards to the departing troops. Men of the Ontario counties' battalion then travelled east to Port Perry, south to Whitby, by boat across Lake Ontario to Niagara, and overseas to Britain in July 1916. That fall, at Bramshott Camp in England, the Canadian volunteers further trained for their posting to the front lines. Then, as a final act of allegiance, the battalion ceremoniously deposited its regimental colours at Westminster Abbey and departed for France.

In the time it had taken Lt.-Col. Sam Sharpe to recruit, train, transport, and deliver his 116th Battalion to the front lines in France, much had happened to the Canadian war effort. The 1st Division had joined the British Army and withstood the first gas attack at Ypres in the spring of 1915. The 2nd and 3rd Divisions had been organized, trained, and shipped to England also that year, the 4th Division in the new year. By January 1916, there were 50,000 Canadians in the field. The army's weapon of choice was no longer the Ross rifle, but the Lee Enfield. The Canadian Corps had added Festubert, St. Eloi, Mount Sorrel, the Somme, and Courcelette to its battle honours. And the controversial Col. Sam Hughes, once popular Minister of Militia and therefore strong supporter of citizen soldiers in the Canadian Army, had been fired from his cabinet portfolio, allowing a changing of the guard at the top of the Canadian Expeditionary Force.

On February 12, 1917, Sam Sharpe's Ontario County Battalion, dubbed the "baby" battalion by other members of the Canadian Corps, had arrived at rest billets in the village of Haillicourt, about twelve miles from the fighting. Throughout that first day the battal-ion soldiers could hear the guns exchanging volleys over Vimy Ridge. Each man, wrote the adjutant, had nothing but "an ardent desire to get through the 'baptism of fire' with as much glory and as few casu-alties as possible."

That hope was quickly dashed. No sooner had Lt.-Col. Sharpe begun settling his battalion "billeted in a frame barn" just behind the front lines, when he had to send his first note of condolence home. Pte. George Hudges, a battalion signaller who had earlier been drafted into a sister regiment, lost both his arms during a German shelling and died shortly after. Sharpe reported that Hudges, "a smart and gentlemanly young man," had become the 116th's first casualty of the war. Along with that grim task, like any newly arrived officer at the front, Lt.-Col. Sharpe immediately received a reconnaissance tour of the war zone in general and background notes on the military significance of Vimy Ridge in particular.

By the time Sharpe and the 116th arrived on the scene, the third winter of the Great War had settled very little on the Western Front. Bookended by the North Sea in the northwest and the Swiss Alps in the southeast, more than 300 miles of front-line battleground stretched diagonally across western Europe. Entrenched along its length and on either side of a No Man's Land buffer zone—varying in width from several farm fields to less than a football field—the two adversaries had shelled, gassed, mined, attacked, and counter-attacked each other to a stalemate.

Since the outbreak of war in August 1914, several geographic and topographic sites along the Western Front had emerged as strategic positions. Chief among them on the Douai Plain between the Rivers Souchez and Scarpe in north-central France was Vimy Ridge. A prominent height—nine miles long between the towns of Givenchy-en-Gohelle in the northwest and Bailleul to the southeast—the humpbacked ridge offered a most favourable fortress for any army occupying it. The northern end and the escarpment rose abruptly from the Souchez ravine—about 200 feet in half a mile—and included the summit known as "the Pimple," while to the southeast the main

THE WESTERN FRONT

Front Line November 1914

Front Line December 1917

body of the massif rose another 150 feet in a mile to the main summit known strategically as Hill 145.* The heights here offered a commanding view of French soil as far south as the River Somme and as far northeast as the Belgian border.

Both sides had spilled much blood to own that vantage point. In the first week of October 1914, French forces moving onto the Douai Plain collided with the German Sixth Army. By November the Germans occupied Vimy as well as the valuable coal fields around Lens. The next month, the French Tenth Army, assisted by both artillery and cavalry, attempted to drive the Germans off Vimy. The scheme failed and cost the French 7,771 casualties. The spring of 1915 brought a new Allied offensive along the Western Front, involving eighteen divisions of the French Tenth Army, eight divisions of the British First Army, and the 1st Division of the Canadian Army. An Allied force of more than 250,000 men, supported by 1,160 guns and two million shells, advanced a mile and a half on a front of five miles.

They captured towns to the west of Vimy, 24 guns, 134 machine guns, and 7,500 prisoners, but sustained 100,000 casualties. Nine divisions of the German Army suffered 80,000 casualties, but succeeded in holding Vimy Ridge, the dominant and essential feature of the battlefield. A repeat French offensive, including a division of Moroccan troops, gained the Pimple in the fall of 1915, but cost 40,000 French casualties and left the Germans commanding the remainder of the ridge. They consolidated their position in the winter of 1916, pushing the French off the Pimple and seizing 1,500 yards of the front to the west of Hill 145. Vimy Ridge had been in German hands for almost a year when the four Canadian divisions—amalgamated for the first time as a single unified army of about 100,000 men—arrived to occupy the Allied trenches just before Christmas 1916.

---

* In 1922, around the former military location of Hill 145, the French government bequeathed in perpetuity 250 acres of Vimy Ridge to Canada. Fourteen years later, Canadian sculptor Walter Allward completed construction of the 125-foot-high Vimy Memorial, officially dedicated on July 26, 1936.

The battlefield maps that Lt.-Col. Sam Sharpe and other battalion commanders reviewed upon their arrival at Vimy that winter resembled a pie-shaped wedge. At the northern tip of the wedge—the Pimple—the German and Allied forces occupied trench lines that were barely 700 yards apart. To the south, at the wider east-west base of the wedge, opposing trenches sat 4,000 yards apart. It was the bulk of this wedge of land—a No Man's Land that virtually commanded the Western Front in central France—the Canadians learned would become their military objective as part of a wider Allied spring offensive on or about Easter 1917.

When Sharpe and the 116th arrived at Vimy, the battle plan to attack the ridge was only three weeks old. In mid-January, Gen. Henry Horne, the commander of the British First Army, had told Lt.-Gen. Julian Byng that in the spring offensive he and the Canadian Corps would be responsible for wrenching the four-mile crest of Vimy Ridge from the Germans, while the British I Corps and British Third Army would provide support on the left and right flanks respectively.

Byng's Canadian divisions lined up in order from right to left (southeast to northwest)—1st, 2nd, 3rd, and 4th—facing the German Sixth Army, commanded by Col.-Gen. Ludwig von Falkenhausen. In the new 1917 Allied battle plan, at Zero Hour the 1st Canadian Infantry Division, commanded by Maj.-Gen. Arthur Currie, would depart its front lines to engage the German 1st and 3rd Bavarian Infantry Regiments at Thélus and Farbus wood. The 2nd Canadian Infantry Division, led by Maj.-Gen. Henry Burstall, would move against the village of Les Tilleuls and the wooded areas beyond, occupied by Regiment No. 263 (of the Prussian 79th Reserve Division). The 3rd Canadian Infantry Division, under Maj.-Gen. Louis James Lipsett, would mount its parapet and take on Regiment No. 263 and No. 262 in front of La Folie Farm. Meanwhile, the 4th Canadian Infantry Division, commanded by Maj.-Gen. David Watson, would confront Regiment No. 261 and elements of the 11th and 14th Bavarian Infantry Regiments up Hill 145 and the Pimple. According to the battle plan, in the first wave roughly 15,000 Canadian troops would attack positions held by about 5,000 Germans, followed by

12,000 Canadians in reserve to meet 3,000 German reserves. The Canadians—nearly 100,000 men in total—were to take and hold the ridge.

In the days before the assault, Canadian trench raids had yielded a German prisoner who said his commanders knew about Allied plans to attack the ridge.

"You might get to the top of Vimy Ridge," the German POW said. "But I'll tell you this. You'll be able to take all the Canadians back to Canada in a rowboat who get there."

Though he wasn't privy to the German POW's warning, Sam Sharpe of the Ontario County Battalion was learning quickly just how seriously both sides treated possession of Vimy Ridge. Writing home to his sister Martha, Sharpe referred to "an intensely interesting experience." Sharpe told his sister (after the fact) that the 116th Battalion was to be held in reserve with the 9th Brigade as this Easter offensive against German positions on Vimy Ridge took shape. But he then described being given a tour of an extraordinary labyrinth of communication facilities being assembled underground and for great distances behind the front lines. He wrote about "the most wonderful dugouts and tunnels you ever saw all over here. . . . 'A' and 'D' Coys [companies] are in a narrow tunnel, our headquarters in an adjoining dugout and 'A' Coy has its own headquarters. . . . There is room here for a small tramway and it is entirely electrically lighted. We are certainly having some experience."

## March 3, 1917—Tottenham Subway, 4th Division sector, Vimy

When Gordon Thomas left Victoria, B.C., with the 67th (Western Scots) Battalion for overseas, he fully expected his rifle drill during basic training at Clover Point near the Willows Fairgrounds would be the most handy of his acquired skills. It turned out that his army-issue shovel was more important to army planners than his Ross rifle. Even at the Bramshott Camp in England, though they were trained for hand-grenade and machine-gun attacks, stringing telephone wire, and combat with bayonets, the volunteers of the 67th excelled in the art of digging more than anything else. That sealed their fate in the battlefields of Belgium and France.

"We became the 67th Canadian Pioneer Battalion at Bramshott," Thomas said. "Most of us were miners from the Cariboo and loggers from the north end of Vancouver Island. We knew how to use a pick and shovel. It turned out we had to be the pioneers [excavation experts] for the 4th Division."

At age eighteen, L/Cpl. Thomas got his baptism of fire at Ypres. The first night along the battle salient in Belgium, the battalion immediately began digging trenches in the dark. Unaccustomed to the ways of front-line life, including the need to keep German gunners from homing in on any lights at night, Thomas's platoon commander ordered a rest period and invited his men to smoke. Several men were killed in the resulting enemy artillery barrage. Next, the 67th marched to the Somme, where the battalion survived its first gas attacks and learned to repair fighting trenches as quickly as they were either taken by advancing Canadian infantrymen or destroyed by enemy fire. The dirt they shovelled in dry weather turned to oozing mud in rain or snow. They learned to work in hip waders and gumboots until those got sucked beneath the surface of the unforgiving mud; they worked barefoot until clean dry shoes arrived.

Sometimes, however, even such Herculean efforts went unrecognized. In a letter home to his wife, Duncan Macintyre, then a captain in the 28th (Saskatchewan) Battalion, described an encounter with Lt.-Gen. Julian Byng, the British general who was the Canadians' corps commander. Following an action during the battle of the Somme in 1916, Byng had assessed the trench-digging skills of the Canadians.

"You Canadians are a very brave people," Byng told a group of his officers. "You would, I know, fight and die if necessary in the last ditch."

Then, alluding to an aerial photograph taken of the less-than-orderly trenches Canadian pioneers had dug, he raised his voice.

"But I'm damned if I can get you to dig that ditch."

Whether it was out of defiance or the culmination of a year's front-line experience in France, at Vimy Ridge that winter of 1917, L/Cpl. Thomas's 67th Battalion and several of its sister regiments from western Canada moved the science of ditch-digging to a new level of sophistication.

"Vimy Ridge was a big chalk," Thomas said. "Our first job was building a narrow-gauge railway and disguising it so German observation balloons couldn't see what you were bringing in or taking out."

From as far back as six miles behind the lines, the men of the 67th Pioneers entered a network of sunken roads, rail beds, communication trenches, ditches, and service paths—a spider's web of transportation lines covering the same geographical area as downtown Vancouver. Some of these routes were hundreds of years old. Others had been built by French troops during their first attempts to seize Vimy Ridge in 1915 and had been reinforced with sandbags and pieces of metal and timber; French soldiers had named the original communication line Pont Street. The complex maze of routes—some aboveground and as many under it—was vast enough that a soldier could easily lose his way; most needed guides to navigate to and from the front. Among these roads and trenches were transport arteries seven feet deep and wide enough for a narrow-gauge railway to pass through. Mule and horse teams—walking between the rails and over the ties—hauled the loaded cars up the railway to the next stage of the transportation system; then the transport drivers simply unhitched the animals from the front of the train, hitched them to the opposite end, and the empty cars were hauled back the other direction.

Closer to the front, Thomas's battalion went entirely underground into a rabbit's warren of subways (tunnels) and galleys. Again the subterranean passageways had identifying names—Bentata, Blue Bull, Cavalier, Souchez, Tottenham, Vincent, Zivy, etc. Most of these subways—a dozen of them—were at least eight feet underground. Some were completely serviced with tram tracks, lighting, water pipes, side bunkers, even offices and living quarters, the ones Lt.-Col. Sharpe had seen on his tour. Initially built as a safe means of moving troops from rear echelons to the front lines, early in 1917 these

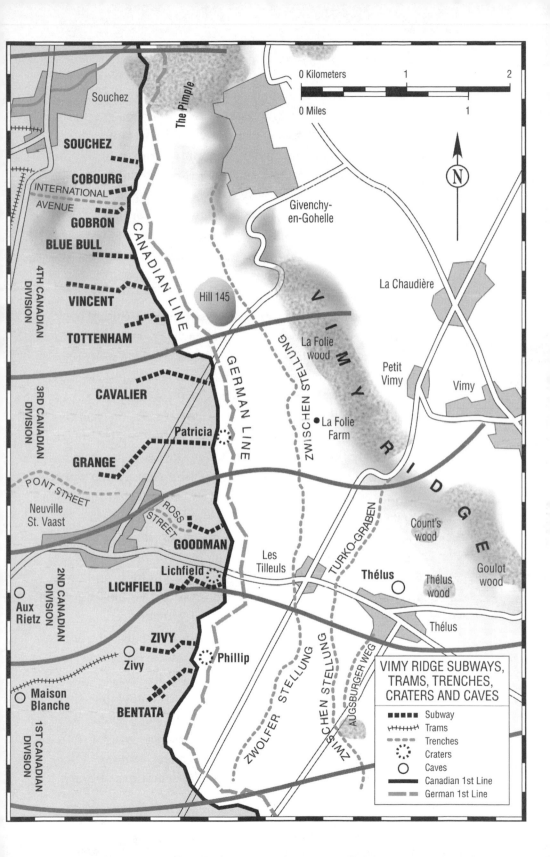

Souchez

The Pimple

SOUCHEZ

COBOURG

INTERNATIONAL
AVENUE

GOBRON

BLUE BULL

4TH CANADIAN DIVISION

VINCENT

TOTTENHAM

CANADIAN LINE

Hill 145

Givenchy-
en-Gohelle

La Chaudière

V I M Y

La Folie
wood

Petit
Vimy

Vimy

R I D G E

3RD CANADIAN DIVISION

CAVALIER

Patricia

GRANGE

GERMAN LINE

ZWISCHEN STELLUNG

La Folie
Farm

PONT STREET

Neuville
St. Vaast

ROSS
STREET

GOODMAN

Les
Tilleuls

TURKO-GRABEN

Count's
wood

Goulot
wood

Lichfield

LICHFIELD

Thélus

Thélus
wood

2ND CANADIAN DIVISION

Aux
Rietz

ZIVY

Zivy

Phillip

Maison
Blanche

BENTATA

ZWOLFER STELLUNG

ZWISCHEN STELLUNG

AUGSBURGER WEG

Thélus

1ST CANADIAN DIVISION

0 Kilometers 1 2

0 Miles 1

N

**VIMY RIDGE SUBWAYS,
TRAMS, TRENCHES,
CRATERS AND CAVES**

▪▪▪▪▪ Subway
⊢⊢⊢⊢⊢ Trams
– – – Trenches
⊙ Craters
○ Caves
▬▬▬ Canadian 1st Line
▬ ▬ ▬ German 1st Line

subways took on tactical importance as Canadian strategists planned the Easter attack. This underground maze of passages and living space would become the holding area for Canadian assault troops. At a given point, when all men and equipment were in position, the faces of some of the subways closest the enemy lines would be blown clear and, it was hoped, the first wave of Canadian attackers would emerge from underground in close proximity to German lines to pounce on the enemy. Behind them, harboured in other parts of the honeycomb of subways, second-wave troops would await their attack signal.

As Zero Hour for the coming operation drew closer, construction and servicing of the twelve subways accelerated. By mid-March 1917, engineers and work crews had assembled nearly 11,000 yards, over six miles of underground subways. In front of the 4th Division, opposite the Pimple, for example, tunnellers had completed the 290-yard-long Gobron Subway. Meanwhile, opposite the German-held La Folie Farm, in the 3rd Division sector, Allied work parties had finished nearly 1,400 yards of passageways known as the Grange Subway. Its facilities were typical: main thoroughfares, cross streets, galleries for holding hundreds of men, mortar emplacements, ammunition dumps, medical aid stations, cooking facilities, and officers' quarters. Each main line contained electrical trunk lines and a four-inch water main because every day those troops working underground consumed 600,000 gallons of water. Farthest south and across from the German positions in front of the town of Thélus, the Zivy Subway and caves would house as many as 500 Canadian troops of the 1st Division; its neighbour, the Goodman Subway, was broad and deep enough that the narrow-gauge railway ran through it. All underground.

Beyond the well-organized subways and their city-like services, there was one more underground world. Past the lighted and populated zones, holes in the chalk disappeared into a distant gloom, waiting for the experienced hands and tools of the newly arrived pioneers to finish them. These last passageways were known as "saps" (meaning "an undermining") or unserviced tunnels deep and far underground; they were close enough to the enemy's positions to listen in, plant explosives, and blow him up. These tunnels were the domain of experienced and hardened Canadian sappers such as Gordon Thomas and the 67th Pioneer Battalion.

"This time we weren't digging trenches, but chalk tunnels, and we lived in caves in the side of the ridge," said L/Cpl. Thomas, whose battalion's job it was to extend and improve the saps beyond the front lines for a coming operation. "The battalion built a latrine, but if you didn't get there, you didn't get there. We were lousy constantly. We were in there for weeks at a time."

## March 15, 1917—Saps, Grange Subway, 3rd Division sector, Vimy

Where the job of digging deeper into the heart of the ridge and closer to the German lines ended, the job of keeping the whole elaborate affair invisible fell to other work parties, including L/Cpl. Gavin McDonald with the Princess Patricia's Canadian Light Infantry (PPCLI).

"Our job was to work at the face of the tunnel," McDonald wrote. "As the miners picked the chalk loose we would put it in sandbags. They started the tunnel about a mile back and dug it underground up to the front line, so men and supplies could be brought in [secretly]. . . . We worked eight hours on and eight off for meals and sleep. Then back for another eight hours."

Like the peacetime miners and loggers of the 67th Pioneers, L/Cpl. McDonald felt pretty much at home with earth and digging tools in his hands. In 1903, his father had staked claim to a 160-acre homestead in Saskatchewan territory (before it was a province) near Craik and moved the family there from Ontario. As a boy of twelve, Gavin helped his father build their first house and barn, ploughed some of the first furrows for planting and raised livestock to help the family survive and keep the homestead. Of necessity, McDonald became a jack of all trades—sodbuster, carpenter, horse wrangler, crop thresher, and even firefighter when prairie wild fires threatened farmers in the district.

"In the fall of 1915, after the work on the farm was finished, I decided to enlist [in the army] as there was a bunch of boys . . . going," McDonald wrote. "About thirteen of us left Craik on the third of December to join the 68th Battalion in Regina."

It seemed wherever L/Cpl. McDonald was posted in France, he found himself assigned to work parties—digging trenches, stringing barbed wire, or building corduroy roads. Still, the pall of war was never far away. At Ypres a shell casing grazed his chin. Outside the city of Albert, France, his company sergeant major had both legs blown off. In the early days at the Somme, his good friend Jim McLean was paralyzed by shrapnel. But indelible memories resulted from the battalion's attempt to hold its Regina Trench position in the face of a German artillery barrage in the fall of 1916.

"A shell came over and landed on a post next to where I was," McDonald said. "I knew a man had been buried by the shell. I grabbed a shovel . . . and started to dig. The first shovel full told me it was no good, as it was all blood, torn flesh, and mud. We uncovered him. His clothes had been blown off to the belt, but above the armpits there was nothing. . . . There was a fresh shell hole nearby, so we turned it into a grave and buried him there . . . a young man from Calgary and his first trip to the line."

A shovel was never far from his hands when McDonald was assigned to lead a seven-man work detail into the tunnels in front of Vimy Ridge in March 1917. Each day his work crew filled sandbags with the chalk subsoil that the miners were digging from the saps. They piled the bags at the mouth of the tunnel and waited for darkness. Then to complete the operation, each night McDonald's crew pulled the sandbags out of the trenches and quickly dumped the contents into nearby shell holes. They made sure to camouflage their work, so that the Germans couldn't see—even from air surveillance—any of the chalk-coloured earth that the tunnellers had excavated from underground that day. Sometimes, to distract German observers, Canadian machine gunners fired over the heads of their own sappers as they unloaded the chalk into the craters. Canadian work parties at a dozen separate sites followed this ritual day and night for weeks, mostly undetected by the Germans.

During those same winter months of underground preparation at Vimy, Calgary machine-gunner Wilfred Darknell, from the 50th (Alberta) Battalion, was also seconded to excavate saps. Pte. Darknell and his platoon would make their way up the six miles of roads and trenches past the villages of Carency and Souchez to the tunnels that led underground toward the German-held heights of the Pimple.

"Our first trip into the line," Darknell remembered, "was as a work party down in the bowels of the ridge. . . . The Royal Engineers were digging out chalk and putting it into sandbags, which we passed up the line to each other. We lay on our sides in this wet, chalky area all night. Silence was vital in this work because the Huns were also digging close by and we could hear them. We were not allowed to talk. It was a gamble—who was going to blow up the ridge first!"

Darknell and his sister-battalion comrades, Thomas and McDonald, had joined the subterranean battle for Vimy Ridge. For months, as the battle for territorial supremacy raged above the ground in No Man's Land, the best mining and engineering brains and brawn—hundreds of miners from England and Nova Scotia—waged a battle of stealth below the surface of the ridge. Here the objectives were not necessarily territorial, but psychological. Allied engineers and miners dug these saps four feet by four feet, with room inside for no more than about twenty men working at a time. Teams used lanterns or candles to light the digging area. No one spoke and the air was so bad, crews positioned at the sap entrance used blacksmith's bellows to pump in fresher air from outside. The object was to finish a sap under the Germans' trenches or locate German saps before being detected and then stem enemy digging before he located Allied mining and tried the same. When British and Canadian crews located a German sap, they would carefully cut holes through the timbers, man these underground listening posts, and finally pack enough explosives into the area to blow the German shafts, their occupants, and the adjoining trenches sky-high.

A fellow private with the PPCLI, Alfred Pearson, recalled those critical final moments as the sapping expedition reached its climax.

"It was a very trying time," he said. "They knew we were tunnelling and we knew they were. It was a question who could advance their tunnels far enough and blow them before the other. . . . So when [our commanders] decided it was time, we blew. The tunnel was loaded with 11 or 12,000 pounds of explosives. Then, they blocked up the tunnel so it didn't backfire and blew it up completely."

Sometimes these mine blasts signalled Zero Hour of an attack* or were coordinated with manned assaults, as Canadian troops charged through the dust and debris of the demolished area to consolidate the resulting crater above in No Man's Land. These tactics became part of the territorial ebb and flow between opposing lines underground, while their explosive results changed the very face of Vimy itself.

"I had the honour, you might say, of blowing one of the saps which we had dug under the German lines," Capt. Pearson recounted. "It was a horrifying thing really, hearing those poor devils on the other side going down shrieking. And the crater itself was a mass of flame."

## March 16, 1917—Communication trenches, 1st and 4th Division sectors, Vimy

Excavating was no picnic at the best of times. Levelling earth for a railway bed, shoring up trench walls to prevent cave-ins, burrowing maiden subways and shafts into chalk, and hauling sandbags while lying on one's side all night, were back-breaking enough. But sometimes the physical exhaustion paled in comparison with the mental stress. Work parties sometimes dug through virgin unbroken earth, but most often picks and shovels and hands clawed through filth— soil that had been a previous army's garbage dump, sewage pit, or unmarked grave. It was not unusual to unearth human body parts

---

*At the battle of the Somme in 1916, the British detonated a number of mines beneath enemy trenches (using from 15 to 50 tons of explosive per mine) at Zero Hour, the exact time at which the infantry went over the top and into battle.

or rats feeding on them. In addition to the squalor, the anxiety of being machine-gunned, shelled, gassed, or blown to pieces by enemy sappers tested every man's mettle in the trenches. British-born Percy Twidale had little problem working outside in the cold and dark. He and his brother had herded cattle on open ranchland south of Calgary before the war. In the 16th (Canadian Scottish) Battalion at Vimy he was assigned to an entrenching unit working under cover of darkness. When he arrived at Vimy, he was posted to Souchez dump. Trucks arriving there with fresh ammunition and trenching supplies on the return trip would carry away the dead to burial grounds. That first moonlit night Twidale stood watch as a sentry "guarding the dead from rats."

So as not to draw attention to their activity, members of the 16th Battalion trenched and graded the new railway bed at night. The narrow-gauge line, which originated in a forested area known as Bois de Bruay, ran about twenty miles and was designed to transport shells forward to gun locations. Once the battle for the ridge began, the rails could then accommodate pushcarts designed to carry the wounded to casualty clearing stations behind the lines. Despite working under cover of darkness, the railway trenching crews frequently drew fire from German artillery. Each time the Germans appeared to bury the rail bed with tons of mud and slush, Twidale and his work parties returned at night to unbury it. It became a nightly amusement shifting the mud on and off the railway line. Until one night the Germans caught the work crew out in the open. When the shells began falling, Twidale was the last man into a nearby sap for cover. He came to, bleeding from his ears, eyes, and nostrils and was rushed away to a dressing station.

The accelerated digging schedule in the spring found Pte. Twidale and his entrenching battalion assigned to communications duty, conducting what had lately been dubbed "the six-foot bury." Again they worked at night, but on this detail 500 men worked in pairs, digging trenches and burying cable deep enough that it would lie below the range of falling German artillery shells. This was the main trunk telephone line along the front, so that when the Easter attack took place, advancing units could tap into the line to report on the progress of the operation. But all the work—digging the trench, laying the cable, and burying everything to look as before—had to happen at night.

"Many times as we dug down the six feet to bury these communication lines," Twidale said, "we had to go through the bodies of French troops that had died there but had never been buried in the previous campaign."

Despite the gruesome nature of Twidale's work, sometimes he and the entrenchment crews had unique company during those nighttime work parties. On occasion, they were joined along the front by groups of British and Canadian engineers and signallers, attached to Allied intelligence. On those early spring nights leading up to the big Vimy attack, they crawled out into No Man's Land and planted insulated copper earth pins or laid out I-TOC lines in circles about a hundred yards in diameter. Introduced at Ypres in 1915, but refined by 1917, these wire devices were the latest listening apparatus. When connected to wireless tube radios (some known as Woolich sets, others called French Pianos) back behind the lines, the pins and loops often picked up and amplified any Morse code signals and German telephone conversations. Signaller Bill Laurie was among the first to hear those interceptions. He worked with fellow interceptor Oscar Davidson and Jack Sturdy, who translated the German and then passed their discoveries along to divisional headquarters.

"The Germans didn't have valves [tubes] then," he recalled. "We were a jump ahead of them. . . . We picked up on any loose conversation in the German trenches."

Born in the Ontario township of Scarborough, Laurie had always known a fascination for communications. A ham radio enthusiast before the war, he had served as a wireless operator on Great Lakes shipping from 1914 to 1915. He even knew a little German since he had intercepted messages from a German wireless station on Long Island, N.Y., before the U.S. government forced the station to close. At age nineteen he had enlisted in Toronto with the Canadian Engineers and arrived in France with the 3rd Division as a signaller in mid-1916. At Vimy, the ear on the ground method of spying worked so well that Allied gunners could time heavy barrages when the Germans were most vulnerable—as they rotated regiments from reserve to front-line positions and vice versa.

Just as during his days aboard Great Lake steamers and intercepting those signals from the Long Island wireless station, at Vimy Bill Laurie was rarely more than a few steps from his radio equipment. He worked, often around the clock, in a wireless dugout in a forward trench with the radio mast just outside the dugout entrance. The wireless gear sat on a bench right next to his bunk bed, and when the gear went silent he would rest in his bed.

"This one night I came to and I couldn't move," L/Cpl. Laurie recalled. "I started hollering, but I had a lot of competition from the shelling going on. Nobody could hear me. I don't know what hit me, a *Minenwerfer* or a shell. In any case it demolished this place I was in. Eventually, somebody heard me and . . . I got hauled out somewhere around daybreak. The only thing wrong was my eye was swollen shut. So they gave me a walking wounded tag and . . . I got reassigned to the 3rd Division in time for big the attack."

## March 23, 1917—Mont St. Eloi, France

At least twice during his service with the Canadian Expeditionary Force in France, Charles Keeler witnessed things he never would have believed possible. To start with, he almost didn't make it into the army at all, because his older brother caught him in the enlistment line in Edmonton and told the recruiter that Charles was only seventeen. Ten weeks later, however, he turned eighteen and got in. By 1915 he was in France with the 49th (Alberta) Battalion and managed to make it through Ypres, the Somme, to Vimy in December 1916.

The first real eye-opener for Keeler, by now a sergeant in "C" Company of the 49th, occurred that Christmas. It so happened his platoon—consisting of about fourteen men—was assigned the job of guarding the front line at the end of Ross Street, a communications trench in the 3rd Division sector. The watch seemed uneventful that December 25, until one of his corporals approached him on the run.

"Come up here, sergeant," the man said as he motioned with his hand.

"What's wrong?" Keeler asked.

But the young corporal just turned and quickly led Keeler to the parapet overlooking a nearby crater in No Man's Land. "You've got to see this," he continued.

Having survived two years in France and Belgium, Keeler wasn't about to leap over the top of the parapet. He cautiously peered over the lip of the communications trench. About 50 yards out, at the bottom of the crater, he saw six soldiers—three Canadian and three German—seated, in some sort of conversation and exchanging German cigars for Canadian cigarettes. Though fraternization was forbidden, it appeared one of the men had carried a white flag of truce out of the trenches, which had undoubtedly precipitated the Yuletide exchange. Keeler quickly ordered the corporal to break up the confab and retrieve the men. He did as ordered and nothing more was said. Although Keeler never reported the incident, it stayed with him.

Equally amazing to the young sergeant, in March of 1917 he and his battalion received orders to pull back from their positions in front of La Folie wood for some special training. When they reached their bivouac in a wooded area near what was left of the town of Mont St. Eloi, they first got their requisite baths and clean set of underwear. While this was rare, that's not what surprised him. Next day, the 49th Battalion received notes, maps, models, and battle plans for the planned Easter assault on Vimy Ridge. Then they were taken to a farm field nearby.

"They had marked with tapes [a replica of] all of the German trenches in front of us and all points of interest," Keeler said. "We were shown all our objectives, [even] the trenches we were to capture. And it was laid out right down to company objectives and platoon objectives. Everything."

For the next six weeks, five days a week, six hours a day, the Albertas repeatedly walked over the replica craters, wire, and trenches they would encounter between the Canadian front line and the German front line in the coming battle. The instructors emphasized that they should "walk" because this would not be a raid. It would be a timed, synchronized, and precision attack protected by artillery and machine guns like never before. But what amazed Keeler most was the openness with which the information of the attack was shared by the officers. All tactics were offered. For the first time he could remember, nothing was hidden from rank and file soldiers.

"You could brief the lowest soldier, any private," Keeler went on, "and from memory he could say just where he was going. He could point to the map and he could tell you where he was going and what he was supposed to do."

As simple and basic as it seemed, this free flow of strategic information turned out to be the turnkey to the coming operation. In the first two years of the Great War, Allied army commanders had staunchly held onto orders like peerage, passing them along on the eve of battle and then only to the next level of the officer hierarchy. During the rehearsals for the Vimy attack, however, Lt.-Gen. Julian Byng invited brigade commanders into the same briefing rooms as platoon sergeants. As much as possible, Byng wanted every member of his fighting team to have access to topographical maps, Plasticine models, and battle plans. What's more, he demanded that every officer and NCO do his homework and know every man in his command—from snipers to Lewis gunners to rifle grenadiers and scouts—so that the same dissemination of information would happen in the dugouts and trenches long before troops marched to the front lines. In effect Byng was undoing generations of British army protocol—sharing the tactical plan. That, the corps commander deduced, would be the difference between defeat and victory.

This new approach to combat preparation had come from the French experience at the battle of Verdun in 1916. Following that campaign, Julian Byng had dispatched Arthur Currie to retrieve positive battle strategies. Currie learned that French Gen. Robert-Georges Nivelle had allowed every French soldier in the campaign to be acquainted with the battlefield he was expected to cross, where there might be resistance, and who would be on either side of him. Currie also deduced that each division, each battalion, each company, but especially each platoon, had to be selected according to the job each was to carry out. To ensure greater success at the grassroots level of the corps, Currie made platoons more self-sufficient—each now consisting of an officer, several sergeants, fifteen riflemen, eleven bombers, an equal number of grenadiers, a Lewis machine-gun crew of six, a couple of scouts, and stretcher bearers. Each member of the new fifty-man platoon knew how to perform his job and the jobs of nearly every other man in the unit. The reorganized platoon not only improved its military efficiency, but by its very structure it engendered a natural esprit de corps.

The 1st Division's C.O. also reintroduced elementary "fire and movement" tactics to the training syllabus during each battalion's run-up to the Vimy attack. The concept seemed incredibly simple— use a portion of a platoon to preoccupy the enemy with intense firepower, while the remaining sections manoeuvred to the flanks of the enemy's position to catch him off guard and overwhelm him from the side or behind. Put aside during the frontal, stationary campaigns at Ypres and the Somme, a resurrected fire and movement technique, to Currie's way of thinking, made practical sense when facing machine-gun nests, isolated dugouts, or elevated gun emplacements such as those across No Man's Land at Vimy. Currie also recognized that to achieve these objectives, the training of each unit should be done on ground laid out to look the way it would on the battlefield.

The rehearsal areas were prepared well behind the lines at Bois de Bruay, Chateau de la Haie, and Mont St. Eloi, among other locations. Each battalion—just the way Sgt. Charles Keeler and the 49th Battalion had—got practice time on the course away from the front lines.

When he got to Mont St. Eloi, Duncan Macintyre, now a major commanding the 4th Brigade, had to contend with incessant rain downpours or snow squalls made worse by constant chilling winds. During their time behind the lines as many as 600 horses and mules died of exposure. Nevertheless, Macintyre's 18th, 19th, 20th, and 21st

(Ontario) Battalions got their replica training too. Day after day, the men walked over tapes on the ground. Each tape line represented a strategic trench, firing position, or line of advance on the Vimy battlefield. First by platoon and then with the entire brigade conducting the exercise together, the men walked the training fields with their rifles at the ready and bayonets fixed, attempting to reach the tapes marking the German objectives at the precise moment prescribed.

Troops in these training sessions learned—many for the first time—that more than just destroy enemy guns' positions, their own guns would protect them during the advance. Allied artillery would fire over the heads of Allied infantry. The tactic, known as a "creeping" or "rolling barrage," would tie the enemy down, inflict heavy casualties, and demoralize him at the same time it prevented him from using his rifles, machine guns, or trench mortars. The barrage would screen the Canadian infantry advance with a wall of exploding shells, dust, and smoke. In the Mont St. Eloi rehearsals, officers on horseback carried flags representing where the Allied shells would be falling at each moment in the attack. Timing was essential.

Periodically, Macintyre needed to reassure himself that any given man at any given time knew exactly where he was and what he was doing vis-à-vis the real Vimy battlefield. During one rehearsal, upon reaching the Red Line, the final objective of his 4th Brigade, Macintyre approached a rifleman in his battalion: "Where are you supposed to be?" he asked the young man.

"On the Red Line, sir," he responded.

"Right," affirmed Macintyre. "And now what are you going to do?"

"Stay right here and hang on like hell."

The rehearsals over the tapes were working. Each participant, through repeated dry runs of the attack, was absorbing not only the scale of the battle immediately around him, but also a sense and spirit of the bigger picture. The practice seemed to signal to everyone that if an officer or platoon commander were lost during the fight, any other NCO could carry on and complete the operation as designed. Macintyre was confident that "all ranks would give the attack all they had . . . even life."

When the battalion's six hours of daily instruction across the training tapes ended, where possible the men received some welcome R and R. After hours at the training sites in Mont St. Eloi, Bois de Bruay, and Chateau de la Haie (the former residence of stage and film star Sarah Bernhardt), some of the troops took part in friendly boxing or soccer matches. Still others attended concert parties presented by Jack McLaren and the Princess Patricia's Comedy Company (PPCC), a group of Canadian Expeditionary Force soldiers who dreamed up comedy sketches, songs, and monologues about sick parade, the *estaminet* (French pubs), the dugout, or the orderly room. Originated behind the lines at Ypres in 1916, the PPCC created and performed the first "girlie beauty chorus" using female impersonation.

"Of course we had to have ladies in the show, which meant we had to have wigs," McLaren wrote, "and all that could be seen for miles . . . were battered houses, cathedrals, and other ruins. But where there's a will there's a wig."

Suddenly, in the back of a forgotten garden, members of the comedy company found a pair of abandoned chairs, both of which contained black hair for stuffing. Next, they discovered a newly hung cow hide and "with the aid of darkness and a jackknife, little pieces of red coat was secured and fashioned into excellent comedy moustaches and beards." One routine, called The High Dive Act, featured PPCC performer T.J. Lilly as Miss Vera Skinny supposedly diving from a platform eighty feet high into a tank of water on stage.

"After much stage business accompanied by circus music, Vera Skinny went up the ladder and disappeared in the flys, allowing enough time for Vera to come down backstage unseen by the audience, and get around into the tank," McLaren wrote. "A dummy girl diver, dressed exactly like Vera, plunged down and splashed into the tank, accompanied by a sustained loud drum roll and crash of cymbal. A can full of rice was thrown into the air . . . to simulate the splash and Vera with her mouth full of water, which she sprayed all over the stage, leapt out of the tank onto the stage bowing profusely, to the accompaniment of loud sustained musical chords and drum rolls."

Eventually, Jack McLaren and some of the six-man Princess Patricia's Comedy Company joined forces with the Dumbells (the name coming from the crossed red dumbells insignia of the 3rd Division). Nearly every night behind the lines, these Canadian army entertainers staged singalongs, female impersonation, and skit humour to the delight of their war-weary comrades. For the troops at Vimy, McLaren and the PPCC were the perfect distraction.

"We held the mirror up to these boys," Jack McLaren said, "and showed them what they were accomplishing."

Members of the 44th (Manitoba) Battalion conducted their Vimy rehearsals over the tapes at Chateau de la Haie. During the daily preparations in March 1917, Jim Wherrett joined fellow infantrymen of the 44th going over the tapes on the rolling ground west of the chateau. The simulated attack zone was so accurate that all the fire trenches, communication lines, and mine craters were reproduced to actual size and gave Pte. Wherrett a true sense of the task ahead. Following each day's exercises, Wherrett and his comrades would march a few miles back to Bouvigny in the 4th Division sector for lectures, time to study trench maps and aerial photographs of German positions. Then, for a few hours in the evenings, the troops and local residents gathered in the *estaminets*, where French families provided an ample supply of French beer and wine for the Canadians. Eventually, the men of the 44th returned to billets—homes, sheds, and other farm buildings—to bed down for the night.

"Our billet was a huge barn," Wherrett said. "Very clean and tidy. The family allowed us to use their precious fodder for beds and they often invited us into their homes. They taught us card games. We laughed and had a lot of fun on those days behind the lines."

Just before the final countdown to the Easter offensive, Pte. Wherrett and his comrades learned from the family whose barn they were using as sleeping quarters that there was a crisis at the house. The woman's five-year-old daughter, Maria, had suddenly fallen deathly ill. The twenty Canadians billeted in the barn began searching for medical help in the community. When they came up empty, the men of the 44th found a medical officer attached to a nearby

Canadian artillery unit and convinced him to come to their billet. They claimed there was a medical emergency, so the medical officer raced to the scene.

"Where's the sick man?" the doctor asked.

"There isn't any," Wherrett and his mates told the officer. "But in that house is a very sick little girl. Will you please see her?"

The doctor obliged. Wherrett said he had never seen an army doctor take such care with a patient. When he completed his examination and diagnosis, the doctor produced the required medication and exact instructions as to how to administer it to the girl. Of course, the 44th Battalion troops quickly returned to the front line, but Wherrett said the men were buoyed by the knowledge that Maria made a complete recovery.

Long after the incident and long after the victory at Vimy, Jim Wherrett remembered the 44th Battalion men and the sick little girl, Maria. He likened their saving a life amid all the killing of the Great War to the experience of a gardener. "If you've ever planted a flower garden and then let it go, it is soon taken over by weeds," he said. "But even in the mass of weeds, you will always find at least one flower that survives.

Such was the contradictory world in which the former Boy Scout bugler Lyman Nicholls and commanding officer Sam Sharpe of the community-raised 116th Battalion found themselves. Subterranean warfare and female impersonation were a long, long way from their bucolic Uxbridge, Ontario, homes. In a few weeks, however—the actual date of the attack was the only detail still secret—they would have their baptism of fire. They would lose their "baby battalion" status. Their 9th Brigade would join eleven other brigades of the Canadian Corps, fighting for the first time as a national army. Together they would rise up before the most daunting land form of the Western Front and engage the most battle-hardened foes firmly entrenched on heights ahead of them. They would join a pivotal operation of the Great War, and for Canada a battle for national identity—the assault on Vimy Ridge.

# WEEK OF SUFFERING

## March 17, 1917—No. 60 Sqn. aerodrome, Royal Flying Corps, Arras, France

A S LONG AS he had served at Vimy, right from the moment the Canadian Corps was transferred there from the Somme, Will Antliff adopted a unique kind of front-line body posture when he moved around. The 9th Canadian Field Ambulance medic from Montreal travelled in a perpetual crouch—knees bent, arms loose at the sides for balance, and head down for protection. Unless something distracted his attention, he nearly always faced the ground. No wonder, given that Pte. Antliff regularly hauled medical supplies and because front-line duty required multi-tasking, he also shovelled mud from caved-in trenches, split wood for tunnel reinforcement, hauled water for cleaning and cooking, and did his share of guard duty. However, Will Antliff's downward perspective was altered temporarily one spring evening when, as he wrote in his diary, "we had a little excitement when we noted a Fritzy [German] aeroplane overhead.

"A favourite method to start a scrap and nail your opponent," Antliff went on, "is to hide behind a cloud and then when an enemy plane comes along, pounce down and give him a [burst] from the machine guns. . . . The first indication that anything was up, was a loud put-put-put way up in a cloud. We all looked up and almost immediately saw a machine come falling down like a bit of paper. It twirled around head over heels all the way down. Some of the boys went over to see the wreck. Hardly anything was left of the machine and the aviator who was only a young fellow was all smashed up. . . .

"Fritzy seems to have a plane which puts it all over our men. It's called the Red Devil and simply plays rings around our best machines."

While the ground war that winter and spring of 1917 had reached a stalemate, the momentum of the air war had shifted to the German Air Force,* in particular, because of its formation flying *Jagdstaffeln* or *Jastas* (pursuit or hunting) squadrons. The previous autumn, German fighter pilots had taken delivery of Albatros biplanes, each equipped with two fixed machine guns that fired synchronized bullet bursts through the propeller. Suddenly, the Royal Flying Corps' BE2 two-seater reconnaissance aircraft, the FB5 Gunbus and DH2 single-seater scouts that had previously given Britain air supremacy in France, were being blown out of the sky. RFC squadrons that had flown almost untouched across enemy lines now faced surprise attacks such as the one Pte. Antliff witnessed.

The Red Devil whom he described was very likely *Jastas* ace Manfred von Richthofen in his Albatros DIII fighter aircraft. In March 1917 alone, von Richthofen and his notorious red-painted "Flying Circus" squadron had shot down 120 Royal Flying Corps machines, the "Red Baron" chalking up ten of those victories himself. Following one of his earlier victories von Richthofen wrote in his war diary that he'd had his enemy's "machine-gun dug out of the ground and it adorns the entrance to my room."

Poor air combat numbers were not Field Marshal Douglas Haig's primary concern. The British army commander-in-chief had endorsed the planned spring Allied ground offensive along the Arras front, including the planned Canadian assault on Vimy Ridge, so he demanded that the Royal Flying Corps deliver and maintain air supremacy over

---

* During the battle of the Somme, from July 1 to November 22, 1916, the Royal Flying Corps had lost 308 pilots, 191 observers, and 782 airplanes. The German Air Force had suffered the loss of only half that number.

the battlefield. He insisted that RFC aircraft and crews treat the support of air surveillance—photography of rail lines, trench configurations, troop movements, and gun emplacements—as their first priority, while keeping the German *Jastas* at bay. In response to Haig's orders, Air Marshal Hugh Trenchard increased the number of active squadrons from 95 to 106 in France; 25 squadrons (or 365 aircraft) in the Arras sector alone, thereby outnumbering the enemy nearly two to one. Even so, during the spring of 1917, Royal Flying Corps fatality statistics rose steadily. In April alone, the British lost 151 aircraft as well as 316 dead or missing airmen, to the Germans' total loss of 119 planes. Life expectancy of RFC two-seater crews was three to four months and of RFC single-seater scout aircraft about two and a half months. The month of crippling losses earned the apt title of "Bloody April."

There were, however, some who defied the statistics.

The first air duty of one particular gunner-observer over northern France was unspectacular. In his view, shooting photographs couldn't be as exhilarating as shooting down German aircraft. Still, the young airman from Owen Sound, Ontario, fulfilled his early RFC service for four months with No. 21 Squadron dropping bombs and compiling reports on artillery reconnaissance. His career as an observer ended when the engine of his two-seater RE7 died on takeoff and his leg was severely injured in the crash. Convalescence fortunately kept him in England during the slaughter at the Somme, but he re-mustered for pilot training and returned to France in March of 1917 as a fighter pilot.

That's how Lt. Billy Bishop found himself in the hottest theatre of war in Europe with the busiest Royal Flying Corps fighter unit, No. 60 Squadron, on the eve of his country's most crucial battle of the Great War so far. His very first combat flight yielded his very first combat victory.

"Today I have had the most exciting adventure of my life," Bishop wrote in a letter to his mother.

Bishop piloted a Nieuport Scout. The French-manufactured single-seat fighter aircraft with a 200 horsepower motor was, in

Bishop's view, "the only real aeroplane for offensive work." While it had a slower air speed than von Richthofen's Albatros,* the Nieuport used a similar synchronized mechanism to fire bullets safely through its propeller. Meanwhile, in the compartment-like cockpit with only his head visible above the freeboard, the pilot sat in hardwood-finished surroundings and faced his polished nickel instruments able to comfortably sight the machine gun through a half-moon-shaped glass windscreen.

During this, his first combat patrol in the skies over Vimy Ridge, Bishop's flight of four Nieuports engaged three German aircraft. As he opened fire on one, another fired at him. When his prey fell apparently out of control, Bishop dived after him, dropping down a thousand feet in seconds and crossing the front lines into enemy skies. He levelled off, watching the enemy aircraft crash, but suddenly realized that during the dive his engine had filled with lubricating oil and stalled. He had no choice but to make a forced landing. The question was: on whose part of No Man's Land? Fortunately, he found himself close enough to British trenches that he and his Nieuport were retrievable.

"When I arrived back [at No. 60 Squadron aerodrome three days later], I found myself a young hero," Bishop wrote in his next letter to his father. "The general in command of the Flying Corps wired congratulations. . . . My own C.O. now calls me 'Bish' so I am getting on. Added to this, I was recommended for a flight command. I slept 16 1/2 hours last night. The great thing is that I have one Hun to my credit."

Now in command of C Flight, Bishop again crossed into "Hunland," as he described it. This time the sortie took its toll. One pilot managed to fly his damaged craft back, but died of bullet wounds to

---

* Bishop and von Richthofen tangled at least once, on April 30, 1917, each scoring hits on the other, but not mortal blows. More telling was the 105 percent casualty rate inflicted by the *Jastas* on the RFC during "Blood April." Bishop went on to win the D.S.O., V.C., *Croix-de-Guerre*, and *Croix-de-Chevalier*. Von Richthofen was shot down and killed by Canadian Capt. Roy Brown on April 21, 1918.

the stomach, while another went down beyond the front and was taken prisoner. Next day, Bishop scored his next victory and he anticipated being "mentioned in dispatches." But as the last days of March moved the Easter offensive closer, Bishop's flight learned its next objective was to "clean the air" of enemy observation balloons. The German lighter-than-air craft looked like elongated gas bags, or "sausages," that were tethered to the ground, but floated up several thousand feet allowing observer crews to spy on the Canadian side of No Man's Land. Most balloon launch sites were protected by anti-aircraft guns and "flaming onions," guns that propelled balls of fire at any planes invading the observer balloons' air space. Chasing sausages and dodging balls of fire seemed to inspire Lt. Bishop to the core.

"Over the lines I went all alone at 8,000 feet," Bishop wrote his mother, "placed my balloon on the map and spotted him below me. Down I dived vertically 2,000 feet. Suddenly, the pop-pop-pop of a [ground] machine gun aroused me. I did the first part of a loop, like lightning swerved and dived again just as the Hun [balloon] passed 15 feet below me. After him I went and shot him dead.... Down he went like a stone.... I turned a sharp circle to upset the aim of the people firing at me, spotted my balloon. I dived again absolutely vertical ... commenced to fire flaming bullets at it. At 200 feet it burst into flames...."

Once again, however, Bishop's engine had conked out. He used whatever altitude and speed he had left to put the ten miles of hostile German territory behind him, meanwhile trying every means he could think of to restart his engine. Miraculously it sprang to life again. But rather than risk climbing into anti-aircraft range, he raced the Nieuport at 130 mph just above the ground and successfully dodged German machine-gun bullets, "Archies" (anti-aircraft shells), and flaming onions all the way home. As he received yet more congratulations and eventually word that he would be awarded the Military Cross, Bishop wrote: "My blood was up.... It was a glorious sight and I came home in jubilant mood. After seeing one's pals in flames, this [victory] was a great satisfaction."

## March 20, 1917—Counter-Battery Office,
## Corps Headquarters, Vimy

In additional to the morale boost that No. 60 Squadron's most successful sausage-hunting pilot provided his Royal Flying Corps chums,
these aggressive attacks gave the eyes of Allied artillery a better focus
on the preparation ahead. On relatively clear and calm (non-windy)
days, British air observers climbed aboard their tethered surveillance
balloons and ascended several thousand feet above the battlefield.
Working in pairs and using high-powered field glasses, the balloonists located enemy artillery positions by spotting the muzzle flashes.
They then plotted the opposing artillery and reported their findings
by linking telephone cable to the ground. Their pinpoint spotting
quickly brought an Allied artillery response to halt or eliminate the
enemy fire. Despite their extraordinary bird's-eye value to the campaign, Canadian engineer Clarence Goode recognized the balloonists' vulnerability.

"This one bright day I watched one of these spotting balloons as
a German aircraft pumped incendiary bullets into it right above us,"
said Goode, only recently posted to Vimy from the Somme. As fearsome as the burning balloon appeared, the sight of the two spotters
leaping from the carriage amazed Goode even more. "This was
the first time I ever saw parachutes. There were no parachutes in the
Royal Flying Corps at all then. But the only hope of escape in a fire
like this, was if a strong wind carried the men away from it. There was
no wind. The blazing carriage came down between the men, set both
their parachutes on fire and I saw those men tumbling over and over
to their deaths."

The loss of balloon observers was particularly disheartening for
Canadian artillery commander Andrew McNaughton. Unlike many
senior officers, Lt.-Col. McNaughton was liked by his battery troops
and vice versa. Most referred to him as "Andy." Born and raised in
Moosomin, before Saskatchewan became a province, Andrew was a
crack shot and had a boyhood fascination with blasting powder. He
excelled at the emerging science of electrical engineering during

studies at McGill and later as a gunner with the 29th Battery in the 2nd Division. So much so that he caught the eye of Maj.-Gen. Arthur Currie, who sent him to meet with the French following the Somme campaign. That's where his attention was drawn to counter-battery intelligence and tactics—the science of sound ranging and flash spotting, the latter done most efficiently from some altitude above the battlefield.

"I don't like balloons. I never did," McNaughton explained as he recounted the loss of five balloons and crews in a single day. Aerial work, however, became paramount to McNaughton and his crews after January 1917, when Canadian Corps commander Julian Byng relieved him of every duty but one—crushing both the offensive and defensive capability of German artillery in the coming Easter attack.

"Hundreds of hours," McNaughton said, were spent aboard surveillance balloons. In his first days as the key Allied counter-battery strategist, McNaughton felt compelled to take a hands-on approach to the assignment. During an evening excursion aloft over the Notre Dame de Lorette ridge, however, German gunners suddenly homed in on his balloon. A shell burst nearby. He and his carriage mate contemplated parachuting, but that scared them more than the German shells. So they remained airborne, winching the balloon up and down between rounds of fire from the German gun. During that time they quickly counter-plotted the gun, telephoned its coordinates to the ground, and by nightfall assisted in knocking out the threatening gun.

War on the Western Front had become the domain of artillery. Canadian and British Expeditionary Forces had come to depend on the 18-pounder field gun, the 4.5-inch howitzers and 60-pounder heavy artillery. Early on, the Germans had relied on their great 420-mm siege pieces to knock out the Liege forts during their advance through Belgium. Later, they introduced low trajectory artillery that fired 3-inch shells, known by the troops as "whiz-bangs" for the noise on impact, as well as heavier guns firing 5.9-inch and 8-inch shells. By 1916 the developing war of attrition favoured heavier explosives. Howitzers and heavy artillery on either side were capable of lobbing shells—weighing from 200 to 1,000 pounds each—distances from

10,000 to 16,000 yards, several miles; some 15-inch naval guns on railway mountings fired shells at targets nearly 15 miles away. As an indication of the way gunnery had come to dominate the battlefield, during the 1914 Allied attacks throughout the Arras region only 300 guns took part (19 guns per mile); in contrast at the Somme, the British alone employed 455 pieces of artillery versus the Germans' 400 guns.

If Lt.-Col. McNaughton needed inspiration for his work, the 60,000 Allied casualties at the Somme provided it. On the first day of the summer offensive—July 1, 1916—the infantry, including 780 members of the 1st Newfoundland Regiment at Beaumont-Hamel, had advanced with the mistaken expectation that a week of Allied artillery bombardment had decimated the German defenders and their gun positions. The shelling had indeed struck the enemy's front line, but when the barrage lifted, the defenders simply scrambled up from their deep underground bunkers to man their machine guns and cut the attackers down in swathes. More than 24,000 Canadians had become casualties in the bloodbath at the Somme. The Newfoundlanders were nearly wiped out; in less than half an hour, of the 22 officers and 750 other ranks in the advance, 658 were killed or wounded.

Silencing the threat. That was McNaughton's sole objective. To accomplish that end he assembled a circle of specialists, some military, some with a science background. Harold Hemming, previously with the British Third Army, had explored a means of locating a gun by spotting the flash of its barrel from several positions at once. Lucien Bull had designed the oscillograph, a device that recorded sound vibration to pinpoint a gun the same way visual sightings could. Two physicists—Lawrence Bragg (at twenty-five already a Nobel Prize laureate) and Charles G. Darwin (grandson of the world-famous naturalist)—as well as an adjutant, Lennox Napier, and an air intelligence officer named Davidson, rounded out his counter-battery team, or as McNaughton described them, "these boys who worked for me . . . just a tiny handful of people breaking new ground. We had to build up from nothing. We had to find out. And if we didn't know, we had to bluff and at the same time do a hell of a lot of shooting too. Find our way through."

Among the group's first directives was to fine-tune the technique of firing artillery using "methodical progression from point to point"; in other words, to lay down fire that would move a curtain of exploding shells just ahead of the attacking infantry, so that when the barrage had passed over the enemy position, attackers would be on top of defenders immediately, before they had a chance to react. Allied batteries would perfect this so-called creeping or rolling barrage system—experimented with during the latter stages of the Somme campaign, but now urgently needed—to ensure that more Canadian infantry arrived intact at the line of impact with German infantry than ever before.

Gordon Beatty's experience at Vimy vividly illustrated the problem that McNaughton's group faced. To that point, the greatest challenge in Beatty's life had been fighting fires in northern Ontario. Following enlistment, his mathematical training helped him gain a transfer from the Cyclist Corps to artillery, charting shoots. At Vimy in the early spring of 1917 he recounted an experience he thought taught him enough about the ways practical considerations outweighed theory in gunnery. On his very first night behind the front lines, the 15th Battalion (48th Highlanders of Winnipeg) staged a raid on the German forward trenches. The 3rd Brigade command had ordered the raiding party to probe the German line, determine its strength, and if possible return with prisoners. Beatty's 5th Battery would provide artillery cover for the attack. Prior to the operation, Beatty's superior officer asked him to work out the details of the barrage. He did.

"Have you allowed adequate margin of error?" the major asked.

"Fifty yards," Beatty said.

"Better make it 100 yards."

"We're firing on the second-line trenches," Beatty quipped, "not on Berlin."

"Make it 200 yards, Gordon," the major said. "When you've been in France as long as I have you'll appreciate it's better to miss 100 Germans than kill one Canadian."

After the attack, the 15th Battalion colonel notified the battery that "the raid had been successful and we had not killed any of his men." Clearly good news for both the battalion infantry and the battery crew, but not necessarily for McNaughton's counter-battery team. Firing either too long or too short wasn't good enough. Attitude and exactitude in the gun pits had to improve.

Overnight the Counter-Battery Office men began assembling intelligence wherever they could find it, including information from the French artillery experience at the Somme, stereoscopic photography from RFC aircraft, balloon surveillance, maps and interrogation gained from raids on German positions, and even meteorological reports. At first, McNaughton had a difficult time suggesting to battery crews that wind velocity, barometric pressure changes, and precipitation could alter their ranging calculations and their ability to target the guns of the enemy. Even some of his own battery crews considered counter-battery science some sort of "fandoodle." But McNaughton went further. He gathered evidence that barrel wear in the 18-pounder field gun (workhorse of the Allied artillery) could alter the destination of a shell by as much as 300 yards.

Next McNaughton's staff established a working network to develop Harold Hemming's concept of flash-spotting enemy guns. They set up a series of front-line observation posts, occupied by forward observation officers (FOOs), connected by telephone lines. When an observer spotted a flash, he took a bearing and reported it to other posts. With the next flash, each observer pressed a Morse key that lit a panel of lights at a rear command post, where a central observer confirmed the bearings by telephone for plotting. As the system progressed, its flash-spotting capacity became accurate to within five yards. Similarly, using Lucien Bull's oscillograph (recording device), spotters set up a series of front-line microphones to pick up enemy gunshots—whether machine gun or artillery piece. The oscillograph recorded the mike feeds. Then, based on the time interval of the sound travelling from one mike to another and the interval between shot and shell burst, Bull's technology could locate the gun for counter-battery firing. Soon the Counter-Battery Office became a focal point for officers planning the Vimy attack. Lt.-Gen. Byng visited. So did Maj.-Gen. Currie when he became Corps Commander; one of Currie's dictums had been to "pay the price of victory with shells not lives." As proof of their accuracy piled up, McNaughton's "fandoodle" scientists made believers out of everybody, including artillery signaller Elmore Philpott.

"At first we were just like oil and water," Philpott said. He had enlisted in 1915 with many of his University of Toronto classmates out of a sense of patriotism. By the time his 25th Battery crew reached Ross Barracks near the English seaside town of Folkstone for training, they were as much made up of lumberjacks as U of T alumni. "The fellow who was in the bunk next to me, I can remember, he had arms down to his knees. His name was 'Lion Tamer' Mahoney."

In France with the 2nd Division, Cpl. Philpott and the 25th Battery learned a great deal by watching veteran battery gunners around them. Philpott served as a signaller most of the time, peering through field glasses trying to spot enemy troops and gun emplacements. Even though the opposing lines at some points on the Western Front were mere yards apart, he rarely laid his eyes on any Germans. Suddenly, battery crews were expanded and activity increased; in March there were 480 18-pounder field guns. As many as 200 men worked in a battery of four 18-pounders, including fifty men on the guns themselves—gun layers, breach loaders, fuse workers, barrel cleaners, elevation and deflection men, shell loaders, and cordite workers—and the rest of the battery was made up of mechanics, horse drivers, blacksmiths, and saddlers. The 1st and 2nd Canadian Heavy Artillery Brigades were now made up of 245 heavy guns and howitzers plus the 18-pounders. Each day as much as 800 tons of ammunition came forward to Vimy battery positions. The McNaughton statisticians calculated that there was a piece of artillery for every nine yards of front facing the Germans. If nothing else, all the rehearsals and close contact among so many battery crews engendered a new esprit de corps.

"Our artillery guns were practically hub to hub behind the lines," Philpott said. The new flash-spotting and sound-ranging techniques seemed to gel the crew. Philpott got a promotion. In fact, three men in the battery got commissions. "The careful planning rather than the training was paying off. . . . We were directing fire by very careful mathematical calculations. It was by then a magnificent operation. I suppose it was the greatest thing the Canadians ever did."

The final artillery plan, issued in mid-March by the chief gunner Brig.-Gen. Edward Morrison, was a thirty-five-page document. It divided the run up to Zero Hour and beyond into four phases: Phase I went from March 20 to April 2. Phase II went from April 3 to the hour of the assault, originally planned for Sunday, April 8. Phase III covered the creeping barrage, which would precede the infantry in average lifts of 100 yards. The final Phase IV consisted of the movement of field batteries forward to assist the infantry in achieving and consolidating its objectives on the ridge.

Consequently, beginning on March 20, McNaughton's counter-battery guns commenced the systematic elimination of German targets—all meticulously pinpointed for destruction. The first bombardments homed in on enemy trenches, strongpoints, and batteries. In the same phase, Canadian and British gunners paid particular attention to German barbed wire in No Man's Land and around machine-gun nests. Using a recent innovation—the 106 fuse—much of the obstructing wire was eliminated or severed because the 106's mushroom-shaped head was designed to detonate the high-explosive shell on contact with the wire, not above or below it. At any one time during the first week, only half the Allied guns were firing; they unleashed no fewer than 140,000 shells on German positions. In the second phase, a week before Easter, the guns and howitzers that had remained silent unleashed sweeping fire on the same targets to ensure that none of the German gunners could make any repairs. Howitzer gun crews also pinpointed enemy batteries and railheads in the eight villages occupied by German troops behind the ridge. McNaughton's counter-battery crew estimated the shelling eliminated 83 percent of the Germans' 212 guns. Canadian artillery records reported that "shells poured over our heads like water from a hose."

For those on the receiving end, there seemed no place to hide. Even more stressful, the German troops knew that intense bombardments telegraphed an imminent attack. It could come on any day, at any hour. Since the Canadians also mounted small raiding parties allowing rumours to spread along the line, enemy troops were further misled. The few Canadians captured by the Germans had little to offer in the way of attack times—the exact date was not known until the Easter weekend itself. As a consequence, the German defenders "stood to," remained at the ready constantly for eleven straight days. The strain unravelled even those with the strongest nerves. German troops called the last seven days of the bombardment "the week of suffering."

"Once again trebled is the raging hurricane of fire," one German soldier recorded in his diary. Hunkered down in their deepest underground tunnels and bunkers, members of the 79th Reserve and 1st Bavarian Reserve Divisions took the worst pounding. "Somewhat lesser is the thunder at 14th Bavarian Infantry Division, but there too are noted characteristics of concentrated harassing fire. The thunder of the heavy guns drowns any other noise. The rumble of the unparalleled storm is deeper now than the Somme."

Repeated night firing at battery positions taxed Canadian artillerymen as well. Throughout the bombardment, gunner L.D. Giffin served with the crew of the 85th Battery in the 4th Division sector. Night after night he withstood the cold and damp of working in mud and water up to his knees, as well as the constant flashing and pounding of the battery guns. At age twenty-three, Pte. Giffin was older than many on the crew, but he was a teetotaller. He had continuously refused the requisite reward—a tot of rum—after his eight hours on duty. Following one of those March nights on the firing line, Giffin trekked back to Gouy-Servins where the battery crew billeted in an old chateau. As usual, the men lined up on a set of steps to get into the chateau. In the doorway at the top of the steps stood the quarter-master with a jug marked SRD (Special Red Demerara, 186-proof Jamaican rum) doling out a tot to each man.

"Here, take one," the quartermaster said.

"No thanks," Giffin said out of habit.

"I know you don't drink, but you look like you should have one," the quartermaster insisted.

"Okay," Giffin said finally and he took a Players Cigarettes tin for the tot. He was so cold, the tin was shaking in his hands.

The quartermaster poured in the portion and Pte. Giffin took a quick swallow. But he took too much too quickly and began choking. Someone pounded him on the back to clear his throat. When Giffin finally got to his bunk, he sat on the edge and felt "the rum tingling even down to my toes. Without undressing I crawled in the bunk with a blanket over me and at once fell into a deep sleep, as peaceful as a babe in a crib."

Giffin slept the day through. He missed the meal call completely and woke with only enough time to take a slice of bread with jam and a piece of cheese before returning to the battery position for the next night's counter-battery bombardment.

## March 20, 1917—French Army Headquarters, Chantilly, France

Even as the pieces of the Vimy plan fell into place, the complexion of the war was changing up and down the front lines in eastern and western Europe. Indeed, key players on the world military and polit-ical stage changed on the eve of the Vimy attack. An attempt by U.S. president Woodrow Wilson to mediate "peace without victory" fell on deaf ears in Europe. Germany offered no concessions at all. The Allies in effect demanded the total evacuation of occupied territories and the dissolution of the Austrian-German alliance. The French and British public had seen horrendous loss of life but steadfastly believed in victory; meanwhile a sense of *durchhalten*—the need to "see it through"—prevailed in Germany. A negotiated peace appeared out of the question.

In Britain, Prime Minister Lloyd George pressed for more decisive action than Field Marshal Douglas Haig had delivered. He even attempted to hand over supreme command of Allied forces to a new French military hero. Though that idea failed, Gen. Robert-Georges Nivelle, the recent replacement for Marshal Joseph Joffre as commander of the French Army, had become popular because his *violence, brutalité, et rapidité* approach in battle had won the day at Verdun. Meanwhile, Gen. Erich Ludendorff fanned the flames by pressing for German victory in the east, withdrawing and consolidating German forces behind the new fortified Hindenburg Line on the Western Front and ordering unrestricted submarine warfare in the Atlantic. In March the British lost 600,000 tons of shipping to U-boat attacks. At the same time, continued Russian support of the Allied war effort fell into question; mass peasant riots forced Czar Nicholas to abdicate and a provisional government to assume tenuous control. Then British intelligence intercepted a telegram from German official Alfred Zimmermann, promising German assistance to Mexico should it attack the United States. President Wilson tabled a declaration of war in the U.S. Congress. It passed.

Throughout these tumultuous first weeks of 1917, at French Army headquarters in Chantilly, Gen. Nivelle continued to advance his *rupture* plan as the centrepiece of the spring offensive against Germany. He recommended a combination of intense Allied artillery fire and massive infantry attack on either end of the old Somme battlefield—by the French in the southern Aisne sector, the Chemin des Dames, and by the British and her allies in the northern sector at Arras and Vimy Ridge. To that end, Gen. Nivelle contacted Gen. Byng at Canadian Corps headquarters. While Nivelle apparently had little confidence in the Canadian plans to attack and seize Vimy Ridge, he did, however, want to learn more about a reported innovative machine-gun strategy the Canadians had developed.

"This is new," Nivelle had said to Byng. "It looks interesting and I request that we should be informed of the results obtained."

Byng in turn notified Col. Raymond Brutinel, commanding officer of the 1st Canadian Machine Gun Brigade, saying, "You will have to make a full report on the machine guns for the benefit of our French friends."

The commander of the MGs, nicknamed the Emma Gees, already knew the impact of indirect machine-gun fire. About the same time that McNaughton's staff began formulating its counter-battery battle plan, so did Brutinel and his staff finalize their plans for a remarkable innovation in machine-gun warfare. Up to and including the Somme offensive, Allied strategists considered the machine gun as simply a rapid-fire rifle. In front-line battle, the water-cooled Vickers machine gun on a tripod could fire 450 rounds per minute. The more portable cylindrical-drum-firing Lewis delivered more than 500 rounds per minute. Used directly against infantry, their .303 shells proved deadly. But one-time prospector, newspaperman, and successful businessman-turned-soldier, Raymond Brutinel believed the weapon offered more diversity as light artillery at the front than the British had allowed.

"They thought the range of the machine guns was too limited to be successful in offensive war," said Brutinel, who encouraged his crews to think just the opposite and then invited them to an eight-day course on using machine guns as covering and barrage fire.

In other words, Brutinel proposed, in addition to firing directly at the enemy, that some machine guns arch their fire over the forward Canadian trenches to intensify and broaden McNaughton's artillery barrages. With 358 machine guns at his disposal, Brutinel predicted that these tactics used regularly at night would prevent the enemy from repairing trenches, communication lines, roads, tramways, and barbed-wire barriers. Such "indirect fire" would reduce his ability to evacuate wounded or move reinforcements and rations forward. Brutinel recommended that sixty-four machine guns provide this form of harassing fire along the Canadian Corps' front by day and another sixty-four at night. More than 80 percent of Brutinel's Emma Gees took the course, and several weeks before Zero Hour they went to work harassing the Germans. One of them was a young lieutenant from Portage la Prairie, Manitoba.

"At first we were concerned about the heavy expenditure of ammunition," Gerard Bradbrooke said. "Later on among my eight guns we would fire as many as 350,000 rounds in twenty-four hours."

Bradbrooke's entire First World War career resulted from an innocent bribe in England. Originally a bugler with the 18th Canadian Mounted Rifles (CMRs), at fifteen Gerard managed to get to Shorncliffe training camp in England. It was 1915 and the only battle Bradbrooke faced was pounding keys on a typewriter as the secretary to the machine-gun instruction staff. Eventually, when the commanding officer wasn't around, Bradbrooke paid an orderly room corporal half a crown to put him on the next draft to France. He wound up in the machine-gun unit attached to the 28th (Saskatchewan) Battalion. He trained on Vickers machine guns at Albert, carried machine-gun ammunition at the Somme, and joined the Emma Gees as a lieutenant in time to be one of those involved in the pre-Vimy indirect fire operations.

Lt. Bradbrooke recalled another of the corps experiments—the first daylight trench raid earlier in the winter at Vimy. Morale was high on the Canadian side. Brutinel's Emma Gees seemed to have the upper hand along the four divisional fronts. The raid was the best way to test how depleted the German armament and morale really were. The day they went over the top, they hid their approach with a barrage, managed to bomb the German trenches, and returned with prisoners. These POWs proved extremely valuable in assessing the effectiveness of Brutinel's indirect machine-gun fire tactics. When Gen. Nivelle requested a full review of indirect fire, the commander of the Emma Gees took great delight in sending his report.

"A report from me would be of little value," Brutinel suggested. "The report [will] be made by the Germans themselves as they and they alone could give first-hand information on the subject from the business end of it."

Testimony from German prisoners captured during March was conclusive. The Canadian indirect machine-gun fire had practically halted all overland movement beyond the ridge. It had restricted any carrying parties the Germans dispatched to their fortified trenches.

"The heavy British long-range guns cover the hellish concert of the smaller weapons," recalled a German war diarist. "There is not a second's let-up in the hammering and screeching . . . day and night, without pause or remission rages the infernal symphony with the fury of a never-ending thunderstorm. . . ."

Remarkably, it was only when Canadian gunners reduced their fire later in the month to keep machine-gun barrel wear to a minimum that the first German relief and ration crews were able to reach the *Zwischen Stellung* trench about 800 to 1,000 yards behind the German front line. For his own reference Brutinel's review also concluded that "at all times . . . ammunition supplies had been sufficient, . . . fire discipline was excellent with officers, NCOs and gunners working smoothly, and . . . identifying, organizing and manning machine-gun positions . . . to support infantry was carried out promptly and accurately."

Col. Brutinel's indirect fire tryouts were peaking at precisely the right moment for Allied forces.

## March 30, 1917—5th Battery, Neuville St. Vaast, Vimy

During the "week of suffering" barrages, there was no more crucial link in the chain of command than horsepower. Behind the lines, on every transportation artery leading to and from the front—along dirt paths, corduroy roadways, narrow-gauge railway lines, in trenches and even tunnels—teams of horses and mules kept the paraphernalia of war moving. Every piece of artillery, every box of supplies, every ration, and nearly every shell arrived at its appointed place thanks to the army's four-legged transports. Thousands of heavy and light horses came from across the British Empire—about two million horses in all—surviving days or weeks of ocean transport (with its dark, congested, and poorly ventilated conditions) just to get to an uncertain future in France. Horses were a lifeline to Alberta farmer John Holderness. Though he nearly starved to death—surviving on his homestead near Gadsby by eating rabbits and prairie chickens—he treated his horses as his most prized possession. As a horse driver at the front in France, Holderness found that horses were equally valuable, although he recalled the price many of the animals paid at the hands of abusive soldiers.

"Even though there were guards posted, one night our sergeant-major's horse was stolen from the picket line," Holderness wrote. "It was butchered, just cut up and sold for meat. No trace was found, but some of our men had poker money for a while."

When he joined up in April 1916, Holderness was initially posted to the 187th Battery, but by the time the Canadian Corps arrived at Vimy, the army had assigned him to driving horses with the 5th Canadian Field Artillery behind the lines near 2nd Division headquarters at Neuville St. Vaast. That's where the lives of drivers and horses took on a new urgency and rhythm in the weeks leading up to the assault on the ridge. The men and animals that hauled the field guns learned to jockey each gun precisely until the gunners were satisfied that the weapon sat in the correct range position. Those teams supplying ammunition knew a different routine. For the 18-pounder field guns, for example, crews tacked up the horses with pack saddles and loaded four shells into each pack, two per horse for the eight-mile, eight-hour trip to forward gun positions. If the horse supplied ammo to machine guns, each pack consisted of 2,000 to 3,000 rounds per trip depending on the size of the horse. Since most of the hauling took place at night, artillery and machine-gun crews could get very anxious if horses and crews lingered longer than necessary. The additional noise and taller silhouettes, even in the dark, had gun crews urging horse drivers to unpack and move off quickly.

"I have a lot of praise for those nags," Holderness said. "Most of them stood absolutely still and very close to those guns and never flinched even when they were fired. Those 18-pounders had a sharp, wicked bark."

With as many as 50,000 horses working those busy lanes behind the Vimy Ridge front, casualties—equine and human—were inevitable. Six horses pulling a hitching limber with three drivers and a field gun attached presented too convenient a target for German gunners. When enemy shells found their mark, the crews and the animals paid a deadly price for being tied so close together. For those horses that survived such attacks or that needed medical assistance, the Canadian Army posted four mobile sections of the Veterinary Corps to the front—one assigned to each division. And well behind the lines, at a veterinary hospital in Le Havre, medical teams housed 1,400 horses at a time, every month returning to the front 600 animals that had suffered disease or shrapnel wounds.

As devastating as enemy shellings might be to horses and their drivers, on some trips the guns proved less threatening than the nature of the front itself. One night, horse transport driver James Robert Johnston, with the 14th Canadian Machine Gun Company, was sent with a two-horse team and wagon to retrieve a couple of guns.

"It was dark when I left the horse lines and raining really hard," Pte. Johnston wrote in his memoirs. "I did not think when I started out that it was a very smart thing to do, but had nothing to say about it."

In the dark and rain, Johnston got lost. At times he even welcomed a nearby shell burst because it temporarily lit his way through the gloom. Yet the resulting darkness made it even tougher to see. In time the horse he was riding stepped too close to the edge of an old narrow trench and in it went, Johnston on top of him, and the second horse and the wagon pole on top of them. Fortunately, a leg iron that drivers wore prevented Johnston's leg being shattered in the crash, but the trench mud began swallowing the entire outfit.

"After a lot of manoeuvring," he wrote, "I got some of the harness off the horses and clear of the limber. . . . I found an entrenching tool [shovel] and after a lot of digging finally got the trench tapered . . . so that I could get the horses out."

The nineteen-year-old Maritimer persevered and miraculously managed to dig free both horses and their harness. But he had to leave the wagon behind, with the limber wedged upright in the mud. When Pte. Johnston finally made it back to the horse lines, his sergeant was not at all pleased about losing the rig in the mired trench. The two men made plans to retrieve it after dark. But for German gunners looking down from their Vimy Ridge vantage point, the vertical limber pole looked too much like a newly installed gun barrel. Consequently, when Johnston and his sergeant got to the site the next night, they discovered the wagon had been blown to pieces.

## April 5, 1917—4th Field Battery, Arras to Bapaume Road, Vimy

Another artilleryman who often found himself serving near or with horses at Vimy was former university student Harold Innis. In March of 1916, McMaster had waived final exams so that the graduating class could enlist. Fifteen of Innis's fellow graduates signed up with the Canadian Field Artillery. Though his family urged him to become a Baptist preacher, Innis followed his classmates into war. That April he was an artillery signaller and by mid-November 1916 (just after his twenty-first birthday) he had arrived in France with the 4th Field Battery attached to the 1st Division. Apparently, Innis's superiors took his signals job description to include plenty of horse-keeping.

"Most of the time was spent preparing for inspections," Innis noted in biographical notes later, "which meant polishing harness and grooming horses. I seemed to have fallen heir to the task of looking after extra horses as someone had gone on a pass to England."

Pte. Innis proved a faithful diarist and letter writer home while serving overseas, although the wartime experience wore him down. In a note home from Shorncliffe Camp in England in July 1916, he seemed to be enjoying the training on horseback that reminded him of his boyhood experiences on the family farm in Otterville, Ontario. He even poked fun at his comrades because "there are some here who hardly know any more about a horse than a cow." However, just four days before the massive Vimy attack, front-line life had clearly blunted any sense of emotional involvement in his writing. Part of his April 5, 1917, diary entry read: "Horse developed lockjaw from shrapnel wounds. Had to be shot. . . . Airplanes at night. Dead horses by roadside."

As numbing as the continuous death and destruction around him became, Harold Innis never appeared to lose touch with the crucial role each soldier seemed to play in the overall war effort. Writing part of a university thesis later, he recalled that "in the period before Vimy, working from 4 o'clock in the afternoon to 4 o'clock in the morning, horses were exhausted as well as the men. In the face of that feeling that other men's lives depended to an important extent on how much work we did . . . monotony was one of our worst enemies."

While the horrors of trench warfare traumatized the man who would one day blaze the trail for Canadian studies in political economy and communication, the wartime experience seemed to waken his sense of nationalism. Innis felt uncomfortable with the notion that Canadian volunteers had simply signed up and crossed the Atlantic to defend Great Britain. He recognized that many former English immigrants to Canada had done just that. However, his contact with men he described initially as coming from "industrial communities" having "a hardness such as I had not come in contact with" evolved to a deep respect. These were comrades-in arms who were not necessarily fighting just for "the mother country," but particularly at Vimy, for the first time shoulder to shoulder with fellow corpsmen they were fighting "for Canada, and Canada alone."

Though some, like Harold Innis, were students barely out of universities in Montreal and Toronto, others who were formerly miners from Nova Scotian collieries, still others from the logging country of B.C.'s interior, as well as ranchers and homesteaders from the newly formed provinces of Saskatchewan and Alberta, in April 1917 they were suddenly something more. As members of the Canadian Corps, they had joined weeks of preparation on paper and in reality. Many of the 100,000 Canadian troops at the foot of Vimy had participated in targeted trench raids, albeit not always successfully. They had trained, even studied, the new tools of war—sausage hunting, counter-battery offence, indirect machine-gun fire, communications eavesdropping, and silent sapping. And like actors practising their lines and blocking for a three-act play, they had rehearsed the steps they would follow behind the creeping barrage, the territory they would cover across No Man's Land, and the specific jobs they would carry out upon the capture of their objective. On a battlefield hardly recognizable as countryside any more and an ocean away from their former civilian pursuits in Canada, theirs was to be the first major offensive effort by a Dominion military contingent on the Western Front.

# COUNTDOWN TO ZERO HOUR

### April 8, 1917—Hythe School of Musketry, England

L ESLIE FROST could not have known their numbers. They were overwhelming. One hundred and four 6-inch howitzers, thirty-six 8-inch howitzers, another thirty-six 9.2-inch howitzers, four 12-inch howitzers, three 15-inch howitzers, fifty-four 60-pounder guns, eight 6-inch guns, 480 of the stalwart 18-pounder field guns, and all 358 machine guns pouring murderous fire and steel at the enemy. Frost did, however, hear the distant rumble of the Allied combined firepower against the Germans on Vimy Ridge. At the time, the assistant adjutant with the 157th Battalion (from Barrie, Ontario) was training at the Hythe School of Musketry in southern England. He was over a hundred miles from the front.

"It was a cold, overcast day with flecks of snow," Frost wrote later. "The sound of the guns could be plainly heard."

As awe-inspiring as that distant sound seemed, Leslie Frost had grown weary of the perpetual training and wanted to get closer to the action. Born and raised in Orillia, Ontario, Frost, who would one day become premier of Ontario, had grown up in a typical Victorian home. Bible readings and a strong belief in temperance had shaped his moral character (and that of his younger brother, Cecil), while lively dinner-table discussions and reading *Boy's Own Annual* had given the boys awareness of their country's politics and its role in the British Empire. Both Frost boys had enlisted as volunteers in the Simcoe Foresters—Leslie as a private, Cecil as bugler. By the spring of 1915, Leslie was a provisional lieutenant in the 157th Battalion, and by the following year he'd earned a captaincy while training in England. But he had grown impatient with the waiting, preferring to be "a private [at the front] doing my bit, than in England as a colonel."

So, that spring of 1917, Leslie Frost trained incessantly at Hythe while his brother did the same a few miles away at the Machine Gun School in Crowborough. They felt stuck in England. Adding insult to the injury, the Frosts watched their British commanders begin dismantling the newly arrived Canadian battalions. Instead of keeping all the new battalions intact and in a promised 5th Canadian Infantry Division, the Canadians' British masters had decided to break up the rookie regiments—the so-called Umpty-Umps—and post them, eventually to the front line, as reinforcement units for the older established battalions. Cecil Frost wrote his parents complaining about the arrangements:

> When a unit, for instance the 157th Simcoe Battalion, is broken up it means that eleven hundred men have lost the esprit de corps of that unit. Multiply that eleven hundred men by the number of battalions broken and the result is that we have a generally discontented army.

That Easter weekend of 1917, Capt. Leslie Frost attended church services at Folkstone on the coast of England and listened to the distant thunder of artillery in France. Authorities were disassembling the 157th before either he or Cecil had fired a shot. Worse, the Frost brothers couldn't get any closer than earshot to the looming fight at Vimy.

## April 8, 1917—YMCA hut, Ecoivres, France

Across the English Channel, behind the lines at Vimy, arranging any kind of Easter church services had become an unexpected challenge for one member of the army chaplain service. Canon Frederick G. Scott, the senior padre for the 1st Canadian Infantry Division, had attempted to lead a Good Friday service in Ecoivres, near the training area at Mont St. Eloi. He was told the battalion troops were too busy preparing for the attack to attend. Scott then rode to Anzin and had a service for the 7th Siege Battery in an empty Nissen hut instead.

"Most of the men of the battery were present and I had forty communicants," Canon Scott wrote. "The place was lit by candles which every now and then were extinguished by the firing of the fifteen-inch gun nearby."

During the Great War the Canadian Chaplain Service operated with relative efficiency and posted 447 Canadian clergymen overseas—in Siberia, the Mediterranean, Flanders, and across France. Two days before the war broke out, Rev. Scott had announced to his congregation he would be volunteering for overseas service. He had been the peacetime chaplain of the 8th Royal Rifles of Quebec City; accordingly, he trained at nearby Valcartier, shipped out for Britain, and arrived in France with the 15th Battalion for their baptism of fire at Armentières. Scott served the Canadian Corps right through the war, suffering a severe wound within six weeks of the Armistice.* The reverend and his steed, a supposedly over-the-hill thoroughbred named Dandy, blended in wherever they went, from open-air services to YMCA centres and along every roadway to and from the front.

Before the frantic period of preparations began at Vimy, church parades had been as much a part of a weekly schedule as work party

---

* On September 29, 1918, near Cambrai, France, Canon Scott assisted a Canadian soldier who had lost his hand in the battle; then a shell landed in front of them, killing several men and severely wounding Scott in both legs. At the dressing station the reverend announced, "Boys, I am going to call for my first and last tot of rum."

details in the trenches and subways. As the Vimy training exercises and bombardment program progressed, however, congregations and suitable service locations dwindled. Dugouts and galleries at the front lines grew crowded with men and activity. Behind the Vimy front lines, clergymen with the chaplain service held evangelistic meetings in the evenings in available huts or turned ruined buildings into impromptu chapels, theatres, and service canteens. When he could find the room, Rev. Scott conducted full high-holiday church services; other times he ministered to the wounded and dying over stretchers in field hospitals. Sometimes he had to improvise more than usual.

Just before the Vimy attack, he rode Dandy to a place called Maison Blanche, a large cavern in a chalky hillside used as a billet by one of the reserve battalions. Early in the war, French and German troops had fought bitterly to control this area; as a reminder, months of rain and shelling had exposed bits of faded French uniforms still clinging to skeletons on the ground nearby. Inside the cavern the air was smoky and lighted by candles. Men were cooking in mess tins, "reading their shirts" (running a cigarette lighter along the seams to burn the lice out) or playing cards on the floor. Rev. Scott walked among the troops and invited them to come to the end of the cavern to join him in a service. Some followed, but not the card players.

"Don't make too much noise," Rev. Scott announced to catch the card players' attention, "lest we disturb the gamblers."

One card player looked up and said, "If you will wait till we have finished this hand, sir, we will all come too."

"We will not begin, then, till the players are ready," Scott agreed.

Presently, all the men joined the service.

Then, as it had been for every Canadian in the Vimy sector, army chaplains became cogs in the machinery of the attack. Each padre received reports, itineraries, maps, and timetables so that he knew in advance where to go in an emergency. Depending in which sector a chaplain served, he might be attached to casualty clearing stations, battery locations, or brigade staging areas. When troops went over the top, some chaplains would follow immediately, setting up aid positions as far away as captured enemy trenches and dugouts.

"Easter [Sun]day was originally intended to be the day for our attack, but [on Good Friday we learned] it had been postponed till Monday," Scott wrote. He frantically searched for any place to observe the great Christian feast. He finally found enough space and men around to stage two celebrations of Holy Communion in the local YMCA hut. "The floor was covered with sleeping men. I managed to clear a little space on the stage for the altar. . . .

"What did the next twenty-four hours hold in store for us?" he wrote that Sunday night. "Was it to be a true Easter for the world? . . . If death awaited us, what nobler passage could there be . . . than such a death in such a cause?"

## April 8, 1917—Zivy Subway, 2nd Division sector, Vimy

On the weekend before the attack, there was a massive mail call, the biggest one yet. Appropriately so. Never was morale higher, it seemed, among Canadians on the brink of the Vimy operation. Never was an additional boost from friends and family at home more welcome. Mail arriving from Canada in England moved quickly through the offices of the Canadian Postal Corps, a unit of officers and hundreds of NCOs, who sorted, redirected, and re-bagged the mail by battalion for delivery. Behind the lines, the Canadian Corps had set up twenty-eight mobile field post offices.* Each year of the war, the Canadian Postal Corps was processing nearly a hundred thousand bags of mail and three times that many parcels. Military censors kept a tight rein on the mail troops sent home. Officers either black-marked or excised from letters lines of information about military units and locations. To reduce the problem, the army introduced convenient field postcards. Soldiers could simply check off the "I am well" box or the "I am in hospital" box and enclose the card in a green envelope for speedy processing.

---

* In 1918 alone, the Canadian Postal Corps processed more than sixty-eight million letters between Canada and overseas war zones; in addition, the CPC delivered ten million newspapers and five million parcels to Canadians in the front lines.

In the 2nd Division sector near Mont St. Eloi, Sid Smith had just been re-assigned to a mobile field post office. It had not been under pleasant circumstances. Several weeks earlier, Pte. Smith had moved up in the front line to an 18th (Western Ontario) Battalion position, where German 5.9-inch and 8-inch heavy artillery shells—called Jack Johnsons and Coal-Boxes respectively—began exploding in their area.

"I was in a bit of a trench. There were five of us in it. They dropped a Jack Johnson in it," Smith said. "I got blown straight up ten feet and thrown on top of a bank. My clothes were stripped right off me. I was naked to the waist, but not a scratch on me. I passed out. A terrific explosion and concussion."

Two of Smith's platoon mates disappeared in the explosion. The two others went to hospital—one had had a leg blown off, the other had lost both arms—but both died of their wounds. When he came to, Pte. Smith found himself in one of the underground galley areas, a makeshift field hospital carved from the chalk under Vimy Ridge. After a short convalescence he was assigned to process mail at the field post office near Mont St. Eloi. Then the post office was hit by a German shell and the corporal severely wounded. That's how Smith had become a Postal Corps corporal.

"I got his stripes, I guess."

Unlike many of the others in the 18th Battalion, Ellis Sifton had not received much mail during that first week of April. In fact, when he wrote to his sisters a few days before the attack, he noted that "there have not been any letters from you people for about ten days." L/Cpl. Sifton had written to members of his family several times a week from the moment he enlisted in October 1914 and left the family farm near Wallacetown, Ontario, right up to his arrival at Vimy. In training at Wolseley Barracks in London, Ontario, he proudly announced to his sisters, Ella and Millie, that he'd scored twenty-six out of thirty-five in target practice, "third place in our company" and that army life "seems more a dream than anything else." He dashed off fourteen letters and six postcards during the battalion's transatlantic crossing, posting them when he arrived at Sandling Camp. "If

(ABOVE LEFT) Introduced in August 1916, the small box respirator (SBR) was an effective anti-gas device, unless the wearer began breathing heavily such as in a stressful situation or running across a battlefield. Horse handlers even had a modified gas bag for their animals. (ABOVE RIGHT) Pte. Charlie Venning participated in the aborted gas attack by Canadian troops at Vimy Ridge on March 1, 1917. He was captured, missed the victory at Vimy, and spent the duration of the war in German POW camps. (BELOW) Entrenched German troops prepare for a gas attack along the Eastern Front near Riga, Latvia, in 1916.

(LEFT) One of more than a thousand recruits, an underage Lyman Nicholls dashed from high school French class in Uxbridge to enlist. (ABOVE) Gathered first in Uxbridge's Elgin Park and then (BELOW LEFT) paraded through the streets, the men of the 116th Ontario County Battalion got a hometown send-off complete with a banner: "God bless our splendid men; send them safe home again." (BELOW RIGHT) Lt.-Col. Samuel Sharpe personally took on the responsibility of recruiting, outfitting, and training volunteers for the 116th Ontario County Battalion.

(ABOVE) Practical training began at Vimy behind the lines, where every Canadian assault brigade, battalion, and platoon rehearsed on a detailed mock-up of German defensive positions. Note tapes, trench configurations, and sign (centre) denoting No Man's Land. (RIGHT) After a day's rehearsal "over the tapes" Canadian Corps soldiers enjoyed the evening entertainment from the Princess Patricia's Canadian Light Infantry Comedy Company, including: (l to r) T.J. Lilly, Jack McLaren, Percy Ham, and N.J. Nicholson Pembroke.

(ABOVE) To ensure air circulation where the sappers dug tunnels under Vimy, troops manned an outside bellows to continuously pump in fresher air. (BELOW) The crenellated trench (like the top of a castle chess piece in this aerial view) ensured that an invading enemy had a limited field-of-fire up and down the line. (LEFT) For L/Cpl. Gavin McDonald, the transition from peacetime sod-busting on the Saskatchewan prairie to digging tunnels under Vimy was easy enough, except that the Germans were shooting back.

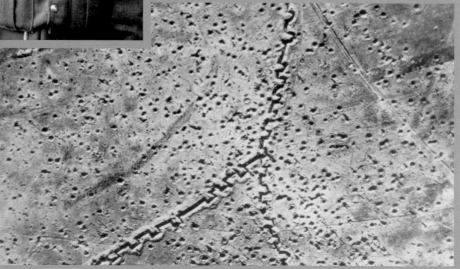

(LEFT) If the bombardment didn't make the ground at Vimy unrecognizable from one day to the next, Canadian engineers did their level best when moving soil or mud for road beds.

(RIGHT) An equal number of work parties laid beds, ties, and rails for twenty miles of narrow-gauge railway behind the lines at Vimy.

(LEFT) And when all else failed, crews used 19th-century corduroy road methods—with wooden planks side-by-side—as the artificial road surface.

(LEFT) All the dignity of
royalty, rank, and responsibility
couldn't get around the mud
that (l to r) King George V,
senior Canadian commander
Arthur Currie, and British
First Army commander
Henry Horne found at the
Vimy front.

(RIGHT) As awkward and
uncomfortable as the
trenches looked, any bivvy
(sand-bagged area) or (BELOW
RIGHT) funk hole (carved into
a trench wall) could double as
a bed for a few moments'
rest. (BELOW LEFT) Sunshine
was rare, but if it coincided
with lunch break beside the
duck board path, somehow it
made the bully beef, biscuit,
and tea delectable.

(ABOVE) Typical of German trenching, beginning in 1916, troops excavated at least 30 metres beneath the surface and reinforced all trenches and dugouts with timber. (BELOW) Rest areas even allowed above ground activities such as chess and card games.

(LEFT) Behind the lines at Vimy, Canadian troops consumed a million gallons of water a day, as well as two hot meals per man and—on combat operations—a tot of rum. Canned meat was a staple, and when possible a slice of bread with jam or cheese.

(RIGHT) Sand bags helped to convert earth and mud into fortified trenches; despite the mud and cold, these 13th Battalion troops continued to work in their kilts.

(LEFT) Keeping clean at the front proved the greatest challenge, so leftover tea, rain runoff, or trench water often became the basic ingredient for daily ablutions.

(ABOVE LEFT) Common on both sides, hunting rats was a sport-like distraction while improving underground hygiene. (ABOVE RIGHT) The result was a nearly spotless trench system where German L/Cpl. Winterhager posed for this portrait in 1917. (TOP) Deeper underground these German troops read in what they called the "Baurin" quarters.

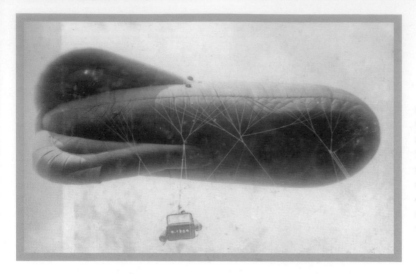

(LEFT) Tethered to the ground and allowed to hover a few thousand feet above the front, surveillance balloon crews became the artillery's eye in the sky.

(RIGHT) While mortality rates among crews were high, they were among the first airborne troops issued parachutes.

(LEFT) Ft.-Lt. Billy Bishop earned the Victoria Cross, Military Cross, and Distinguished Service Order. His first distinction, however, was as a "sausage hunter," knocking down German surveillance balloons.

(RIGHT) Equally helpful in determining Allied troop movements and gun positions, German air surveillance balloonists soared over Vimy just as often.

(RIGHT) Post cards issued in 1917 depict German missions that gave Manfred von Richtofen and his Flying Circus such notoriety.

(RIGHT) During "bloody April" 1917, the German air force shot down 151 Royal Flying Corps aircraft, compared to losing 119 of their own.

(LEFT) Behind the lines at Vimy, as many as 50,000 horses served king and empire in return for water, feed, shelter, and regular shoeing.

(LEFT) Often the most lethal of wounds horse and mule teams sustained came from nails dropped by smithies and others and accidentally picked up by passing hooves.

(FAR LEFT) Most lethal of all was German shelling, which inflicted thousands of equine casualties each month.
(LEFT) Coming from an Ontario farming community, Pte. Bill Hewlett willingly took on the added duty of burying horse casualties following battles or barrages.

(LEFT) A light or narrow-gauge railway transported shells to battery positions in greatest numbers.

(RIGHT) For reliable delivery of these 18-pounder field gun shells, teamsters tacked up the horses with pack saddles—four shells per pack—en route to the batteries at Neuville St. Vaast.

(LEFT) The Germans called the seven days of Allied shelling prior to the ground attack at Vimy "the week of suffering," during which more than a million rounds crashed into German positions. Artillery crews dumped spent shell casings along the roadsides.

(LEFT) These 9-inch guns played a key role in the Allies' counter-battery fire, which eliminated more than 80 per cent of the German artillery before the infantry battle even began on April 9.

(RIGHT) In the first ninety minutes of the Easter Monday battle, Allied guns fired 200,000 artillery rounds. All of the battery ammunition had been stockpiled days in advance.

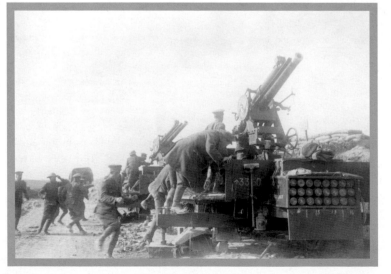

(LEFT) Allied gunners used anti-aircraft weapons against slow-moving air surveillance balloons and fixed-wing bomber and fighter aircraft.

(TOP) One thousand Allied guns—nearly hub-to-hub along the Vimy front—fired relentlessly at German targets day and night for a week. (ABOVE) These Canadian Vickers machine gunners revolutionized use of the weapon by firing over the heads of their own troops and creating an arc of indirect harassing fire against the enemy. (RIGHT) Pte. Harold Innis, with the 4th Field Battery, recorded in his diary that after twelve hours of firing Allied guns, men, and horses were exhausted.

(ABOVE) While the Christmas truce of 1914 is more famous, members of the 49th (Alberta) Battalion witnessed Canadian and German soldiers fraternizing at the Vimy front on Dec. 25, 1916. (LEFT) Though cyclists mostly delivered messages, they willingly took on other duties: digging tunnels, processing prisoners, and acting as early warning sentries for gas attacks. (BOTTOM) At Vimy, some Canadian Corps troops trained to use carrier pigeons as the principal message delivery system. Ninety-five per cent of the messages sent by pigeon arrived safely.

the people of Canada realized how serious it is over here," he wrote, "they would wake up and do about three times what they are doing." And he applauded his British hosts because they "all have a smile for the boys from the maple leaf."

By the fall of 1915, L/Cpl. Sifton was return-addressing his letters according to regulation "Somewhere in France" or "Somewhere in Belgium." He began most letters saying he was "fine and dandy," even when the cold, mud, and lice from living in trenches and dugouts could barely be tolerated. He even sugar-coated his references to battalion casualties with "but we must expect that." Most of the following year, his "C" Company of the 18th Battalion worked in reserve in Belgium and France, as Sifton himself helped with the transport horses, wash wagon detail, handling ammunition, and running rations to the forward battalions—what he called "bomb proof jobs."

Sifton's letters reflected his own experience and that of the Canadian Corps soldiers around him. One moment he chafed at Prime Minister Robert Borden's delay in legislating conscription and the next entreated his family to send a coat, gloves, and boots to fend off the elements. Naturally, when the young lance corporal saw French farmers seeding or haying behind the lines, he longed to be doing the same at home in southwestern Ontario. But most of all he hoped "that the courage will be mine at the right moment if I am called upon to stare death in the face."

In the new year at Vimy (he didn't identify where he was), Sifton explained he had suddenly been returned to his old company and had rejoined "a few of the originals that are left. There have been so many changes." As gently as he could describe it, the winter weather had turned severe, the regimen more strenuous and despite his hopes of getting a respite in England or Scotland, all leave had been cancelled. The 18th Battalion had served eighteen months in Europe, and though his sisters did not know it, their brother was about to go over the top for the first time against the enemy. In the letter he wrote lamenting no mail just before Easter, as he waited for final assembly in the Zivy Subway, Ellis Sifton signed off with the best news he had.

"Do not be anxious if you do not receive any news, as it is not always convenient to write. This is a very short scribble. . . . Good night. Love to all from your loving brother Ellis W. Sifton." And he added, "P.S. They have promoted me to sergeant."

In the neighbouring Bentata Subway, Jay Moyer had also written his family back in Jordon Station, Ontario. Pte. Moyer, with the 1st (Western Ontario) Battalion, had just survived "the toughest night I have ever experienced," a night bombing raid on the German lines to test their defences. The raiding party had struggled its way through mud, wire, and machine-gun fire, delivered its Mills bombs (hand grenades), and returned. But the platoon had suffered other casualties.

"Quite a few of the boys are gone across the Great Divide," he wrote to his mother. He added glowingly and even enviously a note about Ray Howells, the officer who led the raid. "He was a real hero. He is on his way to England with shrapnel in both arms . . . a Blighty," which meant he had received a wound that wouldn't incapacitate him for life, but did require his evacuation from the front line to England, "old Blighty."*

Pte. Moyer explained finally that he had no Blighty, just some scrapes from the barbed wire in No Man's Land. He would stay on with the 1st Battalion at the front for the coming assault.

## April 8, 1917—32nd Battery, 9th Brigade Headquarters, Vimy

That Easter Sunday the weather was spring-like—sunny, balmy, and just windy enough to dry some of the muddy roads. Throughout the day, anybody who was moving was doing so underground, although Royal Flying Corps pilots reported that during a lull in the Allied bombardment that day, they could plainly see German troops scrambling forward to reinforce their support and reserve trenches. By now all the rehearsing over tapes had ended. Most of the counter-

---

* The word "Blighty" actually comes from the Hindustani word bilayati, meaning foreign, especially European.

battery shelling was complete. The horse and mule trains had delivered as many artillery shells for the coming rolling barrage as had been exploded on German defences during the previous two weeks. Railway bed construction, trench repair, subway extension, and sap digging were complete. All twenty-five miles of communication cable were buried. All 2,600 miles of telegraph and telephone wire were laid and tested.

A couple of days earlier, Sgt. Signaller F.J. Godfrey had met with one of his senior officers at the 32nd Battery site, near the 9th Brigade headquarters. The captain had reminded Godfrey he would be responsible for any and all communication arrangements once the main assault began, now set for Easter Monday. Godfrey knew that existing forward observation posts were fully operational. He was, however, worried about the Observation Posts ("O. Pips") with artillery observers who would have to join the infantry advance and go beyond the limits of the installed communication lines. Godfrey deduced that the 32nd and its sister batteries connected with 9th Brigade would need new line laid as their O. Pips men dashed forward with the infantry advance on Monday.

"We need two miles of D.3 wire for the advance," he told the quartermaster at brigade headquarters.

"There is no wire to be had," the man said.

Godfrey was beside himself and wrote in his diary: "Talk about the Israelites having to make bricks without straw. Here was I with an important scrap coming off and a couple of miles of wire to lay forward and couldn't get any at all."

Not ready to be stymied, Godfrey noticed that several hundred yards from the brigade location battery engineers were digging a deep pit. He learned this pit would become the new brigade headquarters. He also noticed plenty of heavily insulated cable on wooden reels lying nearby; the engineers planned to bury the cable as communication lines for the new headquarters. Godfrey suddenly had an idea. Fortunately, the sector was alive with men scurrying back and forth with equipment in last-minute preparations for Zero Hour. So he assembled a section of his signallers and gave them instructions for an emergency mission to liberate the necessary wire from the construction pit.

"Was I in a sweat! There was only a blanket hung up for a door to hide the light and keep some of the cold out," Godfrey said as he recalled entering the engineers' dugout around midnight with a water bottle full of rum in hand. "I had to talk very loud. . . . I could hear the odd grunt and scrape as the signals boys heaved the reels up outside. But all went well and when the necessary time had elapsed I made my adieus to the engineers and rejoined my pals."

No doubt the 9th Brigade engineers eventually discovered the missing extra wire. But by then Sgt. Godfrey and his signallers had lugged those precious reels aboard one of the hundreds of carts rumbling up to the forward lines, trenches, and subways during those last nights just before the main assault. In the dark, they laid the heavy cables across and in the shell-pitted mud holes approaching the ridge. They ditched the cart, buried the empty reels in a shell hole, and made it back to the battery before daybreak. Then on Easter Sunday "away out in full view of Fritzie, my signallers coiled up the lighter wires, brought them in and repaired breaks in the insulation, etc.

"Apart from being exposed all the time to the odd shell and getting smothered in mud, those lads had risked court martial . . . [but] we had made ready for the advance."

## April 8, 1917—3rd Bavarian Reserve Regiment sector, Vimy

Despite such snafus in Allied ranks, those on the other side of Vimy Ridge began playing into the hands of the Canadian Corps' plans for Easter Monday. Not that the Germans underestimated the capabilities of their opponents at Vimy. On the contrary, captured documents signed by German Gen. von Bacmeister indicated "there are no deserters to be found among the Canadians." The difference, however, stemmed from contrasting strategies at upper levels of the German Army.

Operating on the principle that the defensive is often more powerful than the offensive, by March 18, Gen. Erich Ludendorff, German Chief of Staff, had completed "Operation Alberich," a German withdrawal to a "final" position behind the Somme battlefield. This so-called Siegfried or Hindenburg Line would shorten the Germans' Western Front trench system and free up as many as ten divisions for posting elsewhere. In addition, along vital stretches of the Western Front, a new German defensive strategy took shape—deeper, more widely separated trenches, greater emphasis on defensive weaponry, not infantry, but greater accessibility to fresh troops for counterattacks where needed. To that end, Ludendorff strongly urged Col.-Gen. Ludwig von Falkenhausen, commander of the Sixth Army, to move reserves forward to meet a looming threat at Vimy Ridge.

There was no question an attack was coming. Even the overall commander of the German Army Group, Crown Prince Rupprecht of Bavaria, predicted it would come. But when? On March 26, in the first week of Allied shelling, Rupprecht wrote in his war diary that "an attack against the heights of Vimy seems likely." His suspicions seemed confirmed when, again in his diary, he wrote that "a captured Canadian stated that after six to ten days of artillery preparation the attack on Vimy Ridge would be launched." Ultimately, however, he decided "the reserve divisions will remain where they are and will not move without a personal order from me. . . . I am firmly convinced that this year all enemy offensives will fail."

As the German generals bickered, the German rank and file suffered. Early on during the Allied bombardment, members of the 79th Reserve Division—at the very centre of the German defensive line—had counted between 12,000 and 15,000 artillery shells crashing into their forward positions. After that, the troops of the Division's 261st, 262nd, and 263rd Regiments lost count. The commander of the 79th, Generalleutnant Alfred Dieterich, noted that in addition to the defensive trenches and deeply buried communication cables, Allied shelling had smashed villages, roads, and an observation balloon anchorage in German-held territory east of the ridge.

"Since the beginning of April, there existed no more possibility of repairing destruction caused by the bombardment," Dieterich wrote. "In concert with the predominantly wet weather, the positions were soon transformed into a crater-field of thick mud, in which only a few shelters escaped destruction."

Farther to the southeast, in the trenches manned by the 3rd Bavarian Reserve Regiment, infantryman Michael Volkheimer, recorded that after fourteen days of uninterrupted barrage from Allied artillery of every calibre, "the enemy finally levelled our defensive positions—the first line, second line and third line." He described the German defenders' desperate attempts to find shelter from the bombardment as far underground as their dugouts could take them. "But soon," he concluded, "the entrances were blown in and many soldiers buried alive."

## Pre-dawn April 9, 1917—Cobourg Subway, 4th Division sector, Vimy

As the battalions kitted up in Allied tunnels before the attack, every soldier's equipment weight began to increase. Each Canadian Corps infantryman's field service orders required him to wear his helmet and carry a box gas mask, an overcoat or leather jerkin, his Lee Enfield rifle* with bayonet and 120 cartridges, a pick or shovel, four Mills bombs (hand grenades), two unfilled sandbags, a haversack on his back with two days' rations and an iron ration, two aeroplane flares, a Verey light, a candle, a box of matches, and his mess tin slung outside the haversack. The entire kit could add 50 or 60 pounds to his overall weight.

Early Easter Sunday morning, in the damp, crowded conditions of Cobourg Subway, infantryman Ray Crowe prepared an additional load for his eventual charge over the top. A former band drummer with the 72nd (Seaforth Highlanders) Battalion, Crowe had served as a rifleman at the Somme. At Vimy, however, he and another half-dozen members of the 4th Division battalion band had retrained over the tapes at Chateau de la Haie as ammunition carriers. Each

---

* By 1916, the Canadian Corps had discarded the Ross rifle (notorious for jamming in muddy conditions) in favour of the Lee Enfield rifle.

man carried four panniers of shells for the Lewis machine guns in his section. Crowe took some solace in knowing he would not go over the top until the second wave. But then, in the final nighttime hours before the attack, he found himself on an unexpected mission. Suddenly, the battalion's commanding officer appeared in the tunnel and approached Crowe.

"Drummer," Lt.-Col. Jim Clark said, "are you ready?"

"I think so, sir," Crowe said.

"Come with me."

The C.O. proceeded up the subway and out into the jumping-off trenches where the rest of the Seaforths were gathering and preparing for the assault. It was customary that such rounds be made by more than one person, so Clark chose his drummer to accompany him. Crowe followed as the commander made his way along the whole serpentine line of troops waiting for Zero Hour.

"I followed him out into the trenches," Crowe said. "There were places where the trench wasn't any deeper than waist high, so he was down on his hands and knees. I was too, of course. But he went right down the line and visited every man out there on the front line . . . that night."

Even though he was sitting in a tunnel close to the front trenches in the 4th Division sector Easter Monday morning, Art Castle knew he wasn't going over the top in the first wave. His turn would come— in the second wave—twenty minutes after the creeping barrage began. Reassuring perhaps, he thought, but the waiting gave him time to reflect on his time at Vimy. He recalled the fatalistic conversation he'd had with his buddy George Parker, a baseball player originally from Hawaii.

"Parker says to me going over on the boat, 'I'm not coming back. I'm not coming back.' Sure enough when we got up to the ridge, he must have put his head up and got sniped. He was one of the first, if not the first [in our 47th Battalion] to be killed on Vimy Ridge."

The thought of Parker's premonition spooked Castle for a while in the early hours of the morning. The waiting also allowed Pte. Castle some time to carry out what had become a mandatory practice among men of the Canadian Corps. Partly because the troops needed to wear gumboots for extended periods of time, their feet would sometimes swell and they would develop trench foot. The condition had become such a problem that winter, that if a soldier was evacuated for treatment of trench foot, his entire unit would be punished by forfeiting its leave for months at a time.

"Stretcher bearers would come around with a pail of whale oil," Castle said. "We had to massage our feet to get the circulation going. Some of the boys were so tired and didn't obey the orders and went out with trench foot. In some cases their feet were amputated."

So just before Zero Hour, Art Castle killed some of the waiting time by following orders and massaging his feet with the ice-cold whale oil that the stretcher bearers had brought in by the jugful. Twenty-four hours later, Art Castle would nearly lose his legs in a shell-hole explosion during the attack up the slope of the Pimple.

In the pre-dawn darkness, a machine-gun crew made its way forward toward the same 4th Division tunnels and trenches. Like Pte. Castle, Sgt. Ed Russenholt knew he would not have to leap into No Man's Land until the first wave had achieved its objectives under the creeping barrage at dawn. During the Vimy training, Russenholt was assigned to a Lewis gun section of the 44th (Manitoba) Battalion. His machine-gun unit had also practised over tapes at Chateau de la Haie, where they had learned to clear dugouts, bring forward cans of water (to cool the guns) and panniers of ammunition, and establish Canadian sniper posts with each move forward. He had even been to Bouvigny to view a scale model of Vimy showing the terrain, bridges, roads, and villages of the entire area. Now it was time to bring all that training forward to the front and await his turn to fight. Sgt. Russenholt's walk with his crew mates in the middle of the night was a contemplative one. The battalion crossed a farm field where they passed a Canadian-made Frost & Wood binder. Russenholt thought of his Manitoba home.

"For a few quick moments my mind saw the beautiful Swan River Valley, where we had harvested our first grain crop with a little six-foot Frost & Wood binder," Russenholt wrote. He imagined the mid-April thaw with spring runoff everywhere, flocks of geese migrating north and the newly ploughed black soil of Manitoba, "so different from the tumble of yellow mud and battered chalk we were scrambling over."

The period of intensive preparation had clearly buoyed Sgt. Russenholt. After the battering the battalion had taken at the Somme, Lt.-Col. Dick Davis took over as C.O. of the 44th. The cane-swinging commanding officer had told his troops they would become a "fighting unit." The battalion got reinforcements not excuses, intelligence not just orders, and realistic training not parade ground drills. For sergeants such as Russenholt, the new regime had given the whole battalion a shot in the arm. The battalion and the brigade had received one of the toughest assignments—assaulting the Pimple at the far northern end of the ridge. But Russenholt felt passionately that "we had mastered this job and we were the finest troops on earth."

## Pre-Dawn April 9, 1917—Grange Subway Dressing Station, 3rd Division sector, Vimy

Some things about Bill Breckenridge's experience that winter were different from his earlier postings. At Vimy, the former business college graduate now signaller with the 42nd (Royal Highlanders) Battalion got the occasional bath and billet bed behind the lines. Sometimes the sun came out to dry things. And occasionally the rations included fresh food from the nearby countryside. The rest, however, did not change—the strain under shell fire (which he called "windy"), the ubiquitous mud, the sadness of losing "old-timers" who'd been with the regiment from the beginning, and the congestion.

En route to the front he had travelled in a claustrophobic "*8 chevaux ou 40 hommes*" (8 horses or 40 men) boxcar. At Vimy, Breckenridge never stopped feeling cramped. The men slept in tiny funk holes carved into trench walls or over-populated bivvies (huts of sandbag walls and tarpaulin roof). Every trench, tunnel, or roadway to the front—especially just before Zero Hour—suffered from too many people, too many horses, too many supplies, and too little room. War offered nothing but an existence of confinement. Even the French military cemetery near Mont St. Eloi seemed crowded with hundreds of crosses.

In the final hours, it seemed signallers received orders from everybody. Breckenridge carried forward rations for the Black Watch battalion. He helped supply the dressing station in the Grange Subway. Most of Easter Sunday evening, he and a dozen other signallers hauled tins of water to replenish the supply required by medical officers at the dressing station. Every time they passed up or down the tunnel, soldiers were now standing three deep along its walls waiting. More congestion.

In that limited space underground, Breckenridge recalled some of the last-minute rituals and activities in the tunnel and galleys around him. The neighbouring Princess Patricia's Canadian Light Infantry had moved their pipers forward into the front line to play their men over the top. A battalion had brought along nine footballs to be placed on the parapet and eventually kicked across to the German trenches. Finally, Breckenridge overheard conversations that seemed to relieve the tension among his comrades.

"I'm going over this morning," said a corporal, "and I'm not looking for a Blighty or an R.I.P."

"A Blighty will be acceptable for me," another said. "Then a fellow can get away from this mud and water for a while."

"I just want to return," said a third man.

Then Breckenridge recalled the words of his best pal, whom he just called Darky. "When that barrage opens," Darky said, "I'll sure be glad I'm on this side of the fence. Old Fritz will think that Hell has been let loose."

It was Easter Monday. Still dark and growing colder. The moon had slipped below the horizon, and forty-nine battalions of Canadian Corps troops moved silently into their final positions as Zero Hour approached. At a casualty clearing in the 3rd Division sector, Rev. George Kilpatrick worried the dawn attack might be a repeat of his experience at Ypres where the bodies were so numerous "you could only say a sentence of prayer and pass on to the next." Capt. Harry Clyne of the 29th (Vancouver) Battalion, a support battalion in the 6th Brigade, had earlier walked among his troops at their assembly area. There in the protection of a wooded area they had lit small fires and "I saw that night Henry V at Agincourt wandering 'round from little fire to little fire. 'And gentlemen of England now abed, will curse the day they were not here.'" In the 1st Division sector, the paymaster for the 5th Battalion did Clyne one better. F.C. Bagshaw had tried to get some sleep in the subway that last night. Next to him was friend and fellow Saskatchewan volunteer Dave McCabe.

"Bag, I'll tell you what," he said.

"What?" Bagshaw answered.

"I'll recite Robbie Burns and you can recite Shakespeare."

So, in the last hours before the attack, the two men offered any and all of the bards' poetry they could recall. Any of their battalion mates within earshot stopped whatever they were doing and listened.

## 5 a.m. April 9, 1917—Goodman Subway, 3rd Division sector, Vimy

The nervousness underground and jumping off trenches was palpable. Alfred Thomson served with the Trench Mortar Battery attached to the Black Watch. As troops filed into the Goodman Subway around him, he watched them closely. In particular, he noticed the men of the 4th Canadian Mounted Rifles Battalion. They lined up close together and leaned up against the subway walls, and Thomson said he "could tell by their faces, they were apprehensive of what was going to happen."

Pte. Thomson's own nerves were pretty rattled by the tension underground too. His battery crew had spent part of the night preparing its barrels and shells. The mortar-loading process generally left the gunners' hands greasy, so the men had brought a tin of gasoline into the subway to rinse the grease and grime from their hands. In the Goodman Subway—as in most tunnels—electric lights were available only twelve hours a day; then, until gas-operated generators could replenish power, everybody worked by candlelight. During one moment of inattention or haste, somebody knocked a candle over, igniting a small fire.

"In our excitement we upset the tin of gasoline," Thomson said, "and it started running down toward some ammunition boxes. But Askew [one of the mortar crew] saw what was happening, got a blanket and threw it over the flames. He saved a bad accident from happening there."

A short distance away in another 3rd Division holding area underground, David Moir and his 7th Canadian Machine Gun Company crew prepared their weapons. After the guns were sufficiently cleaned and oiled, procedure required the number one gunner to half-cock the gun and press the trigger to release the pressure on the firing spring. The gunner would then half-load the gun so that with one pull on the lever it would be fully loaded and ready to fire. Given the tension of the hour and a tendency to prepare and prepare yet again, a gunner suddenly repeated the process on one of the machine guns, so that when he pressed the trigger to supposedly ease the pressure on the spring, it fired instead.

"At that split second Sgt. Magee happened to pass," Moir said, "and the bullet struck him in the head, killing him instantly. No burial arrangements could be made so his body was placed in a storage room and we all went to bed to try and snatch a few winks of sleep."

To ease the tension he faced, an officer with the 25th Battalion mulled over the battle plan that his regiment had rehearsed again and again at Bruay. Capt. Robert Clements knew that orders had placed his Nova Scotia battalion in the subway system at the centre of the 2nd Division sector directly in front of the ruins of Neuville St. Vaast. Ahead of him outside in 300 yards of moonlit trenches, but not seen by the German defenders, members of the 24th (Victoria Rifles of Montreal) Battalion on the right and the 26th (New Brunswick) Battalion on the left crouched at the ready. At Zero Hour when the creeping barrage began, the 24th and 26th would overrun the enemy front line and press on to their second-line trench, *Zwischen Stel-*

*lung*, as the 25th in close support mopped up the captured ground, brought forward fresh supplies, and rounded up German prisoners.

Clements had written in his notes the critical times and intervals of the rolling barrage—when it would shift and over what enemy ground.

"Zero Hour. 5:30 a.m. April 9, 1917. At Zero, barrage will open and troops will advance to the assault.

"At Zero plus 3 minutes, barrage will lift from German front line.

"At Zero plus 8 minutes, barrage will lift from German support line.

"At Zero plus 32 minutes, barrage will lift from Black Line. . . ."

And so on to the Red Line, the Blue Line, and the Brown Line, if they got that far. As he reviewed the timings associated with each step of the barrage, he contemplated the perils of having to go over the top in the first wave. But he also recognized the real dangers his own battalion in a supporting role might face. "It may seem strange," he wrote, "but in an attack planned this way, there was a brief period when the safest spots were in the leading waves."

Not far from Capt. Clements, in the Goodman Subway, Frank MacGregor prepared himself for the attack too. The rifleman, also with the 25th Battalion, had tried to sleep, but in vain, and had remained awake most of the night, waiting for the final commands. He looked around and recognized that in each trench, in every subway, and in hundreds of roadways and pathways behind them, thousands of Canadian Corps comrades were all conspiring in this extraordinary operation to seize the ridge from the Germans.

"From one o'clock until five-thirty, thousands of men, quiet," MacGregor said. Then he recalled the pivotal moment. "The locking ring on a bayonet is a little loose. When the order to fix bayonets went along the line, you'd think there was a thousand bees humming. The trembling. Waiting."

Four seconds before Zero Hour, the perceptible slackening of the Allied bombardment came to a complete stop. The brief silence was the signal. The waiting was over.

# OUT OF THE HANDS
# OF GENERALS

## 5:30 a.m. April 9, 1917 — Canadian Forward Trenches, Vimy

IT WAS ZERO HOUR. The thunder of a new artillery bombardment was the signal for the infantry battle to begin. When Gus
Sivertz climbed over the parapet on the Canadian side of Vimy
Ridge, several warnings rang in his head. A corporal in the 2nd Canadian Mounted Rifles, Sivertz had come through the training over
the tapes behind the lines well informed. He understood that any
German gun sighted on the open ground ahead of him had a low trajectory, so it was important "to keep right down [and] not let your
buttocks get ripped by bullets." Coming out of the 3rd Division
trenches, he knew he had to move forward with his nose nearly down
in the mud. He and his comrades also knew to move by "column
lumps," not in lines abreast to prevent being cut down in swaths by
German machine-gun fire. Sivertz could still hear Lt.-Gen. Julian
Byng, the C.O. himself, saying, "Chaps, you shall go over exactly like
a railroad train, on the exact time, or you shall be annihilated."
Sivertz understood that he and his comrades needed to walk, and not
run, behind the synchronized creeping barrage. Despite the threats
and warnings, however, Cpl. Sivertz still found this fearsome moment
mesmeric.

"We were dancing a macabre dance as our nerves just vibrated to the thousands of shells and machine gun bullets . . . whizzing over," Sivertz wrote later. "I felt that if I had put my finger up, I should have touched a ceiling of sound."

The ceiling of sound stretched the full length of the Vimy front—nine miles. Nearly a thousand Allied artillery pieces roared almost in unison—a third of them concentrating fire on the forward German trenches, while two-thirds joined the coordinated barrage rolling out ahead of the advancing troops. Adding to the din, 150 machine guns filled in the gaps with indirect harassing fire. A battery sergeant next to an 18-pounder was blown to the ground by the howitzer behind his position, and he described it as "not a bark, or a roar, but like a big cough or whoosh." Men felt the concussion of the shells in their trenches and dugouts, aboveground or below, said a Canadian signaller, "as though a tremendous earthquake was taking place. . . . The battle roared like a mighty furnace." Likening the noise to "a thousand unmuffled motors," a rifleman with the 8th Brigade called it "drum fire [where] there was no intermission of shells large or small." A soldier with the British units on the north flank of the Canadian assault said "the whole atmosphere was rent by screaming shells passing overhead." And for a private soldier writing home to his aunt, "the crash and thunder of the battle smote the senses [and] a light made up of innumerable flickering tongues . . . appeared from the void and extended as far to the south as the eye could see."

Not surprisingly, Nature played a trump card in the stakes for a successful early spring assault. Though Canadian Corps troops had enjoyed clear skies and relatively temperate conditions through Easter Sunday, the pre-dawn hours of Monday brought a sudden downpour and a drop in temperature. Scouts with the 24th (Victoria Rifles of Montreal) Battalion in the forward trenches of the 2nd Division sector reported that the rain had drenched the men—whose battle dress did not permit the use of greatcoats. As the temperature dropped, the winds picked up and the rain turned to a steady snow. Those in the outdoor trenches began to shiver with the damp and cold. There was one saving grace. Unlike the disastrous night of the gas attack on March 1, the prevailing winds were strong and west to east, thus driving the sleet and snow "in the teeth of the enemy." Any German defenders who braved the pounding of the creeping barrage to man their forward trenches faced visibility down to nil.

Despite the deteriorating weather conditions, the number two man on a Lewis gun crew in the 1st Canadian Mounted Rifles witnessed very clearly the quick response of the Germans to the 5:30 shelling. As Pte. Alex Gerrard followed his lead gunner over the top in the 3rd Division sector, the German front lit up ahead of them, not with counter-battery fire, but with a display of coloured flares. In answer to the first curtain of fire from Canadian artillery, troops in the forward German trenches had fired off SOS signals all along the ridge.

"Streaks of reds and yellows and greens—like fireworks," Gerrard said. "It was like a coloured hail storm." The distress signal was designed to bring returning fire from the German batteries down on a gathering infantry attack. But too many German guns located behind the ridge had been destroyed in the Canadian counter-battery campaign of the previous two weeks and only a handful answered the distress call to slow the mounting Canadian assault. In fact, twenty-one-year-old Pte. Gerrard soon realized that his CMR buddies had more to fear from the falling Canadian shells than any German ones.

"Some of the boys got going faster than the shells and they hit a lot of our men with 'friendly' shrapnel," Gerrard said. "They got caught in the barrage from the batteries behind us."

## 5:30 a.m. April 9, 1917—Canadian Trenches, 1st Division sector, Vimy

*The veteran 1st Canadian Infantry Division, under Maj.-Gen. Arthur Currie's command, faced the longest stretch of No Man's Land to cover that morning in the southernmost sector of the Canadian attack. It was more than 4,000 yards to Farbus wood, a forest just beyond the southeastern lip of Vimy Ridge, where the Germans had positioned a number of their artillery batteries. The 1st Division's orders were to overrun the first three German*

*trench lines—the Black Line on their battle maps—then the* Zwischen
Stellung *trench system—the Red Line—then another set of trenches—the
Blue Line—and finally capture Farbus wood—the Brown Line—near the
outskirts of the town of Farbus. The plan called for the 1st, 2nd, and 3rd
Brigades of the division to reach the final objective by early afternoon.*

Just before he entered No Man's Land that morning, Lt. Cyril Jones
with the 16th Battalion in the 1st Division sector, exchanged words
of encouragement with his friends and battalion mates, Mac Mc-
Gowen and Archie Cornell. The three men had known each other
since enlistment and training together with the 113th Battalion from
southern Alberta. Jones had left the Bank of Commerce in Calgary to
join up and was posted to the 16th (Canadian Scottish) Battalion
when he got to France. At Vimy, Jones referred to his troops as the
"moppers-up," those assigned to plug the holes as the first wave advanced. As Jones wished McGowen luck, they both leapt into No
Man's Land; it was the last time Jones saw his friend McGowen alive.

"There came one big crash," Jones wrote, "as the whole weight of
our artillery swept the Hun line and we walked out following under
our barrage. It was a wonderful sight. . . . Lines of Canadian soldiers
with intervals between, and on our right a Scottish division with the
kilts swaying and bayonets fixed."

Several thoughts crossed Fred James's mind when his turn came
to join the assault on Vimy Ridge. As a junior officer with the 2nd
(Eastern Ontario) Battalion, also in the 1st Division sector, even if
he felt scared by the explosions and blinding flashes around him, he
ought not show it. Lt. James had only been over the top two or three
times before. Still he desperately tried to exude in his steps through
No Man's Land what the book prescribed for officers as "a look of
calmness and resoluteness." James also had a passion to record the
events he witnessed this day. As a member of the press gallery on Parliament Hill before the war, James carried with him to France that
drive to record and report. He wanted to put these additional skills
to good use. So, when he had the chance, he recalled his first impres-

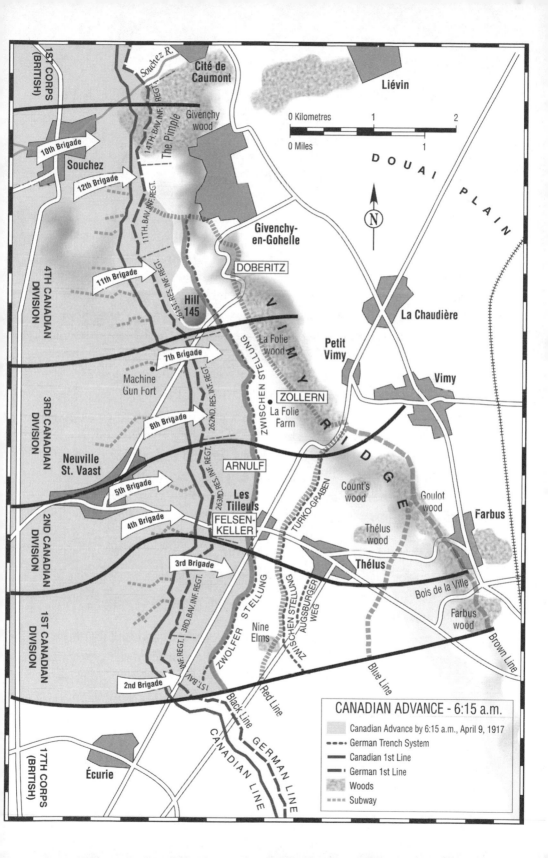

1ST CORPS
(BRITISH)

Souchez R.

Cité de
Caumont

Liévin

14TH BAV. INF. REGT.

Givenchy
wood

The Pimple

D O U A I   P L A I N

10th Brigade

Souchez

0 Kilometres    1    2

0 Miles    1

12th Brigade

11TH. BAV. INF. REGT.

4TH CANADIAN DIVISION

11th Brigade

Givenchy-
en-Gohelle

N

DOBERITZ

261ST. RES. INF. REGT.

Hill
145

V
I
M
Y

La Chaudière

La Folie
wood

Petit
Vimy

3RD CANADIAN DIVISION

7th Brigade

Machine
Gun Fort

262ND. RES. INF. REGT.

ZWISCHEN STELLUNG

ZOLLERN

La Folie
Farm

Vimy

R
I
D
G
E

8th Brigade

Neuville
St. Vaast

5th Brigade

263RD. RES. INF. REGT.

ARNULF

Count's
wood

Goulot
wood

Farbus

2ND CANADIAN DIVISION

4th Brigade

Les
Tilleuls

FELSEN-
KELLER

TURKO-GRABEN

Thélus
wood

3rd Brigade

ZWISCHEN STELLUNG

AUGSBURGER WEG

Thélus

Bois de la Ville

1ST CANADIAN DIVISION

1ST. BAV. INF. REGT.

3RD. BAV. INF. REGT.

ZWOLFER STELLUNG

Nine
Elms

ZW.

Farbus
wood

Brown Line

Blue Line

2nd Brigade

Black Line

Red Line

17TH CORPS
(BRITISH)

Écurie

CANADIAN LINE

GERMAN LINE

CANADIAN ADVANCE - 6:15 a.m.

Canadian Advance by 6:15 a.m., April 9, 1917

German Trench System

Canadian 1st Line

German 1st Line

Woods

Subway

sions of the mighty roar of guns he heard behind him and the flashes of flame illuminating the pre-dawn sky ahead of him.

"It is as if Hell itself has been uncorked," James wrote. And when he saw the German SOS flares he added, "It was a display that made the [Canadian National] Exhibition seem like a joke. It made me think how foolish I had been to pay 25 cents to see some sputtering illuminants."

In the weeks leading up to Zero Hour, Canadian and British sappers and pioneers had detonated no fewer than 200 mines beneath the slopes of Vimy Ridge. Their explosions and implosions had left the already minced landscape of the gradual western slope to the top of the ridge pocked with huge craters, some as big as a house. Some of the older craters had been named by former British and French troops—Duffield, Crassiers, and Durrand. Other craters owed their names to the more recently arrived Canadians: the Patricia crater, blown and seized by the PPCLI; the Montreal crater, captured by the Royal Highlanders of Montreal; and the Phillip crater, which when blown open would put undetected Canadian troops two-thirds the way across No Man's Land. However, the mining troops, who had so painstakingly burrowed beneath the German forward trenches for months, left their biggest show for Zero Hour. Within seconds of the start of the 5:30 artillery barrage, the sappers detonated two massive mines that blew some of the forward trenches of the Bavarian Infantry Regiment sky-high and allowed Canadian troops of the 1st Division easy access to enemy parapets. Among the first into the new craters was George Alliston from the 7th (British Columbia) Battalion.

"Before the stuff had stopped falling, we had to man the lip of the crater that was caused," Alliston said. And he described the racket of the explosions as "ten thousand thunders," while his battalion mate, Arthur Pollard called the curtain of fire around him "Dante's Inferno."

The inferno of Canadian artillery blasts, mixed with those from the German side, quickly took their toll. A shell fell beside Pollard, striking his platoon commander. Pollard stopped long enough to bandage his wounds, but the man soon died. Minutes later, Pollard arrived at the first German trenches and found a Bavarian soldier trembling on the ground. He took the German's rifle, threw it away, and booted him in the backside, directing him toward the next wave of advancing Canadian troops. Alliston also came face to face with a German soldier calling out to him.

"*Wasser*," the man cried.

Pte. Alliston understood the man just wanted a drink of water.

"*Wasser, bitte*," he continued.

Alliston just hurried this surrendering soldier, like other Germans in his path, in the direction of the Canadian troops mopping up in his wake. He said he had a bottle of water, but "I didn't have the guts to give him any water."

Also quickly out of the Canadian forward trenches was Percy Twidale. At age twenty-five, Pte. Twidale was considered one of "the originals," an old-timer, by those still eighteen and nineteen and recently added to the ranks of the 16th Battalion. The Canadian Scottish had drawn a first-wave assignment with the 3rd Brigade in the 1st Division attack. Twidale was fully prepared. After all, he and many of his comrades had arrived at Vimy early in the winter as an entrenching battalion; throughout January, February, and March of 1917, they had prepared the grade for the narrow-gauge railway, repaired trenches left decrepit by previous Allied troops, and buried the main communication lines forward in preparation for the Easter attack.

"We got to know every part of that front," Twidale said, "which was a great help on the day of action. I was in the first wave over and we got across the first trenches to a sunken road when a big piece of shell casing hit my rifle. Bent it over double. So I picked up another rifle from someone that had fallen. . . ."

In the instant that he leaned over to take his dead comrade's Lee Enfield, Twidale felt his leg buckle. A bullet or a piece of shrapnel had gone clear through his shinbone, though he said he didn't feel it right away. Purely on adrenaline, Twidale managed to reach the next set of trenches, where he captured six Germans. Since he was wounded, he was detailed to escort the prisoners back behind Canadian lines.

"After I had delivered the prisoners to the internment area," Twidale said, "I walked into a dressing station and sat down. I didn't know until I tried to get up again that my leg was broken."

Rapid access to ground deep in No Man's Land via the subways, combined with the devastating impact of the creeping barrage, had given the first wave of Canadian assault troops the upper hand. Twidale and others in the ranks of the 16th Battalion reported the effects of the barrage were the "best ever," an assessment borne out by those in the German forward trenches facing Canadian troops in the 1st Division sector. War diarists for the German 268th Reserve Regiment reported that many of their machine gunners emerged from dugouts to find most gun positions destroyed or inoperable. They described having to resort to a hand-grenade battle amid the craters in front of their trenches. Calls for reinforcements went unheeded but the German defenders in this sector fought on stubbornly.

"The first position became impossible to hold," the diary said. "Death had a rich harvest."

It was here that some of the manoeuvres that Canadian Corps troops had rehearsed over the tapes in March at Chateau de la Haie, Mont St. Eloi, and Bois de Bruay came into play—the fire and movement tactics of outflanking enemy positions. Bill Milne, a private with the 16th Battalion, carried the requisite number of Mills bombs in his haversack up from the trenches in front of Zivy Subway. When the machine guns first cut into his fellow Canadian Scottish attackers, Milne went to ground. Using those prescribed flanking tactics for taking out the gun, he crawled through shell holes and around bodies off to one side of the gun emplacement. He managed to remain undetected until he was close enough to use the grenades. He leapt to his feet, hurled the Mills bombs into the midst of the German gunners, rushed the survivors firing his rifle and put the gun position out of action.

By 6:15 a.m., only ten minutes later than planned, members of the 2nd and 3rd Brigades reached their first 1st Division objective—the third German line of defence, the Black Line. As his battalion re-formed and advanced toward the second objective, *Zwischen Stellung*, Milne stalked another machine-gun nest in a similar fashion, saving many more lives. However, while making his way to the third objective, Milne was killed in action. For "conspicuous bravery and devotion to duty" in sustaining the Canadian advance, Pte. Milne earned the Victoria Cross this day.

## 5:30 a.m. April 9, 1917—Canadian Trenches, 2nd Division sector, Vimy

*The 2nd Canadian Infantry Division sector covered the centre of the Canadian Corps front at Vimy. Commanded by Maj.-Gen. Henry Burstall, the division's 4th, 5th, and 6th Brigades had to cover about two miles to reach their final objective. Plans called for the first wave to roll over the forward three defensive German trenches—the Black Line—and through the remains of the town of Les Tilleuls to the* Turko-Graben *trench system (an extension of the* Zwischen Stellung*)—the Red Line—just short of the top of Vimy Ridge. Then fresh troops would pick up the attack at that halfway point and carry the division over the ridge and down the eastern slope as far as the forested areas of Count's wood and Thélus wood—the Blue Line—up to outskirts of the town of Farbus—the Brown Line on their army maps.*

At Zero Hour when explosives blew open the blind end of the sap leading from the Zivy Subway and cave to the Phillip crater, a team of pioneers, signallers, sappers, and officers from the 2nd Division suddenly looked out into a massive open pit. They were hundreds of yards in front of their own advancing comrades. More surprising, there appeared to be no Germans manning the far side of the crater. Moments later, the Allied barrage rolled over the crater and one of the Canadian officers got on the telephone line connecting him to a 4th Brigade communication galley back in Zivy. The man "had the extraordinary experience of seeing our own troops advancing toward him and kept reporting their progress. . . . Some of our men . . . took him for an enemy and peppered him with grenades so that he had to take cover." But as soon as the first wave passed them by, the Canadian pioneers leapt from the tunnel and began another six-foot bury. By nightfall they would have a telephone cable trenched all the way to the Lens-Arras road, nearly a thousand yards inside once German-occupied territory.

Royden Barbour had intimate knowledge of the shell holes and craters in front of his jumping-off trench in the 2nd Division sector. He came to the front line as a reinforcement for the 25th Battalion, made up of Nova Scotians; his company consisted mostly of Cape Breton miners. Within a few days of his arrival at Vimy, the young subaltern from New Brunswick was sent up a long sap tunnel to an outpost on the edge of a crater in No Man's Land. During his twenty-eight-day posting, he had regularly spotted a German sentry—his equivalent—on the far side of the crater. But because of what Barbour called "a gentleman's agreement," neither sentry had precipitated any action against the other.

Suddenly, all that changed Easter Monday morning when he stepped out of the blown sap and witnessed the "curtain of shells" striking the far side of that same crater. He noted the timing and placement of the shells—"the perfection of it all"—and then everything went black. He had taken shrapnel in the side and back of his body, and when he awoke he lay in one of those same craters he'd been assigned to the previous month.

"Nobody found me," he said. "The troops had moved beyond me. And there wasn't much traffic through that particular crater at the time," but eventually Lt. Barbour managed to drag himself out of the crater. Still nobody spotted him. Fortunately, by that time, some of the tunnel entrances had been marked with flags to guide runners, stretcher bearers, and the wounded back to friendly lines. The lieutenant crawled to a tunnel entrance and inside to an aid post where medics finally treated his wounds.

Charles Dale's combat record may well have been even shorter than Barbour's. The eighteen-year-old private had actually arrived at Vimy as a reinforcement for the 26th (New Brunswick) Battalion only nine days before the attack. His crash training course alerted him to the creeping barrage and the need for his 15th Platoon to advance in the "column clumps" style. However, within the first minutes of his advance, a German artillery shell landed two yards from his section. Dale took shrapnel in his right thigh that shattered his femur instantly. The man behind him took shrapnel at the top of his boot. Both soldiers were in great pain. While Dale encouraged the other man to crawl with him back to the jumping-off trench he couldn't, so Dale made his own way there and sheltered himself near some sandbags. It was six hours before he next saw anyone. Suddenly, there were Germans around him. They were prisoners—twelve of them—walking toward the Canadian trenches.

"I'll carry you," said one of the Germans in clear English.

"All right," Dale agreed.

The German then hoisted him on his back and continued walking.

"I can't stand the pain," Dale said. "You better put me back where I was."

The man did exactly as Dale asked. Eventually stretcher bearers happened along, wrapped his leg wound, and carried him to a dressing station. He had a severe Blighty that would take a year to fully heal. But he had survived the first-wave attack on Vimy Ridge. "I got lucky," Dale said. "I never had to kill anybody."

Discomforting thoughts of killing with a fixed bayonet, being wounded in the groin or gassed in No Man's Land without access to a mask—there were plenty of horrific thoughts if a soldier let his imagination play with what he'd seen or heard. But Claude Williams, in command of a gun crew in the 6th Brigade Machine Gun Company, used thoughts of the job at hand as an antidote. He had to ensure that his twenty-five-man gun crew—gun carrier, tripod carrier, spare parts carriers, water carriers (for cooling the gun), and ammunition carriers—all knew the drill once out in No Man's Land. He had to review orders issued to the 27th (Winnipeg) Battalion to which his gun crew was attached. And just before Zero Hour, he had to make sure all watches were synchronized for the creeping barrage.

Capt. Williams could have avoided going over in the first wave with the rest of the 2nd Division. The sector needed stationary gun crews to provide the harassing indirect fire over the heads of the Canadian assault troops during the creeping barrage. But the former medical student from Hamilton decided he had not come all this way to miss "the show." Consequently, he and fellow gunner Jim Stone-hewer agreed to flip a coin. Williams won the toss and chose to go forward with the infantry. Once over the top, Williams discovered the slow pace of the walk, described by some as "the Vimy glide," as the initial difficulty to overcome; the adrenaline in all that noise and light tended to move troops faster. But soon enough, the enemy pro-vided other more tangible barriers to the gun crew's advance—tear gas, some return machine-gun fire, and trench mortars.

"The orders were that under no circumstances was anybody to stop to do anything for the wounded—to help them, carry them out, doing anything—it would break up the line," Williams said. "We came to one deep shell hole and there was a Canadian in there. He was calling out, 'Water, water.' . . . I looked down and here the whole top of his head was off. You could see his brains. He was dying of course. You couldn't do anything for him, not even give him water. You had to keep going. . . ."

## 5:30 a.m. April 9, 1917—Canadian Trenches, 3rd Division sector, Vimy

*The 3rd Canadian Infantry Division, to the left (north) of the 2nd, faced an advance of approximately 1,200 yards to achieve its final objective. With Maj.-Gen. Louis James Lipsett commanding, the division's 7th and 8th Brigades planned to capture a large treed area—La Folie wood—just beyond the crest of Vimy Ridge as well as what was left of La Folie Farm. On a grade that was slightly steeper than the slope in front of the 1st and 2nd Divisions, the 3rd would again cross the first three German defensive lines—including the Black Line—and press on to La Folie wood—the Red*

*Line in its sector. The one hazard that most planners overlooked was Hill
145 and the German guns that could strike the 3rd Division's exposed left
flank.*

Greg Clark lost the hearing in his left ear at Vimy. In April 1916, the
junior reporter for the *Toronto Daily Star* had persuaded his editor to
send him to cover enlistment activities at one of the city armouries.
Calculating that Clark's 106-pound, five-foot-three-inch stature would
make him an unlikely specimen for the army, his editor let Clark go
to get the story. Once he'd arrived at the armoury, however, Clark
found a sympathetic recruiting officer who allowed him to sign up as
a private on the Canadian Army's general list. By the time his training
was complete, Clark had a commission and a posting to the 3rd Division with the 4th Canadian Mounted Rifles. He caught up with his
regiment as it prepared for the attack on Vimy Ridge in early 1917.

The experience changed him physically; the cold and wet front-
line conditions and the noise of machine guns and artillery had deaf-
ened him in one ear. But while the result was physically debilitating,
Lt. Clark claimed the Vimy campaign and the war enlarged him in
mind and spirit. He attributed his individual survival and the overall
success of operations such as Vimy to the community of men closest
to him.

"The grand strategy," Clark wrote, "is all great formations and
groups. Do you know, it isn't even battalions that engage in battle?
A battalion goes in and the sections of five or six men with a lance-
corporal leading them. A little band of brothers . . . The minute the
battle begins—at zero hour—it is out of the hands of generals . . . who
sit back in their dugouts with their telephones, listening desperately
with this catch-as-catch-can signalling. . . . It is the sections doing the
thinking and the planning. . . .

"The battle is won . . . by lance-jacks and their five or six boys."

The first twenty minutes of Jules De Cruyenaere's experience
that morning reflect that "band of brothers" reality. Cpl. De Cruyenaere and a fellow rifleman named MacGregor went over the top
with one of Greg Clark's sister regiments, the 1st Canadian Mounted

Rifles, in the same 3rd Division sector. Their sergeant had doled out a tot of rum to the men in his platoon to ward off the chill in the forward trenches. Whether it was the rum or the adrenaline, De Cruyenaere and MacGregor dashed ahead too quickly and found they had caught up to the trailing edge of the rolling barrage. They witnessed the power of the shelling at close range. One explosion lifted a massive tree trunk ahead of them twenty feet in the air. They did, however, benefit from the element of surprise. The two men quickly came across German trenches abandoned because of the shelling. MacGregor stood guard at the entrance to an adjoining dugout, while De Cruyenaere called on his conversational German to draw out his enemy.

"I give you two minutes to come up and surrender," he shouted in German into the darkness. "Canadian soldiers are here waiting."

In seconds the first German emerged with his hand over a wound. "My arm is sore," he told De Cruyenaere.

"Go back down," the Canadian told the wounded soldier, "and bring up the rest of your comrades, or else."

Eight more Germans filed out. As the two Canadians searched for weapons, De Cruyenaere demanded a souvenir.

"I have a picture of my mother, brother, and sister," he said.

A few minutes later, another group of 1st CMRs caught up to De Cruyenaere and MacGregor, and the two men passed their now thirty prisoners of war along to the mop-up troops.

Meanwhile, a sap face blown open in front of Grange Subway allowed troops of the 3rd Division to pour into Duffield and Durrand craters and advance quickly eastward, while wounded could eventually be evacuated via the tunnel the opposite way. The creeping barrage ahead of Canadian storm troops consisted of the heaviest continuous artillery fire of the war. "We fired two thousand rounds per gun and ruined them in the process," the 31st Battery war diarist said. "The guns were red-hot with oil from the recoil cylinders spurting out. It was the last time gun fire was unlimited." As the Allied barrage from the 3rd Division batteries crashed into the German

*Zollern* sector (in front of La Folie Farm), some of the surviving 262nd Reserve Regiment gunners dashed to their machine-gun pillboxes and began returning fire at the Canadians.

"There is heavy drum-fire," reported one German fusilier facing the Canadian attackers. "The day sentries shouted: 'Outside! The British are coming!' We jumped up, all the tiredness gone. . . . While I was handing out hand grenades, in the trench the shooting had already started. The English—they are Canadian troops—had broken through on our left," but not without taking heavy casualties—30 to 50 percent according to one German account.

In some cases, the members of the 7th and 8th Brigades walked over the first and second German lines of defence without even realizing it. The weeks of Allied bombardment and the additional pounding from the creeping barrage had erased much of the German front lines. Instead of intricate trench works, crenellated like the top of a castle chess piece to prevent any invader a clear line of fire, all that remained were muddy depressions and the smell of expended explosives. Cpl. Gus Sivertz and the rest of his 2nd Canadian Mounted Rifles section came across those former trenches just as an incoming German shell landed and buried itself in the mud a few yards away.

"I felt that I'd be on the road west in a moment," he said, meaning that he thought he was about to die. "Instead, I was just knocked over again and, in rising, got a terrific slam on the top of my head. . . . A huge chunk of chalk that the shell had blown skyward was coming down as I came up." The only damage was a bump on his head where his helmet had been rammed down around his ears "just like a lot of those Charlie Chaplin pictures." However, the episode had delayed him enough that Sivertz was suddenly alone, feeling as if every German gun on the Western Front were pointed at him. So he rushed ahead to catch the rest of his gun crew.

Nearby, another crewman with the 2nd CMRs stood on the former first defensive line of his German opponents and looked back to the Canadian jumping-off trenches in awe. "It put me in mind of an anthill," G. Dorman said. "As far as I could see it was just alive with glittering bayonets, and boy, did I have courage."

## 5:30 a.m. April 9, 1917—Canadian Trenches, 4th Division sector, Vimy

*On the far left of the Canadian Corps front, the 4th Canadian Infantry Division looked at the shortest distance to cross—700 yards—to its final objective, but the steepest run and, as it turned out, the most fortified German defences. Under the command of Maj.-Gen. David Watson, the division's 10th, 11th, and 12th Brigades faced Gibraltar-like opposition. On either edge of its attack sector, the ground rose to two prominent summits—Hill 145 on the right and the Pimple (120 metres high) on the left—both located on the attack map's Black Line. The plan of attack called for successive waves in stepping-up fashion to seize Hill 145 and the ground to the north of Hill 145 and once consolidated there to launch a final assault against the Pimple on the following day.*

Victory in the 4th Division sector depended on the troops' successful ascent to the high ground that bookended the 3,000-yard front line. Battalions needed to be at maximum strength and efficiency. That was not the case here. It had only been slightly over a month since the disastrous March 1 gas attack by troops of the 4th Division. Its depleted ranks—nearly 700 casualties, including two battalion commanders killed—therefore reduced the division's potency. In addition, despite the Allied counter-battery bombardment during the run-up to Zero Hour, Canadian strategists had under-estimated the resiliency of the German positions atop Hill 145 and the Pimple. The concrete-encased positions on the heights remained largely undamaged by Canadian artillery fire. Even during the creeping barrage its defenders could return fire from shielded machine-gun nests.

Adding to the already formidable problems of the attack plan in this 11th Brigade sector, at the last minute, the acting commanding officer of the 87th Battalion apparently managed to convince Canadian gunners not to include the German's second line of defence between Hill 145 and the Pimple in the 5:30 a.m. barrage. Major Harry Shaw reasoned that his Grenadier Guards of Montreal could capture the German line, just 150 yards away, more easily if Canadian guns didn't reduce the position to rubble and make the uphill assault tougher. When captured intact, Shaw argued, the position would offer Canadian attackers shelter from the higher positions to the right and left and a jumping-off point to continue the assault.

The theory was dead wrong and a death sentence to the lower ranks given the job of taking Shaw's objective. German gunners in the unmolested strongpoint saw "dense columns of Englishmen . . . toiling across the muck desert . . . and everywhere Germans came up and opened fire," one German war diarist wrote. Within six minutes the defenders had felled half the Grenadier Guard attackers as "heaps of khaki-yellow corpses piled up in front of the 5th Company."

The intended precision of the Vimy attack fitted Art Farmer's personality. He'd always been a stickler for detail and discipline, whether as a telegraph operator back home for the Grand Trunk Railway or during his time in the front-line trenches trying to stay clean by shaving in leftover tea. Originally a signaller with the 71st Battalion, when they broke up the regiment in England, Farmer chose to serve in signals with the 11th Canadian Machine Gun Company. Eddie Farmer, Art's older brother, had also volunteered with the 71st in Canada, but during his reassignment from the 71st in England was sent to the 102nd Battalion, "Warden's Warriors" from northern British Columbia. Despite attempts to reconnect, from the time each arrived in Belgium and France, the brothers could not reach each other. Until April 9. That morning, just before Zero Hour, the two found themselves in the same trench preparing to go over the top together.

"Going forward, we were loaded down like a Christmas tree," Art Farmer said. "In addition to the pack the ordinary soldier carried, we carried a reel [with] 250 yards of wire. . . . Vimy stands out as the most successful engagement the Canadians ever had."

The Farmer brothers, having both survived Ypres and the Somme, but never side by side during a Canadian attack, once again weathered the maelstrom of fire directed at the 11th Brigade's treacherous climb on the north side of Hill 145. This time they survived together. The Canadian advance in that sector, however, had stalled completely. The German defenders had effectively driven a wedge or salient of resistance into the 4th Division's advance.

For at least one scout in the 75th (Mississauga Horse) Battalion the foundering Canadian attack was déjà vu. Pte. John Quinnell had survived the failed gas attack up Hill 145 on March 1. The brigade and divisional officers, he said, "led us down the garden path" about the disabling effect of poisonous gas and now he feared the same with the "creeping barrage." He went over the top with his sergeant, Teddy Dale, and his best friend, McLaughlin; after weeks of waiting for a tunic to replace the one ruined in the gas attack, McLaughlin had finally received it, and he was wearing it for the first time on April 9.

At Zero Hour, Quinnell heard the Canadian guns "cannonading and the shells going over" and he quickly looked back to see flickering lights of the artillery firing from behind. But a few steps toward the objective—the north slope of Hill 145—Pte. Quinnell watched in horror as the barrage seemed to disappear.

"We were a hundred yards up the hill and the Germans were coming out of the galleries and passages," he said. "They had machine guns and were slaughtering us. . . . We tried to take shelter, but the Germans were too close. McLaughlin was lying against the edge of the depression . . . blood and froth coming from his mouth, dripping onto his new tunic."

Then came the Germans' grenades. Quinnell managed to find some refuge in a German refuse pit, but their "potato masher" hand grenades came hurtling into the crater. The resulting explosions buried him in bodies and debris, "so the war went on around me and I couldn't do anything about it. I was pinned down." He would lie there most of the day until he eventually was evacuated to a casualty clearing station en route to ambulances and hospitals on the French coast.

Farther to the left, in the 12th Brigade advance, where the rolling barrage was allowed to go ahead, the craters that had provided Bill Milne ample cover to attack a machine-gun nest in the 1st Division sector had the opposite effect in the 4th Division sector. When troops of the 38th, 72nd, 73rd, and 78th Battalions emerged from Blue Bull, Gobron, Cobourg, and Souchez Subways, the craters they faced were full of water. The terrain in that area west of the ridge was already waterlogged by nearby swamps. Members of this 12th Brigade advance, heavily laden with extra bandoleers, Mills bombs, and climbing gear, were slowed by the mud and the slippery walls of the craters. Some slid into the craters and drowned. Then, the creeping barrage got so far ahead of them, it didn't keep the German defenders' heads down long enough.

"The few undestroyed machine guns came out of the trenches and craters," reported Alfred Dieterich of the German 79th Reserve Infantry Brigade. "And the riflemen wildly, some standing, shot at the enemy. The bloody attack broke down in front of the regiment. But strong danger threatened on the wings." Dieterich realized that even as members of the 261st and 262nd Regiments stood fast in a salient of the *Doberitz* sector of the German front line, the creeping barrage and the Canadian troops to the left and right of the salient were overrunning many adjacent German positions, encircling others.

Among those closest to the German salient in the opening assault, troops of the 38th Battalion skirted the resistance and carried on toward the German third line of defence, the Black Line. In the confusion of the rush forward, Thain MacDowell got separated from the majority of his Ottawa Battalion. The captain and two privates—Hay and Kebus—destroyed one machine-gun position and chased the crew from another into a long tunnel. MacDowell led the two privates down scores of steps into a pitch-black dugout. At the end of the staircase he turned a corner to face seventy-seven Prussian Guards.

"Come ahead. Take the prisoners," MacDowell called to an imaginary force behind him.

"*Kamerad!*" returned some of the Prussian troops, raising their hands.

Capt. MacDowell and his two privates had bluffed their way into a sizable German surrender. However, he knew that if the Germans discovered there were only three Canadians facing them, he might lose the entire initiative or, worse, his life and those of his two privates. MacDowell continued calling to Hay and Kebus and ordered the German prisoners up the stairs a dozen at a time. Even when several of their captives, including two officers, saw through the ruse, the three Canadians pulled off the charade and brought the entire Prussian unit to the surface and passed them along to the Winnipeg Grenadiers for processing. In this instance, one of Greg Clark's so-called band of brothers had improvised and achieved the objective.

"The dug-out has three entries and will accommodate easily 250 or 300 men," MacDowell wrote in his notebook. "It is seventy-five feet underground and very comfortable. The cigars are very choice and the supply of Perrier water very large. . . ." It turned out there was a greater reward awaiting Capt. Thain MacDowell following his actions this day—the Victoria Cross.

## 6:15 a.m. April 9, 1917—Forward Observation Post, Neuville St. Vaast, France

As risky as it seemed, Royal Flying Corps pilots and observers awoke in the pre-dawn with orders to make low-altitude sorties over the battlefield at virtually the same time Canadian ground troops were going over the top. Stiffening winds, snow squalls, and low cloud over Vimy posed an initial barrier to flight operations. Nevertheless, RFC pilot Charles Smart, flying a BE fighter-observer aircraft, took off from the No. 16 Squadron aerodrome near Bruay into air conditions he described as "bumpy as Satan." The BE's open cockpit and observer seat meant the cutting edge of the snow and wind lashed the aircrew's faces as they flew over No Man's Land. Second-Lieutenant Smart had orders to assist Canadian battery commanders with flash-spotting operations as they pinpointed the few German batteries shelling the Canadian infantry attack. Winds buffeted the two-seater aircraft so badly that after ninety-five minutes aloft Smart's observer got airsick and he landed to change observers.

In addition, the wretched flying conditions forced RFC aircraft down to altitudes of 300 feet and lower so that they could maintain visual contact with German batteries. Such manoeuvres, however, invited an additional danger—flying through both the Canadian creeping barrage and German return fire. Pilots and observers flew in skies peppered with shells for up to three hours at a time. Squadron commander Billy Bishop was airborne in his Nieuport Scout fighter that morning too and witnessed artillery shelling that he described as "a long ribbon of incandescent light." The work grew more terrifying the closer he flew to the battle; he could feel his aircraft shudder and heave as shells passed beneath him. And while Bishop managed to stay out of the direct path of the shells, other airmen did not. A major with the British 51st Highland Division, on the right flank of the Canadian Corps, reported seeing three RFC aircraft brought down by friendly fire. Nevertheless, RFC flash spotting and aerial photography translated to fewer casualties, so the perilous sorties continued.

As distracting as Bishop found the blustery weather and near-miss artillery shells, the sight of his countrymen on the ground below intrigued him even more. He watched the Canadian troops advancing behind the creeping barrage, seeming "to wander across No Man's Land and into the enemy trenches as if the battle was a great bore to them." Of course, he was watching for the first time an attack that Canadian troops had rehearsed for weeks in order to arrive at enemy positions with precision and punctuality.

It was approaching 6:15 in the brightening morning sky.

As Canadian troops of the 1st, 2nd, and 3rd Divisions reached their initial positions—along the 3rd German defensive line, the Black Line—according to the schedule, they looked skyward. Before

long they spotted other RFC aircraft specially marked with streamers and a pair of black bands on the lower wing. The pilots in these
planes flew low enough that the troops could hear the pilot sound
a klaxon horn from the cockpit. In response the Canadian troops
waved flags with the divisional red symbol or fired off flares, indicating to the pilots that the brigades had successfully reached their
objectives.

Leonard Youell witnessed the first phase of the Vimy attack at ring-
side. Posted to a front-line dugout, east of Neuville St. Vaast, on April
9, Forward Observation Officer Youell felt numbed by the entire experience. In 1914, he'd been earning summer wages in Toronto for
university tuition, but then he put his education on hold when he
enlisted. Three years later, as a FOO on the front line in France, his
job was smashing German guns and their crews to bits. For the three
weeks prior to Zero Hour, Lt. Youell had worked shifts—twenty-
four hours on and twenty-four hours off—hunkered down in his
observation post three miles in front of a battery of 18-pounders.
He was the eyes of the 43rd Battery—sighting, plotting, and tele-
phoning back coordinates of the German guns he saw in his field
binoculars. He calculated that his flash spotting likely meant the
demise of dozens of German guns and countless German gunners.
He never witnessed their destruction. He just worked knowing that
"their job was to kill us and our job was to kill them."

The killing had stopped briefly, in those few minutes before the
creeping barrage began. The pause had captivated Youell.

"Just before the start of the show, just before daylight, we [stood]
on the top of our gun pits," Youell said. "There had been an ordinary
amount of night firing, our batteries and machine-gun fire. But
about five minutes before Zero Hour, there had been an eerie, almost
complete silence. Then the most deafening roar and display of fireworks you've ever seen in your life."

Not long after he returned to his gun pit, Youell began to see the
results of his work. The wounded from both sides began appearing

out in No Man's Land. Some were on stretchers. Others were walking wounded, "but you didn't pay any attention. . . . I had no hard feelings toward the Germans whatsoever," Youell said, though he admitted he never had any hesitation turning his battery guns on any target. "I felt very definitely that this thing was going to go on until there was just one man left standing."

# ARTILLERY CONQUERS, INFANTRY OCCUPIES

**7:45 a.m. April 9, 1917—Les Tilleuls, Red Line, 2nd Division sector, Vimy**

EARLY into the day's operation, the crews of the Canadian and British artillery batteries were on time and on target. With every third or fourth field piece laying down the creeping barrage—firing for three minutes at three rounds per minute and then advancing the location of shells 100 yards every three minutes at two shells per minute—many of the first wave of troops apparently felt perfectly at ease "walking into shells that were retreating ahead of us." Equally effective at Zero Hour, the Allied howitzers and heavy guns were either destroying or preventing German machine-gun nests, trench mortars, and rear batteries from inflicting heavy casualties among the infantry. Lt.-Col. McNaughton, the Counter Battery Staff Officer, described the process as "intense neutralization." Meanwhile, Canadian machine guns used Col. Brutinel's indirect firing technique to create a zone teaming with bullets 400 yards ahead of the ground troops.

In addition, Allied gunners even had German guns firing at decoys. Knowing that in daylight the Germans often sighted their guns on church spires behind Canadian lines to strike military targets nearby, in the course of one night just prior to the attack, Canadian gunners carefully dismantled one church tower and rebuilt it identically some distance away. The result: German gunners registering on the reconstructed spire fired shells at non-existent targets, in the middle of nowhere.

Yet, of all the innovations, techniques, and improvisations generated by the Canadian Corps, battle planners of the April 9 attack hoped that one new British invention would carry the momentum of men and equipment to a safe and speedy victory at Vimy. They applauded the steel-plated, machine-gun–armed, and caterpillar-tracked vehicle, only recently introduced to warfare as the tank,* as a means of accelerating the infantry's rush up the ridge. Male tanks carried a 6-pounder cannon, while Female tanks housed machine guns. Eight Female tanks, borrowed from the British Heavy Branch Machine Gun Corps, were assigned to the 2nd Division sector to assist troops crossing No Man's Land between Canadian-held Neuville St. Vaast and German-held Les Tilleuls and Thélus. Beyond the initial climb up the ridge, the tanks would then smash through belts of barbed wire obstructing the infantry en route to seizing its final Brown Line objective, the town of Farbus. That was the plan on paper anyway.

Troops who saw the rumbling steel behemoths felt reassured and emboldened by their presence. German defenders described the onslaught as "masses of tanks [that] rolled forward over . . . the German first and second lines," while, in fact, the eight tanks looked clumsy and even comical to some members of the 2nd Division. Even doing the "Vimy glide," walking at an even pace in synch with the creeping

---

* The term "tank" originated in a secret report on motorized weapons presented by British Army Lt.-Col. Ernest Swinton to then First Lord of the Admiralty, Winston Churchill; three potential descriptions emerged—"cistern," "motor-war car," and "tank"—the latter chosen for its monosyllabic ease. Another version of the origin "tank" says that British commander Field-Marshal Douglas Haig, in an attempt to conceal the arrival of these new motorized and armoured vehicles in the front-line area of the Somme in the summer of 1916, had the railcars in which they were hidden labelled "water tanks" and the latter half of the disguise name stuck.

barrage, Claude Williams, gun commander in the 6th Brigade Machine Gun Company, passed one of the tanks on foot. Capt. Williams noticed that it made progress through No Man's Land, but only with great difficulty.

"We saw this lumbering, growling machine approach a mine crater," he wrote. "Its bow slowly dropped downward as its stern rose in the air. It then suddenly disappeared. . . . Then to our surprise the bow reappeared on the other lip of the crater, pointing skyward for a moment, then dropping to the ground, it continued to amble along."

As he usually did, Williams thought more about the welfare of the men inside the vehicle and the physical punishment this up-and-down-and-up traverse must be giving each tank crew. A Canadian Army sniper, attached to the 27th (Winnipeg) Battalion, also walked past the squadron of tanks a little later in the morning. By this time, "the tanks were mired," L.R. Fennel said. "They had tent posts and everything else wired to their tracks, but [the tracks] were just turning around through the mud and the tanks weren't making any headway." By day's end all eight tanks had bogged down at different spots along the 2nd Division route forward. Three had become so stuck and so vulnerable that German gunners finished them off with shellfire.

Despite the loss of the tanks, however, the light and heavy artillery strategies of the Canadian Corps, at least in the 1st, 2nd, and 3rd Division sectors, were paying off. Gunners were living up to the first half of the military dictum "artillery conquers. . ." Now it was up to troops on the ground to fulfill the other half, ". . . infantry occupies." The first wave of soldiers had moved with the advancing wall of artillery shells to liberate the first objectives. Now it was up to the second wave of men to leapfrog past the first group, to seize and occupy the next enemy positions.

While he likely didn't know about military dictums of warfare, Andrew McCrindle did know what was expected of him. The nineteen-year-old private, who'd left his job as an apprentice draftsman at the Montreal office of the Grand Trunk Railway in 1916, had taken his turn over the practice fields behind the lines at Vimy. This would be his first combat experience of the war. So he absorbed every bit of information, every assignment. By the time his 24th Battalion went over the top he knew exactly what the *Zwischen Stellung*—the strategic Black Line of German defences—looked like. What's more, during his army apprenticeship in March 1917, McCrindle had moved from section rifleman to rifle grenadier.

"We have a gadget on the end of our rifles which holds a Mills hand grenade, which we project using a blank cartridge," he wrote. "By doing so we can throw a bomb much farther than by hand."

During the practice sessions at Chateau de la Haie, McCrindle and his fellow grenadiers in the Victoria Rifles of Montreal had rehearsed fire and movement techniques to knock out machine-gun nests in their path to the *Zwischen Stellung* objective. Each attack required a grenadier to load a blank .303 shell, insert the grenade into the muzzle of the rifle, set the butt of the rifle on the ground at a 45-degree angle, and pull the trigger, projecting the grenade at the target. Not every rehearsal had gone perfectly. In one simulated attack, a member of his platoon decided to increase the elevation of the grenade launch; the projectile flew nearly straight up and down, exploding just thirty feet away, fortunately without injuries. On April 9, McCrindle's grenadier apprenticeship paid off.

"There was a spot of bother just to the left of us," McCrindle remembered about one machine-gun nest near the Black Line. "So we had to crawl over there. Our sergeant deployed us so that we approached the nest from different directions. Then we put our rifles in firing positions and let off a salvo of grenades. . . . We rushed in to find only one German survivor. . . ."

McCrindle had also learned not to think about the Germans he killed in such operations. But as much as he was able to shut the killing out of his mind, he couldn't ignore some of the German prisoners. When he and his battalion reached the Black Line and checked the dugouts for stragglers, they were bemused by the German officer they found in his pyjamas. The man expressed indignation at his capture and demanded an officer of equal rank accept his surrender. The

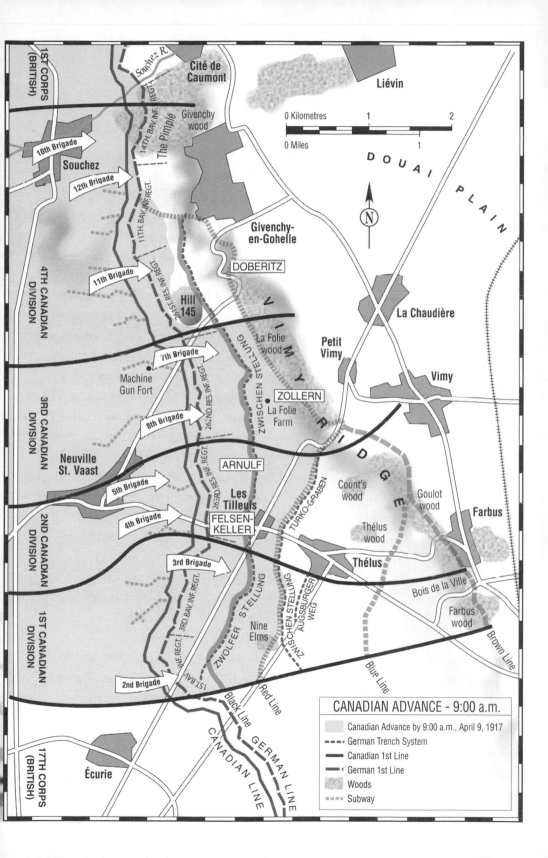

1ST CORPS
(BRITISH)

Souchez R.

Cité de
Caumont

Liévin

D O U A I

14TH. BAV. INF. REGT.

Givenchy
wood

The Pimple

10th Brigade

Souchez

12th Brigade

11TH. BAV. INF. REGT.

0 Kilometres    1    2

0 Miles    1

4TH CANADIAN
DIVISION

Givenchy-
en-Gohelle

DOBERITZ

N

11th Brigade

261ST. RES. INF. REGT.

Hill
145

V
I
M
Y

La Folie
wood

ZWISCHEN STELLUNG

Petit
Vimy

La Chaudière

Vimy

7th Brigade

Machine
Gun Fort

262ND. RES. INF. REGT.

3RD CANADIAN
DIVISION

8th Brigade

ZOLLERN

La Folie
Farm

R
I
D
G
E

Neuville
St. Vaast

5th Brigade

263RD. RES. INF. REGT.

ARNULF

Count's
wood

Goulot
wood

Farbus

4th Brigade

Les
Tilleuls

FELSEN-
KELLER

TURKO-GRABEN

Thélus
wood

2ND CANADIAN
DIVISION

3rd Brigade

ZWÖLFER STELLUNG

AUGSBURGER
WEG

Thélus

ZWISCHEN STELLUNG

Bois de la Ville

1ST CANADIAN
DIVISION

3RD. BAV. INF. REGT.

Nine
Elms

Farbus
wood

Blue Line

Brown Line

2nd Brigade

1ST BAV. INF. REGT.

Black Line

Red Line

CANADIAN ADVANCE - 9:00 a.m.

17TH CORPS
(BRITISH)

Écurie

GERMAN
LINE

CANADIAN
LINE

Canadian Advance by 9:00 a.m., April 9, 1917

German Trench System

Canadian 1st Line

German 1st Line

Woods

Subway

man was hustled off with other Bavarian troops that McCrindle and the rest of the Victoria Rifles captured that day.

Beyond the *Zwischen Stellung* in the 2nd Division sector, resistance of German troops stiffened. The second wave of Canadian troops discovered that more of the enemy positions between the Black Line and Les Tilleuls (in front of the Red Line) had escaped the crippling effect of the Allied bombardment. Nor did the Bavarian defenders surrender easily. German war diaries describe reserve troops desperately rushing forward from the *Felsenkeller* sector, the German command post in the sector, with whatever equipment they could find to try to stop the Canadian advance. "The last two machine guns were brought into action by [German] L/Sgt. Erdmann," the report said. "From the twin entrances of the dugout they fired burst after burst into the lines of advancing enemy. . . . But hardly had they opened up, when they were located and deluged with hand grenades."

As the artillery/infantry dictum suggested, it was not always artillery shells or grenades launched from a distance that silenced entrenched German positions. Sometimes it was the brute strength and willpower of individual infantrymen in the middle of it all. From the time of his arrival at the Belgian front in 1915 until the winter transfer to Vimy, Ellis Sifton had enjoyed the relative calm in what he described as "bomb-proof jobs." As a rifleman with the 18th Battalion, Sifton had served in countless work parties behind the lines— horse wrangling, hauling ammunition, and bringing rations forward to Vimy. In frequent letters home to his two sisters on the farm in Wallacetown, Ontario, he always said he was feeling "fine and dandy," while occasionally revealing his fear that "if this war lasts two years more, I will never see the end."

Sifton went over the top with his Western Ontario Battalion in the 2nd Division sector not long after the opening barrage. His commanders had received a call for relief from their sister regiment—the 21st (Eastern Ontario) Battalion at the Black Line. It had taken 106 prisoners, but had also sustained 215 casualties in reaching the objective. It would need the 18th's assistance in reaching the next German line of defence. Buoyed by his field promotion to sergeant just days before, Sifton advanced quickly to help reinforce the 4th Brigade's push to Les Tilleuls. But even the fresh troops of the 18th began taking casualties from the German strongpoints. Just 100 yards from the objective, a leading officer in "A" Company, Lt. W.J. McLean, was killed. Soon after, Lt. P. Jordan had to take over "B" Company when it lost a commanding officer. Meanwhile, a hidden machine gun had pinned down the men in "C" Company, including Sgt. Sifton.

Between gun bursts, Sifton decided to act alone. He suddenly dashed forward into the enemy trench and overthrew the gun, before its crew could react. He turned on the gunners with his bayonet, killing or wounding every one of them. When a group of Germans charged Sifton from farther down the trench, he fended them off by wielding his bayonet and rifle as a club. Sifton was soon supported by other "C" Company infantrymen. Together they beat back the German counterattack. In the hand-to-hand fighting, however, a wounded German soldier managed to pick up a rifle and shoot Sifton dead.

The twenty-five-year-old farmer from Western Ontario, who had brooded over his own fate, wondered in letters home whether "courage will be mine at the right moment if I am called upon to stare death in the face," had found the courage. And though he had died in the rush, Sifton had, in the words of the Victoria Cross citation, "saved many lives and contributed largely to the success of the operation."

It was nearly 8 a.m. Les Tilleuls was in Canadian hands. Second Division troops had reached their second objective, the *Turko-Graben* trench system—the Red Line.

## 8 a.m. April 9, 1917—La Folie Farm, Red Line, 3rd Division sector, Vimy

Not every Canadian in uniform was eligible to be in uniform. Volunteers had to prove they were eighteen upon enlistment. At sixteen, Fred Claydon left his grandparents' ranch near Elkhorn, Manitoba, to sign up with the 79th Battalion in Brandon. His previous militia experience with the 12th Manitoba Dragoons apparently helped convince the recruiter he was old enough to enlist. He got through training and went to the Western Front as a reinforcement in the 43rd (Cameron Highlanders of Winnipeg) Battalion. Pte. Claydon survived Ypres, the Somme, and Courcelette, all before he was even eligible to join the army. He turned eighteen as the 3rd Division moved to Vimy to prepare for the Easter attack. Now an experienced battalion scout, he hardened to his macabre surroundings.

"When they'd dug up this one new trench at Vimy," Claydon recalled, "they uncovered part of this Frenchman's body. Well, his hand stuck out of the side of the trench. We always used to shake hands with this Frenchie for good luck."

From January to April, like all Canadian Corps troops, Claydon trained for the big show that was coming. They lived through frigid outdoor conditions. Sometimes they slept in what had formerly been graves. And they were always short of rations "except for cheese." Five days before the attack, he scouted for the 43rd on a trench raid against the German positions. Then, soon after the initial barrage on April 9, Pte. Claydon joined the 3rd Division advance. As a scout he wore a green arm band and in the second advance led his battalion toward La Folie Farm. In spite of all he had experienced during two years at war, one sight there stopped him in his tracks.

"At La Folie Farm, the bricks of the foundation were like a little hill of broken brick," Claydon said. "Laying along side one of these was a young Heinie [German], just a young fellow. I looked at him. He'd been killed by the machine guns or artillery. He packed two sacks—one full of bits of rye bread and the other with sausage tied up. It was all the rations he had. He'd probably been a scout . . . just like me."

For his service, if not his longevity as a boy soldier at Vimy, Claydon received the Military Medal.

Harold A. Carter hadn't even reached his eighteenth birthday when the Canadian Corps reached Vimy. He was sixteen, which means he was a boy of fourteen or fifteen when he joined up. Part of a Lewis gun team with the 5th Canadian Mounted Rifles in the 3rd

Division, Carter attempted his first steps into No Man's Land only to slip and fall on two other members of his crew. One of them, a lieutenant, helped him out of the trench but then immediately handed him four canvas bags of ammunition panniers. The sixteen-year-old already was carrying his regulation 120 rounds of ammunition for his rifle, a knapsack, water bottle, and bayonet. This added weight and slowed Carter down.

"I had only gone a short distance," Carter said, "when it seemed the whole German army opened up on me with machine-gun and rifle fire, so I ducked into a shell hole partly filled with water."

Pte. Carter hugged the ground as machine-gun bullets splattered mud from the edge of the shell hole on top of him and splashed into water at the bottom of his hiding place. When the firing moved away, like a scene from a cartoon, Carter put his helmet on his rifle barrel and showed it above the edge of the shell hole. As he feared, it drew further machine-gun fire. Biding his time, he looked up to see an Allied observation balloon that had broken its tether pass overhead toward the German lines. It must have distracted the German gunners too, because when he poked his helmet up again it didn't attract any more gunfire. He gathered his strength and all his gear and crept out of the shell hole. He soon got to the *Zwischen Stellung* and tumbled into a trench.

"I fell in exhausted," Carter said, "but was soon surrounded by machine gunners who let out a great cheer."

While not every soldier in the Canadian Corps was of eligible age, not every member of the Canadian Corps was Canadian. Among those serving at the 7th Brigade Headquarters, also in the 3rd Division sector, was a former civil engineer born in the United States. Hal Wallis grew up in San Francisco, but when his father died, the family returned to his mother's roots near Peterborough, Ontario. At the outbreak of the war, Wallis was working for the CPR, but immediately enlisted at Valcartier, Quebec. Hal joined the Toronto Scottish while his brother Hugh Wallis joined the Black Watch of Montreal. At Vimy, both Wallis brothers found themselves on the intelligence staff of their uncle, the commander of the 7th Brigade, Lt.-Gen. Archibald C. Macdonnell. He was known to most as "Batty Mac."

"He *was* batty too," Hal Wallis said. "He'd go up the line and out into a sap to see what was there. [Once] he looked up, got up a little bit and a German sniper hit him through the arm. He stood up, shook his arm at the sniper . . . and got hit again. Never got killed, but that was Batty Mac for you."

Batty perhaps, but a survivor. A professional soldier through and through, Macdonnell had served with the North West Mounted Police and with the Canadians in South Africa during the Boer War. At Zero Hour on Vimy, in their observation post called Machine Gun Fort, Macdonnell and his young intelligence officers watched the 3rd Division troops go over the top. Eventually, when the Germans began to register their artillery on the former Canadian front line, Machine Gun Fort came under fire. Capt. Wallis moved forward to join the rest of the 7th Brigade. Shortly after 6 a.m. it had reached the Black Line. Within an hour, Wallis had moved the observation post to a former German dugout there and was using already installed telephone lines to observe and report back to Canadian batteries on the accuracy of their artillery fire toward the next objective.

His brigadier wasn't far behind him. Wallis knew to expect that Macdonnell would quickly want to survey the brigade's position and status. The C.O. was wont to making reconnaissance walks and Wallis expected a repeat of an earlier incident. After the battle, Macdonnell and Wallis passed members of the brigade lying face down, dead, on the ground. Macdonnell stopped at each body to pay his respects.

"I salute you," the C.O. said and moved on to the next, repeating his tribute.

So close to the front, Capt. Wallis got nervous about being out in the open and urged the brigadier to seek cover.

"I salute you, my brave highlander," Macdonnell said at the next body.

"Sir, the Germans are shooting at us," Wallis insisted.

Macdonnell didn't flinch.

"For God's sake, sir, get into the trench."

Suddenly, several German shells dropped twenty feet away, but did not explode. Wallis thought, "Thank God they were made by the United States and were duds." Being an American, he probably had the right to think that.

## 8 a.m. April 9, 1917—Augsburger Weg, Red Line, 1st Division sector, Vimy

At two to three rounds per minute, during those first ninety minutes of the Easter Monday battle, nearly a thousand Allied guns had fired more than 200,000 artillery shells. In the first twenty-four hours of the operation, each of the Corps' 358 machine guns required 15,000 rounds. Nearly 40,000 Canadian troops were on the move across a front that stretched for nine miles of front line. In the 1st and 2nd Division sectors, troops advanced by the thousands of yards. Losses were relatively light. In the 3rd and 4th Division sectors, advances were shorter and slower and were taking heavier casualties. Nevertheless, as Canadian brigades leapfrogged past each other, capturing more enemy territory by the minute, they were consequently stretching supply lines to the limit. In order for the attack to continue beyond the Black and Red Lines, the Canadian Corps had to reinforce its infantry units with men and replenish its weapons with fresh ammunition rapidly. Otherwise, the advance could stall. Conveniently, members of the 11th Brigade, through trial and error, had come up with a unique way to keep supplies flowing forward in step with the rapidly moving infantry. They had introduced a backwoods device called the tumpline to speed the process.

"The tumpline is a simple contrivance made of leather and used for carrying loads," wrote F.R. Phelan, a captain in the 11th Brigade. "It has a brow band . . . sewn to a strap seven or more feet long. . . . The load of boxes, sacks, etc., is piled up and the long strap passes around each end of the load. . . . The wide part of the leather band passes over the top of the head just above the brow and the load rests high up on the back. The tumper walks slightly bent forward, [so] the weight is borne on the head and the pressure of the weight is in a straight line down the spine."

Phelan illustrated the value of the tumpline when he pointed out that during the previous autumn, members of his brigade had manually carried extraordinary loads over long distances in short periods of time. He wrote at the Somme that every day for forty-five days an officer, an NCO, and twenty men had transported 1,000 rounds of rifle shells, four boxes of Mills grenades, three boxes of Stokes mortar shells, two boxes of bully beef, one case of biscuits, one bale of sandbags, two coils of barbed wire, a dozen shovels, and a dozen picks over a distance of 4,000 to 5,000 yards. "Any of these loads," he emphasized, "would usually take two men to carry them the ordinary way."

Norman Evans fought the battle of Vimy Ridge with a tumpline. When he joined up for overseas service in the winter of 1916, he left a section gang, tamping railway ties for the CNR, in northern Saskatchewan. He hoped by enlisting in the army the work might not be so menial. He was wrong. His husky, "built like a bull" physique ensured that he would almost always be assigned to labourers' tasks. Because of his strength, at the front Pte. Evans was assigned to carry rations and mail forward, sometimes all night long. On April 9, his platoon went over the top in relief of his 15th (48th Highlanders) Battalion, so his platoon commander put him in charge of carrying ammunition. To make the job more manageable, Evans used a tumpline to manhandle the 250-pound boxes of the machine-gun bullets across No Man's Land.

Evans tumplined ammunition forward with a man he'd befriended in the 15th Battalion. Wherever they served together on the Western Front, Evans tended to stay close to Pte. Joe Lafontaine because he sensed Lafontaine was a lucky charm. On one trip tumping the machine-gun shells forward to the Black Line that morning, Evans was suddenly knocked on his back. Initially out of breath, but then aware of pain in his lower body, he realized he had taken a piece of shrapnel through his groin. Like so many in those early hours, Evans was wounded and alone in No Man's Land. Two medics finally came along and carried Evans back to an aid post. Later in the day, Lafontaine came by to see his friend.

"How come you got hit and I didn't?" Lafontaine asked him.

"I stopped it before it hit you," Evans said.

Despite that undelivered box of machine-gun shells, the 1st Division juggernaut advanced right on schedule. With the Black Line objective in 1st Division hands just before 7 a.m., the creeping barrage in the sector moved across the next thousand yards toward the Red Line objective at *Zwischen Stellung*. The expanse of ground between the two objectives consisted of shell holes and craters, from which the Germans had constructed a network of dugouts, emplacements, and communication trenches leading back across Vimy Ridge to support trenches on the reverse slope. They offered little shelter this morning, however—only a way out. In the face of the creeping barrage and the next wave of Canadian troops, Bavarian infantryman Michael Volkheimer now watched the German defensive line crumble and his comrades in full retreat.

"In this communications trench in front of a dugout was a battalion command post," Volkheimer said. "On the steps leading down sat a sentry, sheltering from the barrage. I called out to him, 'Get out! The English are coming!'"

The young German rifleman dashed to the headquarters of the Bavarian Reserve Infantry Regiment to give the commanding officer a first-hand account of what he had seen. He recommended an infusion of reinforcements to shore up the *Zwischen Stellung* line. But none were available. The result was that the line between Nine Elms, a cluster of battered tree trunks sticking out of the mud at *Zwischen Stellung* in the 1st Division sector, and Thélus to the north rapidly fell into Canadian hands. Only 200 Germans escaped their area successfully—they being mostly rear-echelon work parties, clerks, and kitchen crews.

Jack Pinson made first contact with German troops that morning at Nine Elms. Not that he hadn't faced the enemy before. Since he had enlisted in Victoria, B.C., soon after the war broke out, Pinson had a long list of battle credits, including Festubert, where he first encountered whiz-bang shells; Givenchy, where the British and German front lines sat only twenty yards apart; and Mount Sorrel, where he carried a message across land where "you could hardly step for dead men or pieces of men." At Vimy, L/Cpl. Pinson's 7th (British Columbia) Battalion sustained nearly 50 percent casualties in the first half-mile.

"All that ground was full of German dugouts," Pinson said. "On the way through we'd run into German machine-gun posts. We'd bomb them out or clean them out with rifle fire. . . . We were in a big hurry. We had a timetable to keep to. We couldn't stop to take them out as prisoners, but we couldn't leave them there alive."

By the time he reached the *Augsburger Weg* (trench) at Nine Elms, there were only six left in L/Cpl. Pinson's platoon. Adrenaline pumping, they jumped into what was left of the trench to press their attack. The Augsburger communication trench snaked a long way back into German-held territory. Every fifty feet along its length, doorways and stairs led the Canadians down into a catacomb of galleys and supply depots. Pinson couldn't believe that such a large secure force with such abundant munitions had not risen to stop the attack. In Pinson's view "they shouldn't have been down there; they should have been up fighting."

Another member of the 2nd Brigade merely stopped at each entranceway of the dugout in the trench. He threw bombs down into the darkness and shouted: "Come out, you sons of bitches!" Then, if survivors emerged, the Canadian demanded their wristwatches as souvenirs. Eventually, the run-and-bomb method of dealing with enemy troops in the Augsburger trench broke down. In the first few minutes of their attack along the trench, Pinson and his 7th Battalion mates faced 150 Germans with their hands in the air. The German troops appeared stunned by the barrage and undone when suddenly faced with rapidly advancing Canadian shock troops.

For a member of Pinson's sister regiment, the 5th (Saskatchewan) Battalion, the pile-up of prisoners at the Red Line nearly became a massacre. When Jim Church reached the 2nd Brigade's objective, he spotted a group of German troops—perhaps sixty men in a crater. He had carried sixteen Mills bombs in a sack hung from his neck. So, as a reflex he grabbed a bomb, pulled the pin and cocked his arm to heave it into the crowded crater.

"Don't throw it!" shouted a 5th Battalion officer.

Church didn't realize the Germans in the crater were showing a white flag. Most had gathered around their commanding officer to join a general surrender.

Still holding the grenade, Church told the Canadian officer that the Germans in the crater outnumbered his Saskatchewan Battalion troops and that most were still armed with rifles and bayonets.

"They won't fight no more," the officer said.

Church now faced a unique dilemma. He had pulled the pin on the bomb. It was now armed. "I can't put the key back," he said to the officer. Once he tossed it, releasing the spring lever, the bomb would explode in four seconds. The officer told him to throw it into a different crater. He did, but the moment it exploded, a tide of surrendering Germans came scurrying from that shell hole too.

The accumulating POWs posed a growing problem for men of the 1st Division. Handling prisoners required guards, depleting the manpower of the advance. Where they could afford to assign escorts, 1st Division platoon commanders organized the German POWs into stretcher-bearer units to carry back Canadian wounded. Other prisoners found themselves assigned to work parties, helping their Canadian enemy dig in, to defend against potential German counterattack. Meanwhile, Lt. Cyril Jones of the 16th Battalion came up with his own solution to the rising POW population.

When his "moppers-up" company with the Canadian Scottish moved toward its second objective of the day—the Red Line—he was suddenly surrounded by a swarm of Germans all shouting, "*Kamerad, Kamerad!* Mercy!" and offering watches and other souvenirs in exchange for their lives. Surprised by the mass surrender, Jones laughed out loud. Then he simply pointed them in the direction of "our old lines, and they beat it—couldn't get there fast enough." They began filing unescorted westward to the original Canadian trenches. Meanwhile, Jones noted that some Canadian privates were having the time of their lives collecting prisoners and souvenirs from German dugouts, picking up such items as watches, caps, field glasses, food delicacies, and cigars.

German POWs often summed up their enemies by saying, "The British fight for glory, the Canadians for souvenirs."

### 8:30 a.m. April 9, 1917—toward Givenchy-en-Gohelle, 4th Division sector, Vimy

Some early reports coming back to the jumping-off trenches in the 4th Division sector painted a positive picture of the Canadian Corps' advance. After all, at about 7 a.m. German prisoners rounded up by Capt. Thain MacDowell and other members of the 38th (Ottawa) Battalion near the Black Line began arriving at the Canadian front lines. That was a good sign. Elsewhere in the 12th Brigade attack—in the centre of the division assault—members of the 73rd (Royal Highlanders) Battalion reached their objective, the base of the Pimple, within thirty minutes of Zero Hour. Once there, they had orders to dig in and prepare for the assault on the Pimple scheduled for the next day. Even the 72nd (Seaforth Highlanders) Battalion attack made early gains toward the outskirts of Givenchy-en-Gohelle. The persistent rain and snow, however, began to transform craters and shell holes ahead of them into ponds of muck and water. Ray Crowe, a Seaforth drummer, had gone over the top carrying pans of machine-gun shells in support of a Lewis gun crew. He travelled half the distance to the crew when he slipped into a mine crater with fifteen feet of water at the bottom. He kept himself from sinking right under the water as others had, but his shouts for help were drowned out by the noise of artillery and machine-gun fire.

A fellow Seaforth, Norman MacNeil, heard his cries for help.

"It's Ray," Crowe called up to him.

"Don't move," MacNeil said. Then he flopped down on his stomach and extended his rifle into the crater for Crowe to grab. "Now, just hold on and I'll see if I can pull you up."

It took every ounce of strength each man had to extricate Crowe from the flooding crater. But they finally succeeded. The two men never caught up to the rest of the Lewis gun crew, but still crossed the first enemy lines and began forcing Germans from the support dugouts in order to set up command positions for their 72nd Battalion gunners. Crowe and MacNeil would wait in vain. Since the Seaforths were advancing in plain view of unmolested German gun positions on the Pimple (to their left), more than three-quarters of the battalion became casualties that morning. Flanking fire proved even more devastating to the 78th (Winnipeg Grenadiers) Battalion in the same sector as it went over the top to support the 38th Battalion. A Grenadier lieutenant, pinned down in some of those same 4th Division craters, called his situation "terribly confused."

Lt. Stewart Scott realized the 78th was in trouble when the creeping barrage hadn't knocked out German positions on either the Pimple, to his left, or Hill 145 to his right. When the German gunners opened up, Scott's group immediately took cover in shell holes and watched helplessly as the Allied creeping barrage left them behind. Adding to the confusion, the blizzard-like conditions above them made it impossible for the battalion to spot circling Allied aircraft to notify them of the brigade's progress. One Royal Flying Corps pilot attempted to descend through the low ceiling and was hit by the friendly fire, ending up—like the ground troops—nose down in a shell hole.

"There was no means of communicating back from where we had come to find out where a company commander or another platoon commander might be," Lt. Scott said. "So, we just sat it out in a shell hole and took a fair amount of punishment."

Those Grenadiers attempting to keep up with the barrage to make the objective—the Red Line—on the outskirts of Givenchy-en-Gohelle, got caught in a murderous crossfire enfilade and were nearly wiped out. Gordon Mitchell went over the top in the Grenadiers' second-wave attack. He and two others in his section advanced a few hundred yards until some German snipers who had survived the creeping barrage and the first wave of Canadian troops surprised them. The sniper fire drove the three Winnipeggers into a large shell hole. Presently, a fourth man from another unit flung himself into the same muddy crater. Realizing they were pinned down, the four men began digging funk holes—one-man dugouts—into the side of the crater. They worked in pairs. One man dug while the other hugged the ground out of sight and rested.

"There was an explosion where the other two [men] were working and one of them shouted that he was hit," Cpl. Mitchell said. "I thought that Fritz had spotted us and had thrown a hand grenade, but found that the entrenching tool of one of the boys had struck a buried bomb which exploded right in his face. The poor chap's face was a mass of blood and he was totally blinded."

Mitchell realized the wounded man would bleed to death unless he received medical attention, so he prepared himself for a lengthy retreat. Uncertain of his exact position and of the location of Canadian support lines, Mitchell managed to escape the crater unnoticed and led the wounded man around craters and shell holes back toward friendly lines. It was getting dark when he reached an outpost manned by two forward observers. They directed Mitchell to an advanced dressing station, although they informed him later "that they had seen us coming and thought we were Germans. One of them was about to open fire, but was persuaded by his mate to wait until they could be sure of our identity." Cpl. Mitchell then re-armed and began retracing his steps to the crater in which he'd left his 78th Battalion mates.

Pte. Ernest Morison also went over the top with the Winnipeg Grenadiers in the second wave. He had just spent his twenty-sixth birthday behind the front lines at Vimy. While his chums had come up with a few impromptu gifts to acknowledge his "advanced age," a birthday package his mother had promised to send from home in Roland, Manitoba, had not arrived by Easter Monday morning. Worried that he should write something before the major Vimy action, Pte. Morison reassured his mother that he "had a pretty fair time" on his birthday. He also noted that "quite a few of the boys in our battalion got Distinguished Conduct Medals lately. I haven't been lucky enough to get one myself." He added in the note home that something had arrived for his young brother, Harold, who was serving in the 27th (Winnipeg) Battalion also at Vimy. He said that he looked forward to receiving his mother's birthday parcel and signed off with this: "Well mother, this terrible war is still going on, but I guess it will end some day and we must hope for the best. . . . I ever remain your own dear son, Ernie. Love to all."

Pte. Ernest Morison's letter arrived at his mother's home in Roland on April 30, about the same time as notification that he had been killed in action on April 9 at Vimy, and just three days before her second son, Pte. Harold Morison, was killed in action in the same Arras campaign, on May 3, 1917.

## 10 a.m. April 9, 1917—11th Field Ambulance, Chateau de la Haie, France

While it proved to be Canada's largest military commitment to date, the Vimy Ridge attack, at least for the individual soldier, still came down to the few square yards in front and on either side of where he fought. Certainly, the attention paid to battalion rehearsals over the tapes, the extraordinary breadth of the trench and subway system behind the Canadian lines, the massive stockpile of war munitions lining the roads and choking underground passageways, and finally the thunder of the barrage at Zero Hour, opened many soldiers' eyes to the extent of this Canadian Corps operation. For Douglas Emery, a private serving at an advanced dressing station with the 11th Canadian Field Ambulance, the magnitude of the day translated to the number of tetanus shots he administered to the wounded.

"It was a great big needle," Emery said. "And these poor guys—they were calling me 'Doc' because I was going to give them the needle—they'd say 'Doc, don't touch me,' but I had to give it to them."

Beginning about 10 a.m., when the first troops arrived at the dressing station, Pte. Emery jabbed every wounded soldier in the chest with a tetanus injection. By mid-afternoon he had administered 700 tetanus shots, by day's end over a thousand—all with the same needle!

Pte. Cyril Smith joined one of those lines to get his anti-lockjaw shot. He had gone over the top in the morning with the 54th (Kootenay) Battalion, but had been hit by shrapnel from a German grenade. He came into the field ambulance station as one of the walking wounded. He saw men fainting in front of him, but realized the reason only when he reached the front of the line.

"The needle was about six inches long . . . and blunt," he said. "If you got one half, the other guy got the other half. When the doctor pulled the needle out, my skin went with it, wouldn't let go. It was worse than the wound."

Medics such as Pte. Emery worked feverishly with their tetanus needles, of course, to combat the threat of infection. Every open wound ran the risk of becoming contaminated by the soil of Vimy, which for generations had been fertilized for agriculture by human and animal manure. Emery served as one of nearly 19,000 members of the Canadian Army Medical Corps (CAMC), including 1,500 medical officers, 1,900 nursing sisters (at hospitals behind the lines), and the rest working as first-aid medics, operating room assistants, and field stretcher bearers.

Each day of the war, including the battle at Vimy Ridge, medical staff coped with horrific casualty situations. Triage medics met inbound stretchers to find men with respiratory gas burns, limbs and body trunks lacerated with machine-gun bullet holes, and severe head wounds caused by flying shrapnel. One medic noted the preponderance of wounds to the femur (thigh bone), likely the result of enfilade (roughly the height machine-gun bullets travelled above the ground from the flanking gunfire). Fewer than 1 percent of soldiers' wounds resulted from edged weapons (i.e., bayonets), while approximately 70 percent resulted from shell explosions. Limb amputations were more common than in the Second World War since the practices of bone-grafting or bone reconstruction had not yet come to the operating theatre. Nor were there antibiotics available to assist surgeons facing head, chest, or deep abdominal wounds.

"The carnage of war was assembled here scarcely distinguishable from the mud in which it lay," observed one medic.

Remarkably, by the time of the Vimy attack, the CAMC had moved battlefield medicine to tolerable levels of efficiency and treatment. Fewer casualties died of gas gangrene (infection from soil organisms) because medics cleaned wounds with antiseptics more rapidly. Surgeons often made incisions deeper and wider around shrapnel or bullet wounds to allow oxygen in the air to assist killing bacteria. This concept of "debridement," removing damaged tissue from around the wound, was introduced in 1915. Such wounds were more often drained and attended to regularly after surgery. Medical teams even experimented with the earliest methods of blood transfusion. Despite his foresight preparing the 8th Canadian Field Ambulance for the attack—padding splints, collecting stretchers, and assembling field dressings—J.N. Gunn still felt unprepared when the flow of wounded began overwhelming his medical staff shortly after Zero Hour. His clipped diary entries from April 9 attest to the frenetic state of his dressing station:

> First walking wounded arrived at 6:45 a.m. and first stretcher cases at 7:15. We cleared approximately 2,000 wounded . . . many of the 2nd Division, some of the 4th Division. . . . Shortage of stretchers on account of Aux Rietz [an advanced dressing station in a cave] becoming congested. I sat in my dugout and cleared the field like working a switchboard. . . . My men cleared the front line. . . . They worked like heroes for thirty-six hours without rest. All night long over the wilderness of shell holes strewn with Germans and Canadians. Water in shell holes brownish red with mud and blood. . . .
>
> We captured an advanced dressing station and two German medical officers and had them working in our dressing station at White City cave. We used hundreds of prisoners to carry

stretcher cases and push trucks to Aux Rietz. We got out the cases so fast we congested Aux Rietz. Tram line that was to clear [wounded] there, broke down . . . 300 cases lying on stretchers.

When Maj. Gunn's thirty-six hours came to an end, he and his field ambulance staff were exhausted. He also noted in his diary that his pulse rate was up and he had a temperature of 100 degrees. He got two hours' sleep and then cleared 300 stretcher cases the next day. To speed the process of clearing the wounded, field ambulance medics augmented their stretcher supply by using canvas stretched over two-by-fours as well as sheets of corrugated iron in place of standard stretchers. Sometimes the medication a wounded soldier needed most didn't come from a field dressing or a tetanus shot at all. Fred Hodges served with a trench mortar crew in the 2nd Brigade. His mobile battery was about to go over the top to join other 1st Division troops at the Black Line, when some of the unescorted German prisoners came trudging through the mud and accumulating snow.

"I remember one [German] fellow coming up," Hodges said. "He was wounded and trying to get down into the trench. I gave him a hand. In his own language, I knew he was expressing thanks—he squeezed my hand. . . . Human kindness is just the same in a German as it is in a British subject."

Gavin McDonald dispensed a similar kind of medication that Easter Monday. He served the Canadian Corps neither as a medic nor a stretcher bearer. The former homesteader from north of Regina did, however, have a common-sense perception of the men around him. A member of the Princess Patricia's Canadian Light Infantry, L/Cpl. McDonald had come through Ypres and the Somme. Then, during the winter of 1917, he had led work parties removing soil from secret sap tunnels under Vimy. On April 9, the PPCLI adjutant gave him orders to assist the regimental secretary, Mickey Egan, at a transport post behind the lines. Alone with the secretary during the barrage that morning, McDonald watched Egan freeze with fear on a bunk in the corner of the outpost. Weeks of tension and stress had suddenly pushed the young secretary over the edge. McDonald sent for an ambulance. But when Egan saw medics coming to take him away, he broke down.

"Don't let them take me away," Egan pleaded.

"I'll look after you," McDonald said, trying to calm the man. He put an arm around Egan's shoulders and held him close. Then, he gently rolled the shell-shocked man into a hug.

The ambulance driver looked at McDonald initially in disgust, but then realized the problem and quickly slipped the stretcher under Egan to carry him away. Even as the two men lifted the regimental secretary into the ambulance, Egan called to his friend "Mac," entreating him not to let them take him away. McDonald watched the ambulance disappear down the road. Shaken, but confident that he had prevented Egan's condition from worsening, Gavin McDonald said, "I had to take charge . . . [but] that was the last I saw of him."

# "CHASING HUNS TOWARDS THE FATHERLAND"

## 9 a.m. April 9, 1917—Hill 145, 4th Division sector, Vimy

I F EVER THE FOG OF WAR descended on a unit of fighting soldiers, it shrouded the 4th Division sector battlefield soon after Zero Hour on April 9—figuratively and literally. The checkered nature of the creeping barrage at the base of Hill 145 (because the commander of the 87th Battalion had insisted that his objective not be shelled) had resulted in catastrophic losses to the first wave of his Grenadier Guards troops. The unexpected strength of German gun positions on the highest points of Vimy Ridge had scattered even those 72nd Battalion troops behind the artillery's creeping barrage and left them in disarray. In addition, the atmospheric fog caused by a curtain of snow right after Zero Hour in that sector actually hid 78th Battalion ground troops from friendly aircraft and vice versa. All these elements conspired against the thousands of Canadian Corps troops entering No Man's Land from the 10th, 11th, and 12th Brigade front lines.

Hill 145, the prominent height off to the right in the 4th Division sector, was familiar ground to many troops in the 11th Brigade. Too

familiar for some. In the pre-dawn hours of March 1—five weeks earlier—members of the 54th ( Kootenay) Battalion and 75th (Mississauga Horse) Battalion had followed a protective cloud of phosgene
gas up Hill 145. The wind changed suddenly and overcame many of
the Canadians even with gas masks in place. Those not asphyxiated
by their own poison gas weapon became easy prey for alerted German gunners. Of 1,700 Canadians involved in the attack, nearly 700
became casualties. Eedson Burns, a signals officer with the 11th Brigade, had witnessed his commander, Victor Odlum, attempt to have
the gas raid cancelled and then, after the brigadier was overruled,
listened as the debacle unfolded that night.

Burns must have experienced déjà vu early in the April 9 assault
up Hill 145. On the phone to the brigadier, Burns learned that the
102nd Battalion—"Warden's Warriors"—had used the creeping barrage to clear the German first-line trenches and mount the slope. He
was also told that, according to plan, the 54th Battalion was now
leapfrogging through the 102nd position to pick up the attack. What
he didn't know was that the Warden's Warriors' advance had stalled
halfway up the hill (most of their officers were casualties) and the 54th
had also fallen back among the 102nd ranks, stymied by German gunners from above. Burns began moving his signals crew up the slope
expecting, when it was taken, to establish telephone communication
from the top of Hill 145.

"We got as far as the first line of trenches, the old German front
line," Burns said. "As soon as we got up to go on, we came under quite
heavy fire. Several of my men were hit. That's as far as we got. . . . I
tried to see if there was any way to get around this block. Several Germans were standing up and shooting at us as if we were rabbits."

What concerned Eedson Burns even more than being shot at like
rabbits was realizing his men were "about as warlike as rabbits." One
straggler with his unit strolled into the former German trench and
looked to Burns for guidance. Within seconds the young soldier
collapsed in front of him, shot dead by a sniper up the hill. When he
instructed another man to return the German sniper fire, the soldier
admitted he didn't know how; he had just arrived as a replacement. It

began to dawn on Burns that the bungled March 1 gas attack was still hurting the 11th Brigade. Reinforcements, filling the ranks of the seasoned troops lost in the gas raid, had arrived ill-trained, unrehearsed, and without baptism of fire. Inexperience might stunt the brigade's advance before the Germans did.

The situation went from bad to worse. Burns now noticed a section of troops en route up to his position to reconnoitre the scene. He realized they were wandering right into the German line of fire from up Hill 145. He dashed out to stop them and redirected them toward the 3rd Division advance off to the right. Attempting to clear German dugouts adjacent to his position along the hillside, Burns ran into another frantic Canadian soldier, who claimed the Germans had mounted a counterattack. It turned out to be German prisoners under escort going back to Canadian lines. No sooner had he calmed the frantic soldier than a German shell crashed into the prisoners and escort, tossing several across the mud like dolls. Each time Burns and his signals crew tried to move forward, however, German machine-gun fire chased them back. During one attempt, a bullet struck Burns's helmet, during another his gas mask was hit. That finished any hope of establishing phone lines atop Hill 145—at least for now.

Hopes of extending the Canadian Corps' reach up the north side of Hill 145 proved no brighter. When Alex Jack, a sergeant major with the 54th Battalion, reached the leading troops of his Kootenays group, he found them all jumbled together with advance troops of the 102nd Warden's Warriors, through whom they were supposed to leapfrog up the slope. Sgt. Maj. Jack was now dealing with flashbacks of the disastrous March 1 raid too. Was this a sick repeat performance? But the stalled advance wasn't the only shock that awaited him when he reached the sharp end. He discovered that about ninety men were huddled together in those forward craters and that all of the officers of both battalions had become casualties.

"So, as a young fellow of twenty-five," Jack said, "I found myself in command of the remains of two battalions, with our left flank up in the air and the Germans all around us at the back."

Alex Jack put thoughts of disaster out of his head. There was too little time and too few men to cope with the mission at hand. First, he sent a runner back with information about his position and then sorted out his hybrid battalion, sending 54th troops to defend the exposed flank, and 102nd men to advance to the right.

The two Farmer brothers were among those 102nd troops now suddenly under Alex Jack's command. Eddie and his younger brother, Art, had spent the first two and a half years of the war fighting in the same man's army, but never in the same part of the battlefield. Until today. Eddie Farmer, a rifleman, had gone over the top in the first wave at 5:30 a.m. with Warden's Warriors. Art Farmer, a signaller with the 11th Canadian Machine Gun Company (supporting the 102nd), had decided they should stick together and climbed the Canadian parapet with him. Then, later in the day, as the brothers attempted to move ahead to a new shell hole, a sniper shot Eddie Farmer through the wrist.

"We dropped into a shell hole," Art Farmer said. "I was able to give him first aid and after a few hurried goodbyes and words of advice, I realized I couldn't stay any longer."

As the younger brother made a dash for the next piece of ground that could provide some protection, he heard a shot go past him. He turned and realized his brother had pulled himself high enough in the shell hole to keep an eye on him, but also high enough to become a target.

"I heard the shot land and turned round to see him fall," Art Farmer said. "I'll never know whether that shot was intended for me, [but] when I got back to him a second time, he was gone."

The heights of Hill 145—claiming more Canadian attackers every minute—remained in German hands.

## 9 a.m. April 9, 1917—south of Hill 145, 3rd Division sector, Vimy

On the battlefield the Canadian Corps appeared like an army of privates. Partly as a means of protecting its officers from snipers, but also as a psychological lift for the rank and file, Canadian Army officers in

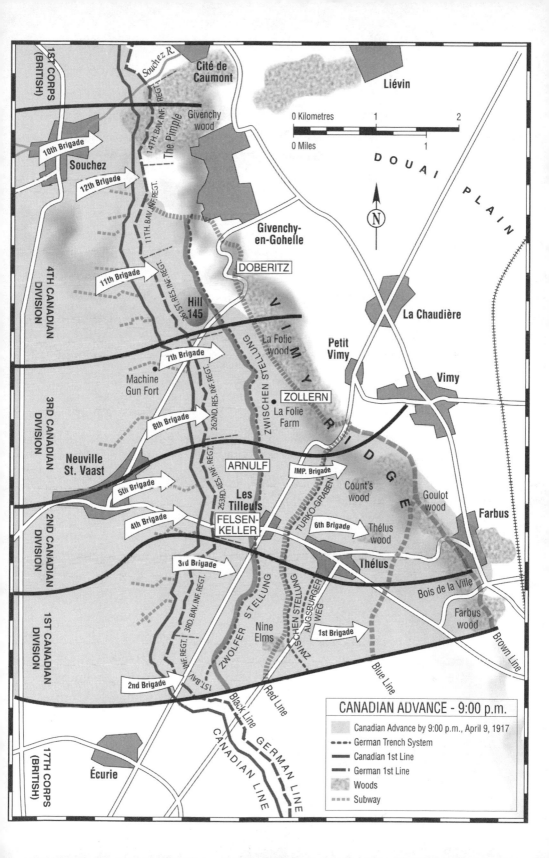

1ST CORPS (BRITISH)

Souchez R.

Cité de Caumont

Liévin

Givenchy wood

10th Brigade

12th Brigade

Souchez

14TH BAV. INF. REGT.

The Pimple

11TH BAV. INF. REGT.

0 Kilometres 1 2
0 Miles 1

DOUAI PLAIN

Givenchy-en-Gohelle

11th Brigade

4TH CANADIAN DIVISION

261ST. RES. INF. REGT.

DOBERITZ

Hill 145

La Folie wood

La Chaudière

Petit Vimy

Vimy

N

7th Brigade

Machine Gun Fort

262ND. RES. INF. REGT.

ZWISCHEN STELLUNG

ZOLLERN

La Folie Farm

3RD CANADIAN DIVISION

8th Brigade

Neuville St. Vaast

5th Brigade

263RD. RES. INF. REGT.

ARNULF

Les Tilleuls

IMP. Brigade

Count's wood

Goulot wood

Farbus

2ND CANADIAN DIVISION

4th Brigade

FELSEN-KELLER

TURKO-GRABEN

6th Brigade

Thélus wood

3rd Brigade

Thélus

Bois de la Ville

1ST CANADIAN DIVISION

ZWOLFER STELLUNG

Nine Elms

ZWISCHEN STELLUNG

AUGSBURGER WEG

1st Brigade

Farbus wood

Brown Line

2nd Brigade

3RD. BAV. INF. REGT.

1ST. BAV. INF. REGT.

1ST BAV. INF. REGT.

Blue Line

Black Line

Red Line

CANADIAN LINE

GERMAN LINE

17TH CORPS (BRITISH)

Écurie

CANADIAN ADVANCE – 9:00 p.m.

Canadian Advance by 9:00 p.m., April 9, 1917
German Trench System
Canadian 1st Line
German 1st Line
Woods
Subway

No Man's Land this day only wore rank insignia on their lapels. The only other aspect that differentiated officers from enlisted men was that they carried revolvers, not rifles. Eric Finley, a major with the 42nd Battalion, recalled "it was the first time that officers wore privates' uniforms."

Initially his battalion—the Black Watch of Montreal—moved forward in the first wave of the 7th Brigade attack in the 3rd Division sector. With the creeping barrage ahead of them "we were conscious of the fact that we were all bending our heads down," but the only resistance they encountered came from the left, where the Germans used enfilade fire from the top of Hill 145. It was further evidence that the German resistance atop Hill 145 was hampering the Canadian advance in both the 3rd and 4th Division sectors. About a third of a mile into the enemy lines, Finley took a flat piece of shrapnel in his back and was knocked unconscious. When he eventually came to, and caught up with his battalion, his men were charging German gun emplacements with bayonets, while Germans fought back with potato-masher grenades. In the fighting, Finley emptied his revolver into enemy troops, but was then struck down by a blow to the helmet. The next thing he knew, he was lying in a shell hole. Snow was falling and a Canadian was leaning over him.

"Well, they've got you at last, Eric," Rev. George Kilpatrick joked.

Finley smiled back at the familiar face of the regimental chaplain, who was in the battlefield assisting stretcher bearers and medics with the 3rd Division.

"Can you make it home?" Kilpatrick asked.

"I've got to try," Finley said.

"The fire is very, very bad," the reverend pointed out as he linked Finley up with another wounded Canadian so the two could lean on each other en route back to a first aid station. Before they began limping away from the battlefield, however, the two Canadians offered assistance to a wounded German—just a boy, Finley remembered—and pulled him between them as they walked. They had barely made it away from the original shell hole when a shot blew through the young German.

"The boy was killed right under our noses," Finley said. "His heart was shot out of his body by a dumdum bullet. All he said was 'Errr' and he was dead before he hit the ground."

Throughout the day, Rev. Kilpatrick continued moving about the battlefield, assisting medical staff as they treated the wounded. At every step the Canadian medics also seemed to gather more and more German prisoners. At one point Kilpatrick joined a doctor going "down into a German dugout, armed with nothing but a flashlight and a pair of scissors and [we] brought up five husky prisoners." The closer he got to the northern edge of the 3rd Division sector, however, the more the chaplain found deadly evidence of the German crossfire from the top of Hill 145. Kilpatrick was in the middle of binding a splint to a soldier's wounded leg when he was summoned to where Charles Owston, a medical sergeant with the 42nd Battalion, had been hit.*

"I went to a shell hole and found him with a bullet through the jugular vein," Kilpatrick said. "He died in my arms in about fifteen seconds. Just like a blind being pulled down, his life was gone."

To the south of the 42nd Battalion position—in the centre of the 8th Brigade advance—members of the 2nd Canadian Mounted Rifles had moved more quickly toward their objective, La Folie Farm. Though he didn't have to contend with the German enfilade from atop Hill 145, Cpl. Gus Sivertz and his comrades faced numerous machine-gun nests—each of these strongpoints was encased in concrete with a slot of steel through which the German machine gunners could fire an arc.

"I figured that if I could get around them with a Mills bomb," Sivertz said, "and drop it behind them, they could share it among them and we could clean it up."

---

* Sgt. Charles Owston, whom Rev. Kilpatrick describes as "the greatest gentleman I knew," had been an orphan, a Barnardo boy; originally an officer with the 42nd Battalion, Owston got into trouble, resigned his commission, rejoined the Black Watch as a private, and became a sergeant just before Vimy. He was twenty-six when he died April 9, 1917.

Sivertz got to within sixty yards of his objective and decided to have a quick look to gauge his position. He was later thankful that his hand, poised to pull the pin of the bomb, wasn't touching the pin, because as he raised his head above the shell hole for a look, the machine gunner made a sweep of fire across Sivertz's location. The crash of bullets against his helmet knocked him down and out cold. A while later, when he came to, the rain had stopped, but his face was still damp and salty tasting. He put his hand to his face, looked at it, and realized his face was bloody, but he had also touched a bandage there.

"By God, I'm hit," Sivertz said aloud. "I've got a Blighty!"

There was blood in his mouth, blood in his gas mask container, even blood in his boots. His left temple artery had been cut and had gushed profusely until somebody had bound it up before moving on. Alone in an otherwise empty battleground, Sivertz tried to determine his position. He spotted the double spires of the ruins of Mont St. Eloi's church in the distance and turned to get there, but he felt so lightheaded that he just stumbled over the muck as if "I was taking great seven-foot steps and going over the ground without any effort at all." Closer to the spires, he paused to study the barrage now blocking his path to the old Canadian trenches. The Germans were firing with limited artillery in one sector, then lifting to another, then another. Sivertz waited until their artillery had lifted from the 3rd Division sector to make his move. He still wasn't sure where he was.

"And I saw a piece of wood, white painted wood, a triangle about two inches sticking out of the mud," he said. "I took it out, wiped it on my pants. It said on it 'Ross Street.' I flung it up in the air. That was the point from which we had started that morning before dawn."

Within a few hours, as he suspected, Cpl. Gus Sivertz was out of the line, into a dressing station, wearing a blue indelible ink cross on his forehead, receiving cigarettes from an eager-beaver YMCA officer, then a packet of Wrigley's gum from a nurse on a hospital train, and eventually a ligature operation on the artery at a hospital near Southampton—in Blighty.

The army telegram, dispatched to his family's home in Victoria, B.C., had a typographical error. It said that Sivertz had a "gunshot wound in hand," which bewildered his parents until they received another message from Gus himself saying he was in hospital with a wound to the head, but all right.

## 11 a.m. April 9, 1917—262nd Reserve Infantry Regiment, Zollern sector, Vimy

Contradictory reports, mistaken predictions, overreaction, and assumption driven by bravado rather than by fact affected the German commanders' understanding of the battlefield too. Some saw the Canadian barrage being directed entirely by aircraft using Verey lights to mark targets, so they believed that if the planes were eliminated so would the accuracy of Allied artillery. Others feared when the Canadian infantry broke through that Allied cavalry and other mobile troops would put German defenders on the run as far back as the Hindenburg Line. German war diarists did record, however, that the Canadian assault had opened up a twelve-kilometre-wide gap along the Arras front. For fusilier Otto Schroeder, fighting in the 262nd Reserve Infantry, however, the battlefield in his immediate vicinity generated enough desperation and myth for an entire lifetime.

When Canadian Corps troops of the 3rd Division began appearing in front of his trench, Schroeder was sent to retrieve additional hand grenades. But the opposing soldiers overran the trench so quickly, by the time he returned to a position along the parapet, he was alone next to the body of a dead comrade. Everywhere he looked beyond the trench "left and right and forward, I saw only Britishers, who in their straw hats [steel helmets] looked as if they were hare-hunting." To save himself, Schroeder pulled the nearby body into the trench and got down beside it, acting as if he were dead too. Most of the Canadians raced past him, but one stopped and bayoneted his dead comrade. Schroeder flinched, fearing he would be next.

"Come on!" the Canadian soldier shouted at him.

Schroeder climbed out of the trench, saying a silent goodbye to his trench mate, just as the Canadian put his bayonet to Schroeder's chest.

"You wounded, no?"

The German shrugged his shoulders. He really didn't understand.

Then, just as quickly, the Canadian and his threatening bayonet were gone, in hot pursuit of the ever-moving advance over the German trenches. Schroeder decided not to wait around for another close call and began running toward the neighbouring 261st Reserve sector. A Canadian rifleman spotted him and shot him in the forearm. He kept moving, but the next man Schroeder encountered was another German infantryman. They moved on together "amongst the dead which had been mowed down by machine guns," until they found the top stairs of a dugout to shield themselves from German artillery shells now landing in the area. Schroeder took this to mean a German counterattack was underway and it would be best to stay put. They would soon be back in friendly territory. The two Germans were thunderstruck, however, when a dugout door opened and a Canadian stepped out. Escorted inside, they found a half-dozen Canadians (apparently medical orderlies) playing a game of cards.

"Hello, Fritz, are you wounded?" one of the orderlies asked, pointing at Schroeder's injured wrist.

He nodded and watched the orderly examine his arm.

"Not good," the Canadian said. Then he bandaged the wrist and gave Schroeder and his comrade food and water. Once he had his strength back, Schroeder was led out of the dugout and—along with other German prisoners whom Schroeder recognized—escorted to a Canadian dressing station where a doctor treated his wounded wrist.

"I realized then," Schroeder wrote, "that [the Canadians] meant to hold Vimy Ridge at all cost."

Otto Schroeder had departed a battlefield that changed with all the speed Allied strategists had expected. The 7th Brigade, spearheaded by the Black Watch (42nd) Battalion, the Princess Patricia's Canadian Light Infantry, and the Royal Canadian Regiment, had taken the first German trenches in twenty minutes. They had blown through the Black Line and on to the shattered tree trunks of La Folie wood forty-five minutes later. By the end of the morning, when Otto Schroeder was captured, the 49th (Alberta) Battalion had joined the advance as the second wave. Members of the battalion were providing support for the first wave with trench mortars, carrying parties, rifle reinforcements, stretcher bearers, and mop-up troops. When he arrived at the first German trenches that the PPCLI had attacked, Byron Morrison found stretcher bearers attending wounded Canadians and scores of German prisoners filing through the battlefield back toward Canadian lines. But something odd was also happening.

"I'd hear a shot nearby and suddenly see one of our fellows drop," Sgt. Morrison said. "I looked around," but he couldn't figure out where the shots were coming from. Then, when another nearby shot was fired, Morrison spotted a German "playing possum. He was wounded alright, but he was picking these [Canadian] boys off one by one. Did I burn up! I was carrying a Colt .45 and I had a full clip. I ran up to the guy . . . and just emptied the full clip into his belly."

In contrast to such outbursts, a medical officer at Aux Rietz dressing station saw human kindness between battlefield enemies. All morning long, Capt. Andrew Macphail had rounded up extra blankets, stretchers, and dressings in anticipation of the rush on his supplies. Wounded arrived at Aux Rietz cave on stretchers for transfer to the narrow-gauge tram and transport farther back to casualty clearing stations. Even as random shells continued to fall outside the cave, Macphail watched everybody pay full attention to tending the wounded.

"There were more prisoners than our men and they were working as well as any," Macphail wrote. "One German prisoner, wounded in the leg, had his arm around the shoulders of a Canadian who himself was wounded in the arm. And they walked along like two [brothers]."

About an hour after he left the Canadian trenches, beyond the Black Line in the 3rd Division sector, Pte. Harold Barker was hit by shrapnel. The scout in the Royal Canadian Regiment had moved too quickly and suddenly realized he'd walked into the Allied creeping barrage.

"When we were going over the [rehearsal] tapes at Bruay in the rear," Barker said, "we had to wait so long for the barrage to lift, but I didn't think anything about that. I kept on going. I was too fast."

Shrapnel hit him in the mouth, chest, leg, and back. The impact of so many hits on his body knocked him down and into semi-consciousness. Sometime later, when he began to focus again, he discovered that he'd lost some teeth and part of his gum. But he didn't know where he was. Men were passing him by the score. He realized they were Germans. He didn't notice they were without rifles and helmets. The last two Germans in the passing column of men stopped beside him.

"Do you need help?" one of the Germans said.

"I can't get up," Barker answered.

"We'll help you."

Barker was surprised that the German spoke English so well. Still dizzy and disoriented, he concluded that he was now a prisoner of war and the Germans were escorting him to a prison camp. Eventually, the column of Germans arrived at the entrance to the Grange Subway. A Canadian officer recognized Barker, and he was taken from the line of Germans and given first aid.

"They took the Germans away," Barker said. "*They* were the prisoners. I thought *I* was the prisoner."

German prisoners moved to the rear echelon of the Canadian lines all day long. Estimates varied as to the exact number of enemy troops captured at Vimy that first day, partly because wounded prisoners went to dressing stations well behind the lines, while those not wounded were herded into holding cages and processed closer to the front. Consequently, POW totals varied. Some suggested fewer than a thousand Germans were captured. The war diary of the Canadian Corps of Cyclists claims its troops "processed over 4,000 of them," while Capt. Macphail wrote that he watched the cages "filling with prisoners. We have in the 2nd Division alone taken 2,050 prisoners." In the 1st Division sector, transport officer Evan Ryrie reported 3,000 prisoners being held and Canadians "lined around the cages . . . trading cigarettes and bully beef for watches, compasses and any other souvenirs the Boche has."

## 12 noon April 9, 1917—Crossroads near Thélus,
## 2nd Division sector, Vimy

In addition to members of the signal corps, the cyclists corps, despatch motorcycle riders, and all the signals crews burying telephone and telegraph lines or experimenting with wireless radio equipment at Vimy Ridge, there was another corps of men—and their accomplices—who helped defeat the Germans at Vimy. Beginning at the Somme in 1916, at least two men in every company in the Canadian Corps received special training in the use of carrier pigeons to send and receive messages along the Western Front. Throughout the lead-up to the Vimy attack, members of the Canadian Mounted Rifles, among others, took one-day courses with British specialists in the Carrier Pigeon Service (CPS) and learned the efficient use of pigeons for sending messages.

"For distances up to fifty or sixty miles, pigeons were practically infallible," wrote Col. W.H. Osman, founder of the CPS. "More than ninety-five per cent of the messages sent by pigeon post were safely delivered."

All armies in the Great War recognized the value of attaching a thimble-sized message carrier (canister) with a message inside to the leg of a carrier pigeon and releasing the bird to fly to its home loft. The Italians had more than 50,000 birds in service. When the United States Army arrived in Europe in June 1917, it included a pigeon service of 9 officers, 324 soldiers, 50 mobile lofts, and 6,000 trained birds. During the Verdun campaign in 1916, when the French commander was surrounded at Vaux, France, his last bird flew through enemy fire with the distress call. The bird dropped dead upon delivery of the message, but was recognized with a French Legion d'Honneur diploma. The French Army used 5,000 birds for sending messages at the Somme alone; only two percent of the birds failed to arrive at their destination lofts. By 1917, Osman and his CPS staff of 400 had built the British Army flock to nearly 22,000 birds. They operated 150 mobile lofts, each looking like a double-decker bus with human quarters on the lower level and bird housing on the upper. During the Arras campaign that year, with artillery shells and machine-gun fire filling the sky, this message was dispatched via pigeon:

> Messages now received from all Companies in Brown Line. Just about to advance to Blue at proper hour. Artillery fire a bit short. Shovels wanted. Have seen Colonel Campbell and shall proceed myself to village. Resistance feeble.
>      Place: Green Line. Time 2:45 p.m.
>      Sender's Signature: R. McCalmont.

The CPS pigeon carrying this message arrived at its home loft at 3:10 p.m. just twenty-five minutes after it was written and the bird sent aloft. On this day on the Western Front alone, over 400 operation messages came back from tanks and attacking forces. The Germans also employed carrier pigeons and even attempted to bomb the main British pigeon loft on Doughty Street in London.

"We often captured [German] pigeons," Osman wrote, "but few of their message holders."

At Vimy there was an exception. When Canadian Corps soldiers of the 1st and 2nd Divisions moved beyond the Red Line, through the town of Thélus, they began clearing basements, dugouts, cellars, bunkers, and nearby caves of any German stragglers. About midday on April 9, Charles Lindsey, an intelligence officer attached to General Staff operations behind Canadian lines, received notification of a unique discovery in a cave near the crossroads outside Thélus.

"They found a pigeon with an undelivered message still strapped to its leg," Lindsey wrote. "It simply said that the Germans needed reinforcements immediately," which was no surprise to the Canadians who invaded the cave. They had captured both the messenger and the sender all in one place.*

---

* Lt.-Col. Charles Lindsey, a member of the Queen's Own Rifles, realized there was a standing order that all captured documents, including pigeon dispatches, had to be turned in. Despite that requirement, he said, "I kept it" and later donated the pigeon canister and message to the Royal Canadian Military Institute in Toronto.

Those same crossroads in front of Thélus held a different surprise for Pte. William Pecover. As the Allied barrage quickly rolled
up the ground in that 2nd Division sector, the 4th and 5th Brigades
reached the *Turko-Graben* trench—the Red Line. At that point, the
men of the leading brigades paused. The second wave of the 6th
Brigade, including Pecover's 27th (Winnipeg) Battalion, was then expected to leapfrog over the Red Line and follow the creeping barrage
as it crashed through the village of Thélus. However, at the crossroads
the Winnipeggers realized an enemy barrage was blocking its path.

"German artillery were shelling the Lens-Arras road, which we
had to cross," Pecover said. "We wondered how anybody could get
through it alive. The officer leading us was from the southern States.
In his broad southern dialect, he said that we had to get through it. It
was every man for himself."

Pecover and his best friend, Argyle McMurchie, ran the gauntlet
and came through the barrage safely. Many others in their battalion
didn't make it. Then the second wave of Winnipeggers started bombing the German dugouts around Thélus. Sometimes the bombs persuaded the Germans to come out calling, "Mercy, *Kamerad*, mercy."
Other times Pecover used his high school German and called into the
darkened dugouts: "*Kommen Sie hier. Kommen Sie.*" It did the trick.
The Germans would emerge from their underground hiding places
offering souvenirs and asking for clemency. Pecover and McMurchie
rounded up dozens of prisoners through the midday this way and
directed them to the rear.

As in other divisional sectors, behind the 2nd Division assault
troops a colour-coded army of second-wave soldiers—each wearing
different-coloured arm bands—carried out specific tasks. Scouts wore
green arm bands for guiding the advancing troops. Those wearing
red bands were running messages back and forth. The mop-up troops
were marked on the sleeve with white bands, while those carrying
supplies—picks and shovels, water, bombs and mortars—had yellow
arm bands to distinguish them from the rest.

Gordon Shrum didn't wear an arm band, but he did feel a bit like
"a tourist on the battlefield." Leading up to the April 9 attack—his

baptism of fire—the gunner had served in the Royal Canadian Artillery principally as an ammunition carrier. For two weeks solid he had hauled individual thirty-five-pound howitzer shells from the end of the narrow-gauge railway to the 29th Battery behind the front lines. Then, at 7 a.m. on Easter Monday during the creeping barrage, his howitzer fired prematurely—the shell went off before leaving the gun barrel. Miraculously, no one was hurt, but the premature explosion tore the gun barrel and put the howitzer out of action.

"You guys are of no value around here," an officer told Shrum and his crew mates. "You're no good in a war without a gun. So we'll give you a roll of wire" to carry up the ridge for the signals soldiers. Back to his old carrying-party job, he and a fellow gunner hauled the wire across the battlefield up Vimy Ridge. When they rested, they talked to wounded soldiers, offering what help they could. By afternoon, when they'd caught up with the 4th and 5th Brigade troops, they were ordered to help dig gun pits for Canadian guns when they arrived at the new positions.

"We started to dig in the rain and snow," Shrum said. "It was almost pure chalk, so greasy and slippery [whenever] you drove the pick in it, it didn't come out. We dug these gun pits . . . fairly deep, so that you could stand up. And this was my battle at Vimy."

### 1:30 p.m. April 9, 1917—Blue Line, 1st Division sector, Vimy

Youthful enthusiasm in most Canadian Corps troops during the Vimy Ridge attack instilled an air of confidence, if not a sense of invulnerability. Some soldiers just exuded confidence as well as fatalism this day. Roy Henley often said of his 5th Royal Highlanders battalion, "We knew we were good. We knew we were the best." That sort of bravado was not uncommon among members of many Canadian battalions, including Henley's 13th Battalion. What even Pte. Henley's superior officers didn't realize, however, was that the boastful Lewis gunner who had enlisted in Toronto, was perhaps the youngest soldier at Vimy that day.

"I had put my birth date down as 1898 instead of 1901," Henley said. He'd been thirteen when the war broke out, fourteen when he signed up with the Royal Canadian Dragoons to become a trumpeter, and barely sixteen at Vimy Ridge. And nobody but Henley knew. As for his confidence, he chalked that up to his rum ration. "George Oak, my platoon sergeant, would come along with the rum jar. I didn't take it straight. I dipped it in a hunk of bread. But you could go and lick your weight in wildcats after that!"

Whatever it was on April 9 that powered him through the elaborate tunnel system, into the forward trenches, and over the top in the second wave that morning gave Henley good fortune as well. In the 13th Battalion's push across the forward German trenches to the Black Line just after 6 a.m. and the Red Line trenches of *Zwischen Stellung* just after 7 a.m. Pte. Henley had barely a scratch on him. His water bottle had a bullet hole in it. His kilt had two shots through it. A bullet had also torn his sock and bruised his foot. Otherwise, Henley had nothing to complain about. At the Blue Line, several hundred yards farther east, counterattack shells began landing in the sector and shrapnel hit Henley in the back.

"If I'm wounded seriously," Henley said, "okay, I get to Blighty. If I'm wounded seriously enough I may get sent home. And if I'm killed I'm not going to know bugger all about it anyway. So why worry about it?"

By noon, stretcher bearers had carried Henley back to the tunnels and into a casualty clearing station in the neighbouring 51st Highland Division (British) sector. Wounded but not out of action completely, Pte. Henley would be back in the line in time for his seventeenth birthday and the battle at Passchendaele. Meanwhile, his battalion continued to make history at Vimy. Linking up with 2nd Division troops as they chased the last German troops from the village of Thélus, 13th Battalion troops swept over the crest of the ridge. The sun broke through the clouds at that moment and there were "Tommy" helmets left and right and behind as far as the eye could see. Ahead of them the Montrealers focused on Farbus wood and, again following the creeping barrage, they entered the small forest to find German gunners, killed by the barrage, and otherwise intact but abandoned artillery. It marked the first time in the history of siege warfare on the Western Front that Allied forces had advanced rapidly enough to capture German artillery.

At about noon, the 4th (Central Ontario) Battalion passed the crest of Vimy Ridge with the Black Watch troops en route to Farbus. The Allied creeping barrage still had as much punch at midday as it had at 5:30 a.m. Bill Green, a private in the 4th Battalion, still found the carnage around him hard to stomach. The bodies of German troops had been mangled and torn open by the barrage explosions. Then, just past the Blue Line, members of his battalion seemed to pick up speed behind the barrage. Pte. Green was walking steadily ahead with several men from his platoon and without warning witnessed the brutality of the falling artillery shells first-hand.

"One of our shells—a dud—cut the head off a machine gunner and took the leg off a lance/corporal beside him. The machine gunner actually walked two steps with his head off and the machine gun on his shoulder. . . . The head struck the man next to him in the chest. . . .

"The rule was no armed troop in action could stop and help wounded. They were to stick a rifle in the ground and put his steel [helmet] on top for the medical corps to see. They would look after him. . . . The lance/corporal bled to death before help could get to him."

### 2:20 p.m. April 7, 1917—Farbus wood, Vimy

Another group of soldiers that had thus far only been observers of the battle also entered the ruins of Thélus about midday. Two troops of cavalry came forward with the second wave of infantry awaiting orders to attack. Each unit of the Canadian Light Horse (cavalry), when it was at full strength, included an officer, two sergeants, and thirty-two other riders. With the crest of the ridge occupied as far as the Blue Line by troops of the 1st and 2nd Division, the opportunity seemed ripe to press home the attack deeper into German territory on horseback.

As a German infantryman stationed at *Zwischen Stellung* had noted, "had the enemy used faster troops, such as cavalry or motorized units, our front would have been torn open even wider." Canadian Corps commander Julian Byng, however, could not send in the cavalry until he had permission from British First Army headquarters, that is, from Field Marshal Douglas Haig himself. Given the green light, the Canadian Light Horse (CLH) was ordered forward—3rd Troop to charge German positions at Farbus wood and 4th Troop to veer along the road to German-held Willerval.

Nearly all the circumstances at Vimy conspired against a cavalry charge almost before it began. Traditionally, cavalry in the Napoleonic Wars or even more recently the Boer War covered open gaps in combat zones where other troops were absent. The Vimy front was so congested with armies, there literally wasn't room for cavalry to manoeuvre. A soldier on horseback presented such a large and obvious target in such a denuded landscape, any surviving German gunners could easily spot and stop any threat. Even if the rider reached his objective quickly, he lacked the firepower and armour to hold it until ground troops arrived. And if such strategic factors hadn't undermined a cavalry charge already, ultimately the weather and the mired condition of the ground would. One former CLH trooper, George Hambley (who was manning a Vickers machine gun at Vimy), wrote in his diary that "our regiment of horses were of little or no value whatever in the actual victory over the enemy." Nevertheless, the two CLH cavalry charges—with swords drawn—went ahead.

Though Canadian infantry had entered Farbus wood about midday and scared off some enemy troops, the 1st Brigade troops had then pulled back to Thélus to consolidate their position. Consequently, any German gunners reclaiming Farbus wood that afternoon quickly homed in on the 3rd Troop cavalry as its horses bogged down in the chewed-up ground in front of the wood. German artillery shells brought down on the charging cavalry sent horses and riders somersaulting through the air. Machine-gun bullets felled many of the rest. Only half the troop—barely sixteen men and their mounts—made it to the wood to continue the assault. There they had to dismount to take on the enemy, but the battered woods of fallen and splintered trees inhibited any forward momentum. The troop decided to sit tight and wait for the 4th Troop to return from farther up the road at Willerval.

That attack disintegrated just as disastrously. Though most of the 4th Troop riders had formerly worked as cowboys, ranchers, and farmers in Saskatchewan, not even expert horsemanship could get them past the quagmire en route to the village. Meanwhile, German reinforcement troops were arriving. They had set up a hidden machine gun and began scything down the remains of the 4th Troop at the entrance to the village; only ten of thirty men reached Willerval. In spite of the beating it took, the troop initially took some prisoners, but in the hail of return fire suddenly it became every man for himself as the troop retreated. One trooper, F.M. Morton, described his horse falling on top of him and breaking his leg. His sword had gone flying, his rifle remained stuck on his saddle, and with bullets ricocheting off the cobblestones around him, Morton was forced to limp away armed only with a bayonet.

When the remains of the 4th Troop rejoined the remains of the 3rd Troop at Farbus, the group was spotted by the pilot of a red-coloured fighter aircraft—a member of Richthofen's Flying Circus—who strafed them and then called down more German artillery to pound the position again. Though only a handful of troopers returned from the afternoon's attack, they were cheered by Canadian infantry-men for their courage and initiative. The charge of the Canadian Light Horse had been a morale booster, but a tactical disaster. Typical was the experience of Sgt. Steve Keay. His horse had sustained eighteen bullet wounds in its neck before dying. His troop's trumpeter "was picking horse's guts from around his neck and face. . . . A shell had landed under a horse running beside him. No doubt the horse had saved his life," Keay wrote. Of about a dozen riderless horses returning from the charge, most were destroyed right there at Thélus.

## 5:45 p.m. April 9, 1917—Hill 145, 4th Division sector, Vimy

Although he was ready for front-line duty, J.C. Uhlman spent Easter Monday morning with a shovel in his hands, not a Lee Enfield rifle. The twenty-year-old infantryman, serving with the 85th Battalion, watched and listened from behind the lines as sister battalions of the 11th Brigade went over the top to attack Hill 145. Somebody had to be a work party on D-Day at Vimy. Uhlman's Nova Scotia High-landers were it. Whether they liked it or not, Uhlman and his com-rades in the 85th had been relegated to rear-echelon duty, digging a communication trench behind the Souchez Subway, well out of harm's way.

"We were proud to belong to the Canadian Expeditionary Force [CEF]," Uhlman said, "[but] we remained in reserve that morning."

J.C. Uhlman came from Carlton, Nova Scotia. His father had spent most of J.C.'s youth away in the woods, supervising log drives, running sawmills, and locating spruce timbers as masts for the wooden ship industry. After completing high school in Yarmouth, J.C. went off to the United States to seek his fortune. Then he got married and was prepared to settle down back home in Nova Scotia when "a pal of mine in the Canadian Expeditionary Force, was killed overseas and I thought it was time I did something about it." That year—1916— Uhlman responded to recruitment calls for a new Highland brigade that would become part of the proposed 5th Canadian Infantry Divi-sion. The initiative fizzled. Mounting casualties overseas meant new recruits would become reinforcements in old battalions, not part of a new division. And though the 85th Battalion remained intact, other Maritimers sort of dismissed the 85th as "the Highlanders without kilts."

Kilts or no, Uhlman and his fellow Nova Scotia recruits came through the same training regimen as anybody else in the CEF, and then some. They were kitted with khaki uniforms, putties, and boots, and then underwent intensive PT (physical training) and bayonet drill, as well as army discipline exercises. Uhlman took an NCO course and achieved lance/corporal level, "but my voice wasn't as strong as these sergeant-majors with the bellowing voices [so] I was a lance/corporal without a stripe." By October, the 85th had arrived at Salisbury Plain in southern England for more training, lectures, indoctrination, and instruction on machine guns, signals, and gas masks, including one exercise through gas chambers without wearing masks. By the time Cpl. Uhlman and the Nova Scotia Highlanders got to France, he was a sniper. But the battalion was still doing route marches, bayonet training, hill scaling, and scattering manoeuvres, "lying down, getting buried and making ourselves as small as possible." As the battle plan for the Vimy attack on April 9 began to filter down from divisional and brigade levels, there appeared to be no front-line role for the 85th Battalion.

"I think I just accepted things and went along," Uhlman said. "There was a tremendous amount of gunfire and artillery that day. Awesome. . . . It never entered my mind I'd be killed. I just accepted that we were in reserve and out of the fighting that day."

All that changed suddenly on Easter Monday afternoon.

In spite of eight hours of fighting, the Canadian advance up Hill 145 remained stalled. German resistance from the heights meant that the creeping barrage up Vimy Ridge had left most of the 11th Brigade troops far behind. The brigade's brute-force attempts to scale the slope had failed. The two principal assault battalions—the 54th and the 102nd—remained pinned down unable to advance a yard. Meanwhile, the follow-up signals crew simply made the shell holes that were full of infantrymen even more crowded and confused. Making matters worse, Brig.-Gen. Victor Odlum had received only a trickle of accurate information. Of thirty scouts sent out to bring back news, only one had returned safely. Hill 145 was a hinge on which much of the battle at Vimy Ridge depended. Well into the afternoon of April 9, it remained solidly in German control and the potential for its use as a jumping-off point for a German counterattack remained high.

Another deliberate attack was needed, this time preceded by a precision barrage.

Just before 3 p.m. Odlum summoned company commanders with the 85th Battalion—Harvey Crowell and Percy Anderson—to his 11th Brigade quarters in the Tottenham Subway. The "C" and "D" Companies of the Nova Scotia Highlanders would mount a new attack on Hill 145 later that afternoon, following a box barrage that would cordon the hilltop with intense artillery fire. Zero Hour for the artillery shelling was 5:45 p.m.

"I didn't have much faith in [the accuracy of] a box barrage when the artillery had been lifting their sights all morning, chasing the Germans in the back lines," Capt. Crowell said. "But those were our orders."

All afternoon, the Highlanders assembled underground and in the forward jumping-off trenches. They were wading through galleys and trenches that had filled with the runoff of melted snow, so even before their baptism of fire on Vimy Ridge, all members of the battalion were soaked to the waist. As it was, Cpl. Uhlman was already drenched from hauling water to the work party all morning. Now he was weighed down by the extra ammunition, digging tools, and rations he was carrying for a frontal attack on the entrenched German positions on Hill 145. Just before the start of the box barrage, everybody was hunkered down in the jumping-off trenches, waiting. Capt. Harvey Crowell, commander of "C" Company from Halifax, looked to the west.

"I remember seeing the brassy setting sun hanging just over the broken spires of the church at Mont St. Eloi," Crowell wrote. "And this same sun was blazing in the eyes of the Germans while we were advancing."

When 5:45 arrived, however, there was no box barrage. Watches had been synchronized, but at thirty seconds and sixty seconds past Zero Hour, there were no Allied shells softening up the German gun emplacements atop the hill. At the last minute Brig.-Gen. Odlum, on the advice of Lt.-Col. A.H. Borden, C.O. of the 85th Battalion, had cancelled the barrage. Borden feared the box barrage might further damage the leading battalions part way up Hill 145. Odlum's cancellation message did not reach the jumping-off trenches in time. Capt. Crowell checked his watch again and looked to his left. The commander of neighbouring 9 Platoon, Lt. Frederick Manning, was standing and looking equally bewildered by the absence of the promised artillery. Both men decided simultaneously they would attack, barrage or no barrage.

"We hadn't gone fifty yards before a shell landed right in our midst," Crowell said. "We found that on our front we had three or four machine-gun emplacements. [The Germans were hiding] forty to fifty feet down in dugouts. When the bombardment was on they went down, but when it was over they came up."

Cpl. Uhlman and his platoon had crossed the old German front line. He was now officially in No Man's Land again. Then he felt a whack on his leg "like somebody throwing a rock at your knee." To the first wave of Highlanders headed up the slope, it seemed as if a waterfall of shell shrapnel and bullets was now pouring down from the German positions above. With much difficulty, Crowell encouraged his company to press ahead. Then, at the moment the Nova Scotians needed some inspiration the most, a corporal in their midst provided it.

"At a range of about one hundred yards, Cpl. M.H. Curll put the wind up the Germans with rifle bombs," Crowell wrote. "I had never drawn my own revolver and no man was even thinking of Mills bombs . . . and Curll's action in firing off a rifle bomb from the hip while advancing really saved many lives."

Watching Curll sending in rounds of the grenades this way caught the attention of other rifle bombers in "C" Company. Some of them had recently taken special training for this style of assault. They followed Curll's example. By the time the men were within fifty yards of the German second line—with five machine guns still firing back— the line of Canadians all firing grenades at the positions turned the tide. Crowell saw some of the German gunners beginning to abandon their position.

"I was twenty yards away from one of these guns," he said. "The gunners were starting to race back down over the hill. [But] they had to climb up out of their slippery trench. . . . Three Germans. The top man started to slide down and he whacked into the face of the man behind him. And the three of them came right down the hill there at our feet. I was almost on the point of laughing when I felt as if a mule kicked me in the back."

Crowell had been shot through the shoulder. Uhlman had been hit by shrapnel in the knee. Manning had a broken leg from shrapnel and bullet wounds to his head; he died of internal bleeding in hospital six days later. But Curll's bold action had spurred the rest of "C" Company to finish the job at the crest of Hill 145. The 85th Battalion men barged into the gun emplacements and either overpowered or killed seventy enemy troops inside the bunkers. "I couldn't stop my boys," Crowell said. "We were then on our objective and I had to pull them back."

Nor could Capt. Percy Anderson. As Crowell and "C" Company took one side of the hill, Anderson's "D" Company from Cape Breton had roared over the other. Capping the advance, Anderson entered the stronghold with his men and shot the first German he met. He demanded that the next German drop his ammunition belt, and when he didn't comply, Anderson tore it from the man himself, as other "D" Company troops killed or captured the others still manning the gun emplacement.

"The ordinary man was overcome with the lust to kill," Crowell said, "chasing Huns towards the Fatherland."

Lester Giffin had a special mission late that evening of April 9. A reserve member of the 85th Battalion, he joined a work party carrying food rations up Hill 145 that evening. Each man in the group of thirty-five Nova Scotia Highlanders carried portions of bully beef and bread in sandbags slung over their shoulders. When he emerged from Tottenham Subway on his way forward, Cpl. Giffin was shaken momentarily because "on the barbed wire just outside the tunnel in the pale moonlight, splayed back looking up into the sky, was a dead soldier. . . ."

Giffin tried to ignore the body and pushed on. He had a personal interest in getting the rations through to the top of the hill. His brother Randolph Giffin had fought with "C" Company during the attack. Lester soon discovered his "hero" Randolph had made it safely through the battle.*

Meanwhile, at 9 p.m. Captains Anderson and Crowell reported to Maj. J. Layton Ralston, the adjutant of "the Highlanders without kilts," that Hill 145 was in Canadian hands. In turn, Ralston (later defence minister in the Louis St. Laurent government) wrote, "I was proud of the battalion before. I'm a thousand times more so now. At the last minute, they were given a tough nut to crack. . . . Our name is written down now."

---

* Randolph Giffin was killed in action as the CEF worked its way from Cambrai to Valenciennes, France, on October 22, 1918, just twenty days before the Armistice.

# THE PROMISED LAND

**2 p.m. April 9, 1917—Red Line overlooking Douai Plain, Vimy**

NEWS of the Easter Monday attack and the Canadians' early success made its way behind the lines by word of mouth initially. On April 9, a member of the 25th Field Battery was travelling to the front. During a midday stop at Houdain, fifteen miles northwest of Vimy, the officer sat for a meal with some French Army officers just as the first news of attack on Vimy Ridge arrived. The French scoffed at the suggestion that the Germans were retreating from the ridge. "*C'est impossible!*" they told the artillery officer. When he pointed out that the Canadian Corps was responsible, the French officers changed their tune. "*Les Canadiens*," they said. "*Alors, c'est possible.*"

A fellow officer with the 25th Field Battery may well have provided the grist for such conversations that day. Elmore Philpott, a gunnery officer with the 25th, had not expected a posting to the crest of Vimy Ridge the first day of the battle. According to the master battery plan, after the morning barrage, he anticipated getting the call to begin moving his battery guns forward to new positions to pursue the Germans. However, when a forward observation officer with a sister battery was wounded, gunner Philpott received orders to pack up his gear and join the exodus of support troops from the Canadian trenches advancing toward the summit. When he got to the Red Line in the 2nd Division sector, he was told to report on what he saw, including potential new targets for Canadian artillery to keep the retreating Germans off balance.

"We knew we could still give our infantry cover, because we still had plenty of range [from the Canadian battery positions]," Philpott said. "The reports I sent back to our own headquarters telling them what it was like . . . that was one of the real thrills of the war."

Like many of his contemporaries, Philpott was intensely patriotic, "believing in Canada and the British Empire." Too young to enlist in 1914, he had returned to studies at the University of Toronto until he was eligible. He feared the predictions of the "great experts" at his local post office—in the Lake Ontario fishing village of Bronte—that the war would be over by Christmas 1914 might come true. The entire Philpott family—three brothers and a sister—joined up to serve and not miss any of the action. Elmore got all the action he ever wanted—at Ypres, Courcelette, and then Vimy. Despite his two years at the front, however, Philpott had hardly ever seen the enemy or the territory he occupied close up. At two o'clock he got his first look.

"I got to the crest of Vimy Ridge," he said. "I don't know what made me think of it, but 'the children of Israel looking at the Promised Land' [came to mind]. Here, as far as I could see, miles after miles after miles, here was this visibly beaten German Army. You could see them going forwards and backwards. It was a scene of the most hopeless confusion."

Unlike some, Elmore Philpott felt no deep-seated animosity for those retreating German troops. He understood the hatred one of his senior officers expressed since the man's mother and sister had died in the U-boat sinking of the British ocean liner *Lusitania*. But for Philpott and his battery mates, the view of the enemy was limited to impersonal song lyrics—"Keep your head down, Fritzy boy, keep your head down"—and occasional glimpses of German prisoners captured during night raids across No Man's Land. One POW had even spoken English to his Canadian captors, talking about his employment with Bell Telephone before the war. For Philpott, those bodies rushing about in the Douai Plain in front of him were just that—a confused enemy army.

A young infantry private, writing home from Vimy, took a slightly more impassioned and poetic view. Pte. Lewis Duncan, describing to his aunt Sarah the view from the ridge, marvelled that he could see countryside as much as ten miles away. Everywhere below him, civilian life appeared normal, with roofs intact, smoke rising from factory chimneys, and town clocks actually showing the correct time. Then he described the shells of Allied guns chasing the enemy away.

"For the first time in our experience, we looked down on the Hun," Duncan wrote. "And there was satisfaction in giving him in plentiful measures what he had given us from Ypres to Wytschaete and the Somme. He did not like the medicine and his reinforcements broke and scattered."

In his first awe-inspired artillery reports, Elmore Philpott even had trouble convincing his superiors of what he'd seen. In their confusion, the Germans were pulling back, but Philpott's colonel wouldn't believe him until the gunner confronted the colonel himself and painted the picture first-hand for him. Perhaps unknowingly the enemy appeared to have fooled the Canadian attackers. The Germans were not organizing the anticipated counterattack. Crown Prince Rupprecht had ordered his armies to fall back to the Oppy-Méricourt line beyond the range of Allied guns still entrenched on the west side of the ridge. That meant to battery officer Philpott that "we were put on the spot of having to move when we didn't want to move."

To pursue the Germans, Canadian battery crews would have to stop firing and move hundreds of guns across a wide expanse of former enemy territory. But the very weapons that had ensured victory at Vimy Ridge—the field batteries of 18-pounders, 4.5-inch howitzers, and 60-pounder heavy artillery—were suddenly unable to finish the job. Thanks to weeks of relentless bombardment they had rendered the ground between them and their infantry brothers virtually impassable. Even with thousands of men and horses immediately put to work, the guns could not move fast enough to take full advantage of a fleeing enemy. One battery sergeant reported it took eighteen horses and a hundred men a full day to move his 18-pounder through the mud to its new position on the ridge. When he reached a former German dugout overlooking the eastern slope of Vimy Ridge, L.R. Fennel, a Canadian sniper with the 27th Battalion, witnessed the typical frustration expressed by Canadian forward observation officers.

"Jesus Christ Almighty!" the FOO stormed. "Two fucking years I've been waiting for a chance like this. And now I can't use it."

There was an exception. On their own initiative, members of the 3rd Battery disassembled their gun positions behind the Canadian lines in the 1st Division sector. They limbered up their guns—using eight teams of teamsters and horses—and began hauling the artillery eastward. Axle-deep in mud virtually the entire distance, the men and horses managed to haul six guns 3,000 yards across the *Zwischen Stellung* (Red Line). By four o'clock the next morning—verging on total exhaustion—the battery crews had re-established themselves in gun pits near Nine Elms with 300 rounds of ammunition in place and were ready to fire.

While the battery officer's outburst stuck in Fennel's memory, the sniper found that leaving the front line overlooking the Douai Plain a short time later left a more melancholy impression. His route back across the Canadian lines took him past the Souchez cemetery, "with I don't know how many hundred thousand Frenchmen and Imperial [British troops] buried there. They'd made so many attempts to capture the ridge and hadn't succeeded. And then for us to come along. . . . We walked over. We got [to the top of the ridge] the same afternoon. . . . It was like a piece of cake."

## 6 p.m. April 9, 1917—Red Line, 2nd and 3rd Division sectors, Vimy

For most of the Canadian infantry and artillery crews, until April 9 the only view of the Douai Plain they knew was virtual. They had seen the view from Vimy represented on maps, in table models, on those notorious rehearsal fields, or at best in aerial photographs taken from aircraft or surveillance balloons. When they finally saw it, the view from the high ground stopped many Canadian Corps troops in their tracks. There it was, complete with bucolic villages, country roads, tidy little farms, and unbroken green forest. And on the horizon to the north were the industrial smokestacks of Lens and the slag heaps of the Douai coal mines, which had been so vital to the blockaded Germany. It was "a good view all round," not something Canadian Corps troops had encountered in France before now.

Not something William Douglas had encountered before either. Until Vimy, he had served as just another nameless sergeant in the Canadian Corps. However, on this day, Douglas had come up the ridge with the troops as Canada's official Vimy photographer. The year before, Sir Max Aitken—Lord Beaverbrook, the New Brunswicker with a fortune invested in British newspapers—had become "Canadian eye-witness" to the war. Officially he was Canada's Officer in Charge of War Records in London. As part of his mandate, Aitken had commissioned artists such as Maurice Cullen and David Milne as well as four painters—A.Y. Jackson, Franz Johnson, Arthur Lismer, and Frederick Varley (later members of the Group of Seven)—to capture the war on canvas. He had also offered Sgt. William Douglas the equivalent assignment with his camera. Having lost a hand in the war but not his passion to take photographs, Douglas now climbed the ridge with an assistant and packs of heavy camera gear. On his way to the summit, Douglas shot images of flooded shell holes, overrun trenches, and captured guns, as well as the victories and losses of Canadian Corps soldiers. Then, to crown the day, he'd shot the first-ever Canadian pictures of the Douai Plain from the crest of Vimy Ridge.

Mandated photographs and commissioned artwork weren't the only lasting images to emerge from this historic day for the Canadian Corps. Some had just as much significance, but no official status. None of the War Records officials knew about the watercolour paintings of Pte. Reuben Jucksch. But they too captured aspects of the Canadian experience at Vimy for posterity. Born and raised in Hanover, Ontario, Jucksch was perhaps unique in listing his profession or trade as "artist" on his attestation papers. Still, he had joined the 20th (Central Ontario) Battalion in November 1914 to fight and in the spring of 1917 was serving on fatigue duty behind the lines at Vimy. In addition, when conditions and time permitted, he squeezed in a bit of his peacetime vocation.

"On fatigue all day, loading trucks, etc.," wrote Pte. Jucksch on the Friday before Easter 1917. "In the evening did a little drawing. Big bombardment in the night." Then three nights later he recounted his own view of the 2nd Division attack up Vimy Ridge. "Monday, April 9, the Canadians went over to Heinie today. Attained their objectives in thirty-five minutes. The 20th [Battalion] sure got along jake. Few casualties. . . ."

When his turn came to look over the crest of the ridge at the Douai Plain for the first time, Jucksch was impressed by what remained of buildings and other structures in the valley in front of him. From some of his battlefield drawings later came watercolour images of battlefield equipment, railway bridges, and the ruins of the village of Vimy. He captured some of the war's desolation in paint, the rest in his diary.

"One boy shot a Hun's chin off, then killed him," Pte. Jucksch also wrote on April 9. And the next day he noted, "Numerous prisoners today, over 2,000. Had a talk with some near the fences. Very pessimistic [but] happy to be out of the war." Thinking of himself as part journalist and part soldier, former Parliamentary press gallery reporter Fred James also paused atop Vimy Ridge to record his impressions. Not surprisingly, when he reached the 1st and 2nd Division consolidation position at Thélus, the soldier's view of the moment shone through first.

"To look at the map, the territory captured by the Allies this spring may not look like much, but it is a mighty big chunk, when it has to be marched over with full equipment on, as I can testify to personally," he wrote. And while the vista of the Douai also captured his attention, James stopped long enough to notice that "skylarks rise and soar skywards trilling their tuneful roundelays [not minding] the shells screaming and screeching as they criss-cross between the two lines."

Just recently commissioned, Lt. James made special note of the strategic importance of the *Zwischen Stellung* that he and his 2nd Battalion comrades had just liberated. He noted with amazement the hive of activity covering the former German territory behind him as "the ground captured is rehabilitated for the thousand and one needs of an army. . . . All along the front where the line has been pushed forward, standard and narrow gauge railways [are under construction]; substantial roads span old trenches; transport lines cast anchor in a spot that was in a dangerous spot in No Man's Land; [and] camps blossom like a rash all over the place."

Five thousand Canadian troops swarmed over what had formerly been No Man's Land that afternoon and evening. Each man, each work party had a job to do and, as it had been in the lead-up to the attack, time was of the essence. The ranks of the medical service were bolstered with fresh stretcher bearers. Work parties brought water and medical supplies to the medical orderlies who were establishing new forward aid posts. Engineers directed construction crews grading the uneven ground for a spur line of the narrow-gauge railway. They built new roads the 19th-century way—planks laid side by side in corduroy fashion—to give the quagmire some stability. As soon as they were passable, the roadways carried scores of battery crews and horse-drawn ammunition trains forward to newly constructed gun pits on the ridge. Pioneer crews dug into former German dugouts and trenches and transformed them into Canadian brigade and divisional headquarters. One group of new occupants then posted a sign on the wall outside a former German dugout: "Do-Drop Inn. Working Parties a Specialty. Daylight Parties Preferred. Picks and Shovels are Not Provided HERE. (Proprietors) The Byng Boys."

Despite the apparent wholesale German retreat eastward from Vimy in front of the 1st, 2nd, and 3rd Divisions of the Canadian Corps, some German resistance remained. Orders to the 40th Battery from Toronto had them pulling up stakes late on April 9 and moving forward.

As they left their old gun pits behind near Neuville St. Vaast, gunnery officer Conn Smythe recalled seeing as many as 600 empty shell cases strewn about their position. Now the young lieutenant had the responsibility for moving a wagon of explosives up the ridge to the battery's new position. That's when an operational German artillery battery began firing randomly into the Canadian supply-line area. A shell landed right between the two wheelhorses of Smythe's wagon team. A few feet farther and the entire battery crew would have disappeared in the combined explosion.

"When I looked at the carnage, my first thought was 'What'll we do now?' Everything looked shattered," he wrote. Not even thinking about the possibility of additional incoming shells, Smythe had the two dead horses pulled aside, backed up the two leading teams, hitched them to the wagon, and carried on a few minutes later—four horses pulling instead of six. "I got a lot of credit for that but did not do one lousy thing."

Late in the afternoon of April 9, the men of the 116th Battalion finally got the call they had been waiting for. One company from Lt.-Col. Sam Sharpe's battalion from the central Ontario counties— latecomers to the Vimy front—would go forward into action on the ridge, albeit as a work party. The 116th's four companies had previously drawn lots, each one wanting to be first up the line. "B" Company had won the right to take the first assignment. Before sunset the company moved from its reserve position at Mont St. Eloi to begin laying new wire in communication trenches toward La Folie Farm, at the crest of the ridge in the 3rd Division sector. The adjutant reported on the action for the battalion war diary: "No sooner had our men begun work on the wiring schemes," he wrote, "than a veritable hail of shells was poured into them [from retreating German artillery]. In spite of heavy casualties, the work of consolidation was continued and completed."

By midnight, "B" Company from the 116th had concluded its first major action at the front. Laying communication wire on Vimy Ridge had cost the lives of ten men and wounded thirty more. The unglamorous work-party assignment continued the next day as the

116th made plans to move all four companies forward toward the new 3rd Divisional Headquarters. Again, as the battalion's troops waited in support trenches to go forward, German gunners found them with a volley of 5.9-inch artillery shells. When the 116th then joined the reconstruction of the Lens-Aras road between Thélus and Vimy, the battalion took further casualties. Once again, even before he was able to report that his battalion had actually fought German troops on the battlefield, the hapless Lt.-Col. Sharpe was forced to write home about losses to his battalion behind the lines.

"It was awfully sad about Lt. John Doble," he wrote his sister. "He was killed instantly by a shell when leading his wiring platoon. Two other officers—W.K. Kift and H.L. Major—and six more of our boys were unfortunately killed and about forty more wounded. . . . Old Ontario County is paying its toll in the great struggle."

## 7 p.m. April 9, 1917 — German Reverse Slope, Vimy

Lt.-Col. Sharpe made one other observation in his letter home about the battalion's first trip to the crest of Vimy Ridge. In reconnoitring the 116th's work-party position near La Folie Farm, the colonel and three scouts had come across an abandoned German dugout. The entrance was blocked by a makeshift door, which the men examined. One of the scouts noticed wires attached to the door, so before they dared enter the dugout, "I caused a wire to be fastened to the door and went back one hundred yards," Sharpe wrote. "[I] pulled the wire and two awful explosions resulted."

The same afternoon that the 116th work party moved forward, so did the scout section of its sister battalion, the 60th Battalion. One of its veteran scouts, Arthur Bonner, made a habit of taking matters into his own hands. He'd been active in the lead-up to the Easter attack since his Quebec battalion arrived at Vimy in February—raiding trenches, capturing prisoners, sniping, night patrolling, conducting reconnaissance. Bonner, nicknamed "Bull," had a reputation for improvising whether it was written in the regulations or not. He wasn't the first nor the last to alter the army issue equipment.

"Greatcoats coming down halfway between your knees and your ankles gathered up mud and it would get on there two and three inches thick . . . awfully heavy," Bonner said. "We just took our jack knives and hacked them off into shorter coats to keep them out of the mud. I was fined $1 for destroying government property, [but eventually] they turned a blind eye to it."

As busy as Bonner had been before April 9, on Easter Monday morning he was kept in reserve. Then he was called ahead to bring his expertise into play. "When we started clearing the German trenches on the ridge, it was up to the scouts to check them out first," said Bonner, recalling the number of booby traps he encountered. "Bombs were hidden under boards so the weight of the board would be just enough to hold the clip on a bomb. When the board was removed, the bomb would go off."

As awe inspiring as the eastward view atop Vimy was, what they discovered inside captured German dugouts and in deeply excavated caves left many Canadian troops in a state of disbelief. First, the extraordinary strength of the enemy's fortifications had to be admired. At key vantage points along the ridge, German engineers had strategically placed gun casements—each reinforced with concrete walls and ceilings five feet thick and each shielded by steel doors. The designers had further positioned single-man observation posts adjacent to either side of each casement—each post was encased in steel with movable peepholes encircling the unit. Farther down the reverse slope, in the innocuous-looking village of Petit Vimy, Canadian troops found what looked like a ruined house. It turned out the building's false front had concrete walls a yard thick and two hidden concrete-encased machine-gun nests with a clear view for half a mile. And what looked like a dishevelled haystack nearby actually concealed a concrete fort.

"We had entered into a new stage of the war," an officer wrote, "a stage when trenches had given way to cement and chilled steel."

Second, arriving Canadian troops marvelled at the comforts Germans had enjoyed on the reverse slope of Vimy Ridge. There, in relative shelter, the Germans had constructed a divisional headquarters, an underground network of medical dressing stations and elaborate officers' quarters—looking like a Swiss chalet—complete with beer garden, vegetable garden, and flower garden full of hyacinths, forget-me-nots, and poppies in full bloom. Fred Hodges related to the greenery on the reverse slope; he had his own garden back home in Calgary. Though he came over the ridge in the second wave with a trench mortar crew, he was amazed to see green grass growing, trees in leaf, and violets in bloom there. But his amazement continued when he entered a German pillbox.

"There were various items of ladies' underwear laying about," he said. "The floor was ankle deep in Vichy Water with the empty bottles everywhere."

Hodges and his trench mortar crew had strict instructions not to touch a thing. Their platoon commanders had warned them that the Germans had booby-trapped everything. Hodges admitted that he and his friend were so hungry they were tempted to dig into the fresh meat they found in the dugout. But they obeyed orders and left the dugout contents untouched. When Hodges and his chum finally got permission to bed down that night on the ridge, they found a partially completed German dugout. They were about to tidy up the underground shelter for themselves when two Canadian sergeants happened along. They pulled rank and told Hodges and his friend to move on. A short time later they heard an explosion. The dugout had been booby-trapped and blew up.

"That's where my chum and I would have been if the two sergeants hadn't come along and claimed it," Hodges said. "The sergeants never came back."

When he eventually entered one of these sophisticated underground complexes, the commander of the 4th Brigade, Maj. Duncan Macintyre, found an equally elaborate facility, complete with electric lights, telephone exchange, signs, steps built into the hillside, light railways, and even a ventilating fan that would be run by a man riding a stationary bicycle. What he realized in discovering these hidden quarters was that they had been "fixed up for a long stay." He also understood now "how the Germans had overlooked us for miles while they moved about safely by daylight."

Finally, Macintyre noted, the Germans were so surprised by the advancing troops that a single Canadian platoon commander had managed to capture three machine guns and turn them on Germans attempting to hitch teams to their artillery to haul them to safety.* In addition, the lieutenant had collected no fewer than ten Luger pistols in the Germans' quarters. That night Macintyre joined the rest of his men in an abandoned German dugout near the crossroads at Les Tilleuls, where his 4th Brigade had established a new headquarters on the ridge. Behind a curtained cubbyhole in the dugout, the major found a bunk bed with the added luxury of an air pillow. And since the German had left in such a hurry, Macintyre was also able to make up some of the deficiencies in his own kit, including food, mineral water, and a supply of candles. Such was the plunder of this war.

The knowledge that the Germans in retreat still had the capacity to booby-trap their dugouts and trenches triggered additional precaution. As work parties reshaped the ridge with railway beds, corduroy roadways, and communication lines, some Canadian Corps troops returned to the routine they'd known during those days and nights before April 9. Patrols and probing raids began again. These sorts of manoeuvres down what had been the German reverse slope, however, suddenly posed the same kind of problem Canadian troops had endured on the other side of the ridge. Out in the open against the face of the slope they were as visible as "skiers on a mountain side" and therefore open to renewed attacks by German artillery repositioning farther east. H.W. Lovell, a private with the 8th Field Ambulance, faced this problem.

---

* In the winter of 1917, some Royal Canadian Artillery crews had taken special training in the operation of German guns should any be seized in the fighting. By April 14, some of those Canadian gunners had captured 5.9s, 4.2s, and 77-mm guns and used them to bombard German positions in Avion and Méricourt.

"The east side of the ridge was precipitous, where Fritz had rooms tunnelled into the cliff for his battalion headquarters and stores," wrote Lovell, whose medical group had commandeered the former German dugout as a Royal Canadian Army Medical Corps advanced dressing station. Shortly after the 3rd Division took over the dugout, Pte. Lovell went out to gather medical gear and to discover if water wells in either the village of Petit Vimy or the town of Vimy had been poisoned by the Germans.

"My three comrades and I were coming back with stretchers and blankets to the captured enemy dugout near the front line," Lovell wrote. "We each had the white band with the red cross sewn on our left sleeve. Fritz was watching us as we approached the dugout. Suddenly, a blockbuster with black smoke exploded fifty feet in front of us. Simultaneously, we were flat on the ground, then into the dugout."

It wasn't long after attacks such as this one that Lovell had survived, when the reverse slope earned the unfortunate nickname "Death Valley." Nor was it long before the 8th Field Ambulance decided to abandon the dugout for the safety of its patients and its medical staff.

## 10 p.m. April 9, 1917 — Villers-au-Bois Advance Dressing Station, Vimy

Except for the 4th Division sector, where pockets on Hill 145 and the Pimple remained in German hands at nightfall on April 9, the change in ownership elsewhere along the western slope of Vimy Ridge provided other medical crews with a welcome change. For weeks before the Easter attack, daily routine orders had seconded members of the 9th Field Ambulance to numerous work parties—fixing trenches and tunnels, hauling supplies, and even doing guard duty. Medical clerk Will Antliff repeated the joke circulating among his section: "What's the difference between a field ambulance and a pioneer battalion? Answer: The former does a little Red Cross work."

When April 9 finally arrived, however, Pte. Antliff was fulfilling his intended service at Villers-au-Bois dressing station behind the lines in the 3rd Division sector. His job was to keep track of names and numbers of the wounded, their units, and the nature of their wounds. Antliff wrote to his mother that the most encouraging feature of his job "was the large number of Fritzys who passed through," signalling that the battle appeared to be going in the Canadians' favour. The former commerce student from McGill University then described in some detail the temperament and demeanour of the Germans being treated. Some seemed quite docile. Others appeared unwilling to forfeit protocol even as wounded prisoners of war.

"A [German] warrant officer and forty men were being [helped] in the dressing station," the private wrote. "One of the [enlisted men] went to get a cup of water, which he was just raising to his lips when the W.O. made a motion to bring it to him instead . . . iron discipline to the end."

In addition to counting more German wounded than Canadian, Pte. Antliff later got orders to move up the dressing station in the wake of the advancing troops. The trip forward, Antliff wrote, proved extraordinary. On every previous trek to the front lines, field ambulance crews nearly crawled through the deepest trenches. This time "we kept to the road, which would have been the height of folly a week ago. All around men were walking overland and it certainly looked funny." En route to the new dressing station, Antliff got his first glimpse of a tank "bobbing up and down in the shell craters on its way back from the front line." That night, his six-man squad made it a mile into what had been German-controlled Vimy and then made the return trip with stretchers bearing some of the more severely wounded.

"The man we had was no feather-weight," Antliff wrote. "We had a hard time circling around shell holes, crossing over trenches and pulling ourselves out of the slimy mud. To add to the enjoyment, old Fritz started whiz-banging the trench we had just left for all he was worth"; however, by midnight Antliff's ambulance crew had "dispatched our patient [to] the horse ambulance."

For the wounded, the route to medical assistance at Vimy—just like most other aspects of the operation—was well organized. A dozen field ambulance units had, in the words of the military "room for initiative," which meant the medical crews had the time, supplies, space, and manpower to prepare for the expected casualties. In the 3rd Division sector, where Will Antliff's 9th Field Ambulance worked, wounded men went through triage at regimental aid posts excavated into the chalk close to the front. Ambulance bearers processed them through relay posts farther behind the lines and finally carried them to larger advanced dressing stations at Aux Rietz, where motor ambulance or tramways delivered them to a railway station for evacuation to hospitals on the French coast. By two o'clock on the morning following the main assault, medical crews at the Canadian advanced dressing stations had cleared 5,976 wounded.*

When stretcher bearers found him, Royden Barbour had crawled most of the way back to the Canadian lines from a shell hole in the 2nd Division sector. He had shrapnel wounds in his back and side and needed hospitalization. The advanced dressing station was crowded with wounded when he arrived, so he was set outside in sunshine awaiting motor ambulance to a rail terminus.

"Going back fifteen kilometres in that ambulance, I was on the top shelf of the stretchers," Lt. Barbour said. "Having a wound in the back and going over those cobbled roads . . . was awfully painful. I took hold of two straps and pulled myself up and so rode the whole distance hanging . . . until I got there feeling like I practically didn't have any arms."

## Midnight April 9, 1917—No. 1 General Hospital, Etaples, France

Vimy kept ambulance drivers working around the clock at No. 1 General Hospital in Etaples on the coast of France, sixty miles away. By late afternoon of April 9, the call had changed from a request for

---

* During the four days of the battle at Vimy—April 9 to 12—the Royal Canadian Army Medical Corps treated and cleared 7,350 Canadian wounded and 706 German wounded.

thirty to a call for sixty-five motor ambulances to be ready when the wounded began arriving. The weather at the railway siding at Etaples had been no better than the wintry conditions the Canadians had fought through that day. So the ice and snow on the three-quarter-mile-long road between the railway station and the hospital made the trip more treacherous than usual. The prospect didn't bother one nineteen-year-old ambulance driver from Vancouver. As a rule Grace MacPherson worked twelve hours on and twelve hours off, but when there were big pushes at the front, she might work fifty to sixty hours straight without sleep—good weather or bad.

"I didn't mind the hard work. That's what I went over for," she said. "We had to clean the inside of the ambulances . . . repair flats and pump up the tires by hand. . . . We served an area of over 50,000 beds," in the three major hospitals nearby.

Grace was used to challenges. She had even battled her way through red tape and male chauvinism to get to France in the first place. From the very night in 1914 when she read in the Vancouver newspapers that Britain had declared war on Germany, she announced to her family, "I'm going. I'm going to drive an ambulance." She then wrote to the war office in Ottawa and the Red Cross in Britain. When neither offered any help getting overseas, she took every penny she had and bought her own transatlantic ticket. In Britain, Grace faced another hurdle. The then commander of the Canadian Expeditionary Force, Sir Sam Hughes, had very definite opinions about women in war. Nevertheless, Grace secured an interview with the Minister of Militia himself (and "about ten crossed-swords and generals sitting around this enormous suite") at the Savoy Hotel in London.

"I've come from Canada to drive an ambulance," she announced to Hughes and his entourage in the hotel room.

"I'll stop any woman from going to France," Hughes told her curtly. "And I'll stop you too."

"Well, Sir Sam, I'm going to France," she insisted. "I'll get there with or without your help."

Conditions at the front in France superseded Sam Hughes's resistance to the idea. The war office had decided that men in the ambulance corps could better serve the war effort closer to the front, so the driving jobs around Camiers, Le Touquet, and Etaples, where the major hospitals were located, were re-assigned to women volunteers. Busy shifts, such as transporting the wounded from railway stations to hospitals, took every driver in the ambulance convoy. Their vehicles had no windshields, no lights, and tires that were notoriously prone to punctures. Despite any urgency en route to the hospital, road conditions required ambulances to travel at little better than walking speed—four or five miles per hour. In addition to coping with vehicle maintenance on their own, the drivers often had to provide stretcher-bearer services by themselves.

Beginning late in the evening on April 9, Grace MacPherson made at least ten trips between the railway siding and No. 1 General Hospital, the ambulance convoys working well past midnight. She remembered the Vimy wounded being "a very sorry looking bunch." And yet she never allowed their disabled condition or their frame of mind to affect her.

Whenever a passenger groaned from the back, Grace would say: "You cut that out! Nobody's riding in my ambulance moaning like that."

"Oh, I got a leg off," he might say.

"Look, I bashed my thumb," she'd respond, trying to distract him.

The patient might say, "You're a queer sort of bloke."

"You're going to get the best ride you ever had in your life," she'd say finally. She refused to allow herself to express sympathy openly, for the patient's sake and her own sanity. On other occasions, the wounded soldier might have reacted to the sight of a woman driving an army vehicle. Not a surprise. Soldiers—wounded or not—loved to make conversation with a woman dressed in a blue uniform that included a cape, a short skirt, and high boots. It bothered Grace, however, when she learned that young men fighting for their country "had not been out of the trenches, except for fleas and getting a bath, for so many months." The British Red Cross paid its women ambulance drivers only ten to fourteen shillings a week. It didn't matter to Grace MacPherson.

"When I stepped off that ship [in France] and got into that first ambulance," she said, "I felt as if I had been there all my life."

When he stepped off the ship in France, Jim McKenzie was told the No. 1 General Hospital at Etaples needed volunteers. Though most medics landing in Europe craved the excitement of front-line service, Pte. McKenzie had learned basic first aid at Work Point barracks in Victoria, B.C., and was content to serve in what they described as a "humdrum" orderly position at the French coast base hospital. Not long after he'd arrived at the hospital, a train pulled in to the Etaples siding with a load of wounded after dark. McKenzie and his roommate heard aircraft motors simultaneously. A German bomber had followed the train into Etaples, and when the train stopped, the aircraft veered off to the hospital encampment and began bombing and then returned for a second pass, strafing the hospital workers as they fled the burning camp huts.

"I'd made a bunk out of a wood frame and burlap over top," McKenzie said. "As soon as I heard the plane engines I dropped out of the bunk to the ground. Pieces of shrapnel flew right across the room about six inches above the bed. If I hadn't hit the floor, I'd have been ripped to pieces. You see, it didn't matter. We were all on the firing line."

The bombing raid on Etaples surprised ambulance driver Grace MacPherson too. The first indication of trouble was the German leaflet drop; they warned British and Canadian officials to move their military bases away from the hospitals along the coast. Then, on a moonlit night, the German Air Force flew low over Etaples and dropped about thirty bombs on buildings adjacent to No. 1 General Hospital.

"We got the stretchers filled in the ambulance," she said. "I had two or three sitting on the floor in the back and two beside me in my seat and one on the seat of the ambulance. He had a blanket . . . thick with blood and I was holding him by the shoulder. We got them up to the hospital and went back for more."*

Shortly after the German bombing raids, British dirigibles flew over the bombed-out hospital areas and photographed the damage for propaganda purposes. A working battalion then built protective walls around the hospital. More tightly guarded blackouts on clear nights became the rule. Male hospital staff were moved to tents on sand dunes away from the hospital, and the nursing sisters' lodgings were moved to a nearby castle.

"How I hate the moon, the Kaiser and the Huns," wrote Nursing Sister Rubie Duffus.

## Evening April 9, 1917—Lens-Arras road, Vimy

Reaching the crest of Vimy Ridge that first day of operations proved momentous for many Canadian Corps troops. Some were dumfounded by the clear view to the east. Others felt the emotional relief of having survived, the thrill of achieving the objective, and the exhaustion after the battle adrenaline wore off. When he arrived just over the lip of the ridge at the Lens-Arras road, Pte. George Hancox, with the PPCLI, marvelled at "the most wonderful sight that met us . . . the big slag heaps of the mines, the hoists, the redbrick cottages of the mining villages . . . and one German artillery battery brought their horses up   about half a mile from the bottom of the ridge—and got out. I don't know how they got away without all being killed."

Cpl. Alan Brown had seen a less fortunate German artillery crew. When he and his 14th Battalion platoon got their first view of the German side of the ridge, Brown spotted a complete German artillery piece stuck in the mud. Around it were the corpses of its crew and six horses. One horse had survived—"a little white mare was still

---

* The May 19, 1918, bombing at Etaples killed seventy, including Nursing Sisters Margaret Lowe, Katherine Macdonald, and Gladys Wake. The May 30–31 bombing at Doullens went through three floors and killed three more nursing sisters and, in an operating room, the surgeon, two attending nurses, and a patient.

alive and frisky, her master dead on the ground." As the snow began to cover the scene, Cpl. Brown found some shelter and warmed himself with a ration of mulligan stew.

Evidence of the effectiveness of the Canadian barrage impressed George Walker as he arrived on the ridge. A signaller with the 2nd Canadian Siege Battery, Walker had come forward during the day to prepare a new site on the ridge for his battery crew. En route to the new gun pit, he came across "dead bodies everywhere . . . I [entered] a German pillbox with [a] dead gunner still chained to his post." Preparing his battery for its next targets, Walker stood out in the open and began signalling by semaphore (flags) when a shell burst nearby. "I checked myself, found shrapnel in my right shoulder and no hole in the back so . . . after applying a field dressing I stayed in position," instead of going to the rear for medical evacuation.

Even though the Germans appeared to be retreating well out of artillery range, Pte. Hal Kirkland, on orders from his platoon commander, began digging in furiously. The chalk was partly frozen and difficult to penetrate with his shovel. However, he soon had dug a trench deep enough to crouch in, so he stopped long enough to eat cold bully beef and hardtack. It was the first time he'd eaten since before the 5:30 Zero Hour that day. He drew the night watch, occupying a listening post out in the snow ahead of his comrades' new position. That watch earned him a respite back behind the lines the next morning. He and several others walked back in single file over the snow-covered terrain.

"I must have been only half sensible at the time," Kirkland wrote, "because when I looked sideways I did not see snow. Instead of the rough ground covered with snow, there were white marble statues lying on the ground, most of them broken. And instead of trees, there were colonnades of marble pillars. From then on I was afraid to let my eyes wander. . . . I was probably a victim of hallucination caused by hunger, cold and lack of sleep."

The Victoria Rifles of Montreal reached the top of the ridge along the Lens-Arras road late in the day on April 9. As with most members of his 24th Battalion, Andrew McCrindle found that the vista of the Douai Plain almost took his breath away. He could see three times the distance he and his comrades had just covered coming up the ridge. However, when his platoon drew guard duty that first evening, McCrindle had an even more astounding experience. As he watched over a number of German prisoners before they were escorted to the rear, McCrindle suddenly realized one of the POWs was addressing him.

"The Victoria Rifles," the German said, noticing the insignia McCrindle wore on his uniform, ". . . from Montreal."

McCrindle stared at the man, incredulous at his command of English.

"I know where your armoury was on Cathcart Street," the German continued.

"How do you know that?" McCrindle asked finally.

The German explained that he had worked in the restaurant at Windsor Railway Station in Montreal before the war and that many times after work he would go to Mother Martin's for a beer.

McCrindle was dumbfounded.

"But I guess you were too young to know that joint," the German said. The POW then related to McCrindle that his fellow German officers had warned him never to be captured by Canadians. They were all Red Indians, he was told, and they would scalp him. The man finished his story by saying, "I knew better and so I thought it would be a good idea to be in a place where Canadians would [capture] me. So, here I am."

Most of the prisoners Arthur Goodmurphy encountered passed him going the other way. A scout with the 15th Battalion, or 48th Highlanders, he and his platoon managed to get most of the way with the second wave from Zivy cave to the crossroads near Thélus rapidly and unscathed. By the time they reached the outskirts of the village, his sergeant, Bill Durrell, and Goodmurphy were leading the platoon and flushing the dugouts on either side of the road "to make sure Germans didn't ambush us. We were like guinea pigs," he said, "[but] the only Germans we saw were prisoners coming back, unescorted. It seemed funny to me. They were unarmed and didn't know which way to go. All they could do was go. . . ."

When the Highlanders began to dig in east of the village, Sgt. Durrell got cooking some bully beef, while Pte. Goodmurphy was sent out in search of a well-deserved tot of rum. He found his platoon commander, Lt. Harold Davis, handing out portions of rum to his sergeants for dispensing to their men. Goodmurphy was parched and, though not much of an alcohol drinker, gulped down some brandy offered by one of the sergeants. He then made his way back to the spot he and Durrell had staked out for the night. He reported on the status of the rum tot.

"Our rum's coming up," Goodmurphy said, "but I don't need much."

"Our rum has been up," Durrell said as he poured half a cup for his private.

"I can't drink that, Bill. I've had too much already."

Durrell insisted that Goodmurphy drink his share. He did and then put his head down. The next he knew, it was several hours later and Durrell was shaking him awake for a night march all the way back to their starting point in Neuville St. Vaast. Every step of the way Goodmurphy wanted to lie back down and sleep off the dull ache he was now feeling from head to toe.

As long as Canadian troops worked that first day on Vimy Ridge to consolidate new positions, escort prisoners away, or remove dead or wounded comrades, the Corps' chaplains worked alongside them. At Vimy, like never before, the Canadian Chaplain Service served more time at regimental aid posts (medical stations) than it did offering prayer or counsel. By the evening of April 9, Canon Frederick G. Scott had arrived at the Blue Line beyond Thélus, a long way from his previous quarters at Ecoivres, where he had tried in vain to conduct a Good Friday service. Still, the beloved padre of the 1st Division continued to assist medics on the battlefield throughout the day, and at that key moment when the Canadians rushed across the top of the ridge, he too had paused to look at "the villages . . . so peaceful in the green plain. . . . The church spires stood up undamaged like those of some quiet hamlet in England."

His day's journey done, Canon Scott took a flashlight into the growing darkness and used the newly laid light railway tracks as a guide to make his way back to his starting point. The snow intensified and his light proved useless, merely reflecting off the swirling snowflakes in his path. What he feared more than getting lost in the white-out of the snow were the rows of Canadian artillery batteries repositioning on the ridge and beginning to blast away at the Germans again. He slipped and stumbled on the return trip nearly as often as he had coming forward earlier in the day, but finally arrived at Ecoivres at 2 a.m. He prepared a pot of strong coffee on his Primus stove, ate an entire tin of cold baked beans and recorded in his diary: "My heart was full of thankfulness to Almighty God for his blessing on our arms."

Blessed in the 1st, 2nd, and 3rd Division sectors perhaps. But as April 9 came to a close, the 4th Division was still licking its wounds from the costly seizure of Hill 145. More than 5,000 Canadians at the northern end of the attack on Vimy Ridge knew their key objectives beyond the Red Line—Givenchy-en-Gohelle and on the far left of the sector, the Pimple—still lay ahead of them.

# "DISHING OUT
# SOME MORE HELL"

**Midnight April 9, 1917—New Canadian front line, Vimy**

IN THE NEARLY BLIZZARD CONDITIONS this first night on Vimy Ridge, finding a place to sleep proved a difficult task. For those enlisted men not assigned to the elaborate underground bunkers formerly occupied by German officers, it meant carving out a funk hole from the freezing chalk or re-digging part of an almost flattened German support trench. Sleeping quarters for 5th Field Ambulance were different yet again. Earlier in the evening, when sporadic German artillery fire from out on the Douai Plain began hitting the village of Thélus, some of the Canadian stretcher bearers found refuge in the nearby Thélus cave. It too had been a German shelter, but when the 5th Field medics got there they christened it "McGuffin's cave" in honour of their commanding officer, Lt.-Col. C.F. McGuffin. By that time the ambulance troops had been up for forty-eight hours straight, so many of them settled on the crowded floor of the cave to sleep. As he lay down, one of the stretcher bearers, Teddy Blair, tugged on the corner of a blanket wanting to borrow part of it from his neighbour, apparently already asleep.

"In the morning," a fellow bearer wrote, "Blair discovered that his bed-mate was a dead infantryman whose shattered body some comrade had covered with a blanket, but had not had time to bury."

While many members of the Canadian Corps slept on Vimy that first night of the battle, Lyle Pugsley was still on duty. Throughout the daytime Monday assault, the members of his regiment—the 85th Battalion—had stayed in reserve behind the lines building a communication trench. With the advance up the western slope of Hill 145 stalling badly, just before 6 p.m., the brigadier had ordered two companies of the 85th—the Nova Scotia Highlanders—into the battle. They had had no artillery support. No benefit of surprise. Still, about 200 men of the battalion had miraculously clawed their way onto the highest section of the humpbacked ridge and overpowered the German machine-gun positions there. For most of the evening, Pte. Pugsley, a twenty-two-year-old farmer from Nova Scotia, had worked in the wake of that attack.

"They ordered me to assist in picking up the German dead," he said, "[as well as] handling prisoners and mopping up enemy soldiers who remained bottled up in deep dugouts."

As the darkness and snow began to blanket Hill 145, Pugsley ran into three corporals who invited him to volunteer for a brand-new mission. Despite having seized gun emplacements atop the hill, "C" and "D" Companies of the 85th Battalion were now receiving gunfire from farther down the eastern slope ahead of them. German snipers and a series of machine-gun nests had a bead on the Canadians as they attempted to secure their new positions on Hill 145. That's when Pugsley got the special call. Among many things he had learned since coming to Vimy, Pte. Pugsley had trained as a grenadier—launching Mills bombs with blank shells from his Lee Enfield rifle. By the end of the winter he'd become quite a marksman and the corporals knew it. Pugsley and nine other grenadiers volunteered to sneak through the growing darkness and intensifying snow with enough Mills bombs to silence the snipers.

"We were to crawl down close enough to those cement reinforced dugouts to fire grenades into them," he said. "Our first shots would have to be accurate. If we missed, there likely would be no second chance. So, we crept down there and cleaned them out. We did not take any prisoners."

Pugsley finally got a well-deserved sleep behind the front lines late that night. When he awoke and reported for duty April 10, he happened to meet the commanding officer doing his rounds.

"Weren't you one of the ten men out last night in the attack on the dugouts?" he asked.

Pugsley acknowledged that he was.

"You may have won a medal," the C.O. said. And he handed Pugsley an upside-down helmet with slips of paper piled in it. "Draw one of these."

It turned out military awards for the previous night's operation would be determined by lottery. Lyle Pugsley did not draw the appropriate slip and was therefore not given a medal or a mention in dispatches. A fellow Nova Scotian from River Hebert had apparently been "luckier" and pulled the right slip, leaving Pugsley shaking his head "at the way they parcelled out medals. They just came up with the rations."

While Pugsley finally slept in the early morning of April 10 and the rest of the 85th consolidated its position on Hill 145, German troops began to move against the Canadian Corps' 4th Division sector. Col.-Gen. Ludwig von Falkenhausen had ordered in a battalion of reserve troops from the Bavarian Infantry Regiment to retake Hill 145. However, darkness and the closing-in effect of the weather hampered any concerted counterattack. By this time as well, any German offensive had little or no artillery support, and so by the evening of April 9 only seventeen artillery pieces and about a dozen remaining field batteries could muster any concentrated fire. The Germans began their advance from one of their few remaining positions of strength—the Pimple—moving south, across a saddle of land between the Pimple and Hill 145. Canadian machine-gun posts discovered the German advance and fired back. The intended assault also bogged down in the mud, to such an extent that some German troops lost their boots, some returning to the Pimple that night in their bare feet. The counterattack had disintegrated.

## 9 a.m. April 10, 1917—La Folie Farm,
## 3rd Division sector, Vimy

Not long after the 5th Canadian Mounted Rifles reached their objective late in the afternoon of April 9, Pte. George Murray received a promotion of sorts. There were no stripes involved. No pay hike. Not even a softer job. In fact, his new role was just the opposite. Pte. Murray was appointed company runner. It meant he'd have to carry messages as well as direct or lead the company in and out of the line. At first, the new responsibility entitled him to the loan of a pair of field glasses. Like so many others late on April 9, he gazed to the east across the Douai Plain, or what he described as "that forbidden land," to watch the shells from the newly positioned British and Canadian siege batteries begin pounding possible German strongholds out in the valley. Then the company runner had to pass along the call for a night patrol.

"No sign of Fritz was to be seen," Murray wrote, "so come nighttime a patrol party of the 5th was formed to go reconnoitre. That little job was performed after dark, they carefully feeling their way over the ridge. How far they went nobody knows. They never returned to tell the tale."

Several hours later, after midnight, it was clear something had happened to the recce party. Murray and his section surmised that the men had lost their way in the dark and snowy conditions and were captured. Another group was organized and set out in search of the first. The second patrol managed to make its way back with reports that the Germans had entrenched their infantry and artillery on the Douai Plain a few miles from the top of the ridge. With that information in hand, troops in the 3rd Division sector got orders to "make fresh contact" with the enemy. For the men of the 5th CMRs, that meant lugging tons of wire, digging new lines of trenches, laying trench mats, and bringing up supplies of ammunition, while the rest of the Canadian Corps, in Murray's words, continued "dishing out some more hell."

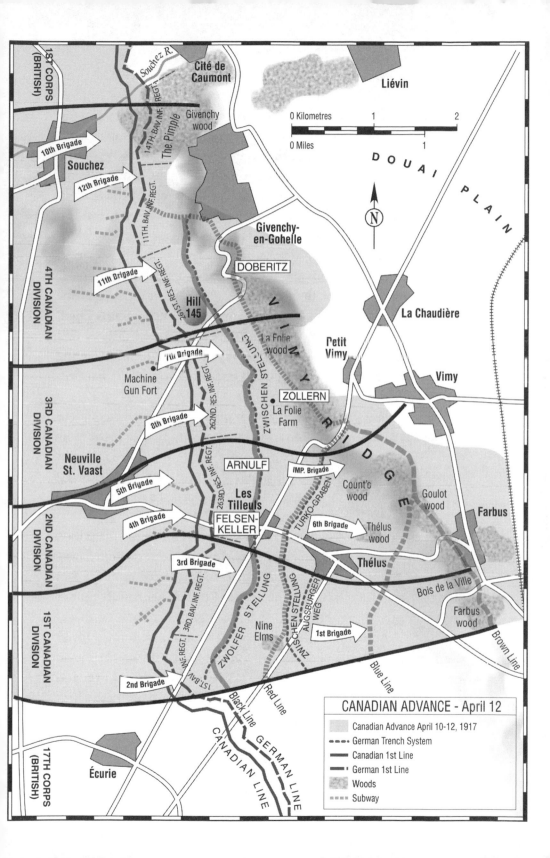

1ST CORPS (BRITISH)

Souchez R.

Cité de Caumont

Liévin

10th Brigade

Givenchy wood

The Pimple

14TH.BAV.INF.REGT.

Souchez

12th Brigade

11TH.BAV.INF.REGT.

D O U A I   P L A I N

0 Kilometres    1    2

0 Miles    1

N

4TH CANADIAN DIVISION

11th Brigade

261ST.RES.INF.REGT.

Givenchy-en-Gohelle

DOBERITZ

Hill 145

V I M Y

La Folie wood

Petit Vimy

La Chaudière

Vimy

7th Brigade

Machine Gun Fort

262ND.RES.INF.REGT.

ZWISCHEN STELLUNG

ZOLLERN

La Folie Farm

R I D G E

3RD DIVISION

8th Brigade

Neuville St. Vaast

5th Brigade

263RD.RES.INF.REGT.

ARNULF

Les Tilleuls

FELSEN-KELLER

IMP. Brigade

Count's wood

Goulot wood

Farbus

2ND CANADIAN DIVISION

4th Brigade

TURKO-GRABEN

6th Brigade

Thélus wood

Thélus

3rd Brigade

ZWOLFER STELLUNG

AUGSBURGER WEG

ZWISCHEN STELLUNG

Bois de la Ville

1ST CANADIAN DIVISION

1ST.BAV.INF.REGT.

3RD.BAV.INF.REGT.

Nine Elms

1st Brigade

Farbus wood

Brown Line

2nd Brigade

Blue Line

Black Line

Red Line

CANADIAN LINE

GERMAN LINE

17TH CORPS (BRITISH)

Écurie

## CANADIAN ADVANCE – April 12

- ▨ Canadian Advance April 10-12, 1917
- ---- German Trench System
- —— Canadian 1st Line
- —·— German 1st Line
- ▨ Woods
- ···· Subway

In the twenty-seven months that he served in France, Pte. Murray saw plenty of that. He had enlisted in Sussex, New Brunswick, in October 1915. At nineteen he had trained in Whitley Camp in England and gone to France as a reinforcement in June 1916. With the 5th CMRs he had survived the Somme and during the winter of 1917 at Vimy Ridge, he had watched German artillery destroy the town in which he was billeted—Mont St. Eloi—brick by brick. In the lead-up to the Vimy attack, he had seen the slaughter of pack animals caught in artillery barrages that left "dozens of mule and horse carcasses in all sorts of grotesque positions and advance stages of decomposition."

On the evening of the first day of the attack, he had glanced back at the battlefield "where not a tree or a house was left standing." Then, as company runner, Murray had gone forward to the railway line near the Lens-Arras road, where he surveyed the destruction that the Canadian artillery bombardment had inflicted on the Germans' reinforced gun emplacements there.

"Our shelling had battered down six-foot reinforced concrete coverings . . . railway lengths having been used to reinforce the concrete," Murray wrote. "And yet they were cut and smashed and split and powdered up as if an earthquake had struck them. . . . Knowing for three solid weeks the bombardment the Germans were subjected to . . . perhaps it's [no surprise] that they retired."

It's difficult to say whether it was friendly or enemy fire that killed the four members of the 4th Canadian Mounted Rifles whom Lewis Robertson found at about nine o'clock Tuesday morning. He had come to Vimy as a reinforcement for the Royal Canadian Regiment about a month before the attack, so he only got to know a few members of "B" Company as the regiment went about building a plank road for the artillery and laying telephone lines. At Zero Hour on April 9, the majority of Pte. Robertson's battalion went over the top in the first wave. He remained at Mont St. Eloi until early the next morning—April 10—when he went forward in a work party to bury the dead. That's when he came upon four men, all dead in the bottom of a shell hole. They were seated in a circle like mannequins.

"They were playing cards," Robertson said. "They had been told to go so far and stop. So they must have been sitting there waiting for the time to go ahead. Each one had their cards in their hands."

Robertson then noticed trails of blood from the men's ears. Otherwise they hadn't a mark on them. The four men must have reached their objective and, with a period of time to wait before the creeping barrage resumed ahead of them, decided to play a quick hand of cards. A heavy bomb must have exploded nearby and the men died from the concussion. Pte. Robertson's burying detail had to follow protocol in each situation: all belongings found had to be bagged and, if possible, noted with name and soldier identification number.

"I had to tear the cards out of their hands. We buried them in the shell hole where we found them and the following day brought crosses up and marked the ground."

Some Canadians buried their dead comrades without orders or official permission. When troops of the Royal Canadian Regiment (RCR) reached the summit of Vimy in the 3rd Division sector late on April 9, they began digging in above La Folie wood. David Moir and three other members of the 7th Canadian Machine Gun Company (CMG) were sent a hundred yards in front of the RCR line to act as an advanced warning group in case of a German counterattack. With only four men, a gun and tripod, and the 500 rounds of machine-gun shells remaining, Moir realized his unit wouldn't likely be able to stop a counterattack.

As it was, before the CMG crewmen had finished setting up their gun emplacement, German gunners spotted them and began firing from farther down the slope. They killed one of Moir's comrades, a man named Walker. After dark, his lieutenant ordered Moir and the remaining two crewmen back to the RCR front line. The CMG gun crew would remain dug in there for four days. However, on April 10, the next day, Moir was approached by a friend of Walker's, the man killed out in No Man's Land. He asked Moir if he would help give his buddy, Walker, a proper burial that night.

"Remembering that line from Robert Service that 'A pal's last need is a thing to heed,' we decided that as soon as it got dark we would venture forth."

Moir considered all the potential problems. He checked any maps to ensure they could find the spot even in the dark. He alerted the front-line RCRs on duty that night not to fire on them when they returned. He gathered the tools they would need and decided not to carry rifles, just sidearms. Then, at the appointed hour, the two men crept out for the impromptu burial. Of course, nothing at night looks as it does in daylight, not to mention in this case the alterations that continuous shelling from both sides had made to the terrain. It took nearly half an hour to find Walker's body.

"We soon realized what an inert mass of nothing a human body becomes once that little God-given spark of life is gone," Moir wrote. "We straightened him out as best we could [and] buried him right in the shell hole where he lay [marking] the spot by mounting his steel helmet on a stick."

Retracing their steps to the friendly confines of the Canadian line in the dark proved no less perilous, and the burial party of two was soon approaching a section of the RCR line that had no knowledge of them or their mission. There were a few tense moments and awkward exchanges of passwords that nearly brought friendly fire down on Moir and his comrade, but they finally talked their way through. The RCRs looked at him as if he were crazy, but he concluded that "no man is braver than the coward who compels himself to be brave."

### 3:15 p.m. April 10, 1917—La Folie wood, 4th Division sector, Vimy

According to the adjusted schedule devised by Canadian Corps command, plans to attack and seize the Pimple were postponed two days, until April 12. The 4th Division C.O., Maj.-Gen. David Watson, decided instead to focus on the eastern slope of Hill 145. He chose two battalions of the 10th Brigade for the operation—the 44th (Manitoba) Battalion and the 50th (Alberta) Battalion—both of which had stayed behind the lines in reserve on April 9. By the afternoon of April 10, the two battalions had quickly moved south to the 11th Brigade front in order to pass through the captured dugouts atop

Hill 145 and then advance east across Vimy Ridge to La Folie wood, seizing about a thousand yards of ground from remaining German defenders. A concentrated barrage would precede the infantry push down the eastern slope of the hill, and a screening barrage on the Pimple would cover the left flank of the attack.

The way Ed Russenholt understood his orders, the operation on the east slope of Hill 145 was designed to "straighten the line . . . where final objectives had not been gained on April 9." The sergeant from rural Manitoba had endured several days of anticipation. His machine-gun crew had waited in the subways and caves as the first wave went over at Zero Hour on April 9. Then officers had told them the attack on the Pimple had been postponed. Now they had been moved to a different front. The proud sergeant, who had expressed to himself and others that the Canadians "were the finest troops on earth," felt that all these delays and detours were preventing them from proving it. So, when he was ordered into the Music Hall trench for this "straightening" attack on April 10, the excitement was palpable. At last, they would finally see the enemy on the battlefield. His first impression of that battlefield, however, was a psychological setback. The waves of Manitoba men in front of him veered to either side of a triangular obstruction.

"That triangle was literally covered with the bodies of our men . . . comrades in the Canadian Corps. They had jumped off yesterday morning while we listened to the opening barrage and they had walked into traversing fire of one German machine gun. . . . They lay, most of them, face down, their rifles with fixed bayonets, pointing forward toward their objective."

Stunned by what he saw, but also spurred on, Sgt. Russenholt noted his progress during the attack: "At 3:15 p.m. intense barrage commenced, remaining on objectives for four minutes. 'C' and 'D' [Companies] moved out and formed under barrage. . . . At 3:31 p.m. 'D' [Company] reached the western edge of Bois de Folie. . . . By 4:15 p.m. 'C' [Company] had established a post. . . . On the right 'D' [Company] had some difficulty in clearing the woods."

On Russenholt's right, in "D" Company, John Spears was getting his baptism of fire. The concepts of creeping barrage, traversing machine-gun fire, the Pimple, and Hill 145 were about as foreign to him as they could be. The eighteen-year-old private with the 44th Battalion had only just arrived at Vimy with reinforcements the night before the Easter Monday attack. His trip through the Souchez Valley and Cobourg Subway to passageways called Banff, Bessie, Beggar, and Music Hall was the first time he'd even seen a trench, much less occupied one. Nevertheless, on Tuesday afternoon, he was assigned to a 44th Battalion machine-gun crew as an ammunition carrier.

"I was carrying four panniers, each with forty-four rounds of .303 ammunition, each weighing about twenty pounds," said Spears, who figured that he had to put them down wherever his gunner decided to set up the machine gun. "We hadn't gone more than a couple of hundred yards when the number one on the gun slumped down, a machine-gun bullet through the chest."

The gun crew halted and looked for cover. Since he was also carrying a shovel, water, and rations—about fifty additional pounds of equipment—Pte. Spears put several of the heavy panniers down while somebody put a field dressing on the wounded gunner. Then, almost as quickly as they had stopped, the section of men continued through German trenches to challenge the guns that were firing on them. Spears recalled seeing the summit of the Pimple and smoke in the distance. As soon as the section leader had found a bay in the trench in which to set up the Lewis gun, Spears dumped his gear and turned to retrieve the extra panniers he'd left behind near the first wounded man.

"That saved my life," Spears continued. "A German shell made a direct hit on that particular bay and killed or wounded every man in it. . . . It was a big shell, about a sixty-five-pounder. It blew three men to pieces. One body had no head, no arms, no legs, nothing but the trunk of his body. . . . His breast pockets were still intact."

With little more battlefield experience than the time it took to walk the lengths of two football fields, Pte. John Spears sat stunned in a shell hole with the remains of three men, another dying and two more suffering from shell shock. Not far from this scene, Frank

Ormiston was advancing with his platoon. He too had just arrived as a reinforcement for the 44th Battalion and admitted to having "butterflies in his stomach," although the tot of rum he'd drunk before going over the top helped him cope. The creeping barrage tended to obscure Pte. Ormiston's line of vision, but he did recognize that men around him were dropping to the ground with machine-gun and shrapnel wounds. "I guess my turn isn't coming," he said to himself, and he kept in step with the barrage. In those first few hundred yards, Ormiston and a comrade took sixteen prisoners, but then "I got a bullet right through the cheek, took my whole jaw bone on the left side of my face and all my teeth."

As he went over the top with the 44th Battalion, D.M Marshall looked to his left and "saw the 50th Battalion going over the top, just like in the book . . . bouncing from shell hole to shell hole, in and out and up and down. . . ." But like the Manitoba men, the first waves of the 50th quickly ran into entrenched German machine-gun fire. Two companies of the Calgary-based battalion were soon pinned down in shell holes on the eastern slope too. Among the riflemen stuck in those craters was a Calgary engineer named John Pattison. At forty-two, he was old enough to have a son in the regiment; indeed, as John fought at Vimy, his eighteen-year-old son was enlisting with the next wave of 50th Battalion recruits en route to France.

Pte. Pattison recognized the perilous state of the attack. While most around him hunkered down as deeply in the ground depressions as they could, Pattison began to move, in short rapid dashes, taking cover on the way in any available shell holes. Before long, he got to within thirty yards of the German strongpoint. He chose his moment carefully.

"He stood up in full view of the machine gunners under their point-blank fire," the battalion war diary reported, "and threw three [Mills] bombs with such good aim that the guns were put out of action and the crews temporarily demoralized. . . . As his last bomb exploded amidst the Germans, he rushed across the intervening space and in a moment was using his bayonet. . . . He had killed them all before his companions had caught him up."

With the strongpoint eliminated, the two companies of the 50th Battalion were immediately sparked to push on to their objective. Within half an hour the Calgarians had reached La Folie wood alongside their 44th Battalion comrades. The attack had taken its toll on the 50th Battalion, though. A quarter of its men—228 troops— had been lost taking the eastern slope of Hill 145. In the hours after the battle, Pte. John Pattison learned that his bold attack had been recognized with a Victoria Cross, the fourth Canadian V.C. won at Vimy.*

### Afternoon, April 10, 1917—11th Brigade sector, Vimy

The month of the Vimy attack had earned the moniker "bloody April." The description could have applied to any April in the ground war between 1914 and 1918. Among military pilots in the struggle for air supremacy over the Western Front, however, the reference could not be more apt than for April 1917. Despite outnumbering the German Air Force nearly two to one in the Arras sector by that point in the war, the Royal Flying Corps lost 151 aircraft and 316 airmen, as against 119 German machines—all in the month of April. But the total number of kills—that is, the number of Royal Flying Corps aircraft downed by German fighter pilots in Richtofen's Flying Circus—may be off in the record books by one kill. And a gunner with the 50th (Alberta) Battalion is probably the man responsible for the discrepancy in the statistics.

Wilfred Darknell had joined the Calgary-based battalion in 1915. He had come through the mud of the Somme only to be seconded at Vimy to a work party digging sap tunnels throughout the night underground below the Pimple. Remarkably, in the weeks of preparation over the tapes at Chateau de la Haie, Pte. Darknell was trans-

---

*The nearly middle-aged Pte. John Pattison never enjoyed the privilege of wearing his Victoria Cross as he was killed in action near Lens, France, seven weeks later. When Pattison's son arrived for service with the 50th Battalion, the commanding officer allowed Pattison junior to wear his father's V.C. ribbon.

ferred from pioneer work to a Lewis gun crew. By April 9 he had become so proficient on the machine gun that he graduated to number one on his crew. His 50th Battalion remained in reserve, however, until the April 10 assault down the eastern slope of Hill 145 to La Folie wood. Orders then moved Darknell's gun crew to the right, in support of the 73rd (Royal Highlanders) Battalion. That sector had witnessed numerous aerial dogfights between RFC pilots and von Richtofen's pursuit squadrons, so Darknell's Lewis gun became a portable anti-aircraft battery. Its first engagement proved a test of will and judgement for the young Calgarian.

"A plane with red, white and blue rings suddenly began strafing us," Darknell said. The Royal Flying Corps roundel was unmistakable on either side of the British fighter plane's fuselage. "We thought the [British] pilot thought we were Huns. He came over again. More strafing."

The apparent friendly-fire mistake was cutting into the battalion. No matter how far into the trenches the Canadian troops sought cover, they sustained more casualties with each of the pilot's strafing runs. Darknell turned to his corporal and got the nod to load tracer bullets in his Lewis gun. And on the next pass, Darknell opened fire and emptied the entire pannier of tracers into the aircraft. The fighter burst into flame and crashed 200 yards beyond the Canadian line. It looked as if both pilot and plane had disintegrated in the fiery crash. Now Darknell and his corporal grew anxious, fearing that they had wrongly brought down an RFC plane. They agreed to quietly search the wreckage later that night.

"Everything, including the pilot, was burnt up," Darknell wrote, "but during the search we found three buttons, each with the German eagle on them. We reported to headquarters that [we thought] the pilot was German. That's when the company commander told us that German troops had recently broken through the British Fifth Army on our far right and captured eight [Royal Flying Corps] planes."

Infantryman Wilfred Darknell had brought down an enemy pilot flying a British fighter plane.

## 5 a.m. April 12, 1917—The Pimple, Vimy

During the run-up to the Vimy attack, Howard Pawley, an officer with the 44th (Manitoba) Battalion, wrote home to members of his family to let them know he was safe and well. At the outset of his letter, he noted that "things are pretty much as usual along the line, with the exception that Heinie [the Germans] get hell at different and unexpected times." He wrote with admiration about the actions of his platoon comrades over several sleepless nights when they were ordered to conduct preparatory raids before the Vimy attack.

In his correspondence, Pawley recalled carrying "a captured machine gun, weighing about 65 pounds . . . and getting it to our own lines" and then when he challenged two Germans in a trench "the chamber [on my revolver] clicked on an empty shell and I darned near went up in the air; but I hopped onto them and knocked their rifles flying by which time the other fellows had caught up." Lt. Pawley finished the letter explaining that members of his unit "got their military medals" and then added facetiously, "I guess my decoration will be along soon." Shortly thereafter, Pawley learned he would have to fill in as platoon commander in the eventual assault against the Pimple—the last German-held position at Vimy.

While it was about twenty-five metres lower in altitude than Hill 145, the Pimple (at 120 metres in height) remained the last bastion of German resistance after three days of fighting along the ridge. By Easter Monday night the farthest objectives targeted by the 1st, 2nd, and 3rd Divisions were in Canadian hands. So too, following a concerted effort by the 85th Battalion, had Hill 145 been gained in the 4th Division sector on April 9. The next day, renewed assaults had advanced the 4th Division to its eastern objectives into La Folie wood and Givenchy-en-Gohelle. But the final prominent feature, on the far left flank of the Canadian Corps' front line, remained an elevated German salient and therefore in the way of any further Canadian advance. The original strategy had called for the British I Corps to capture the Pimple during the main Vimy assault, but eventually that responsibility fell to the 4th Division. In the new plan of attack, medium and heavy batteries would target German communication trenches as well as known Pimple strongpoints overnight. Then just before dawn, the 44th (Manitoba) Battalion and the 50th (Alberta) Battalion would go over the top.

If Sam Kirk had taken to heart the remarks of the recruiting officer in Vancouver in 1914, he might never have made it to Vimy at all. When Kirk and the entire men's club of the local Presbyterian church arrived at the enlistment office, a big Seaforths sergeant took one look at him standing there—all five feet four inches of him—and remarked, "Go on, get out of here. It's men we want!" In 1915, when he tried to join up with the 50th Battalion in Calgary, he got a similar response: "You're a swell-looking guy from the hips up, but you look like hell from there down." The Calgary battalion was about to embark for overseas, however, and needed recruits, so they took Kirk anyway.

At 5 a.m. on April 12, Pte. Kirk carried 120 rounds of ammunition, his Lee Enfield rifle, three Mills bombs, his entrenching tool, bayonet and scabbard, water bottle, rations, gas mask, greatcoat and cape, and the rest of his five-foot-four-inch frame over the top toward the Pimple. Ringing in his head were comments he'd heard from a German POW before the Vimy attack. The man had said there was no way in the world the Canadians could take Vimy. Worse, he had said Prussian troops were about to relieve regiments on the Pimple and "they'll show you what real soldiers are like." Pte. Kirk was in the first wave to capture the Pimple.

Again, the weather had changed dramatically overnight. Despite the date on the calendar, there wasn't a trace of spring this morning either. April 12 dawned with another snowstorm blowing up the hill into the teeth of the German defenders. A combination of the pre-dawn light, the blinding snow, and the effect of heavier shells creeping up the hill and crashing into their gun emplacements meant the Canadians could again use the element of surprise to be on top of the Germans before they could reach their guns. Nevertheless, when the Pimple defenders set off their SOS for German artillery to return fire, Kirk was thrown to the ground by a concussion shell. Twenty minutes later he came to in a shell hole. He was just bleeding from the nose. With only one stretcher bearer per platoon and none in sight, he realized it was up to him to carry on.

The information Kirk had overheard was accurate. The Germans had reinforced the Pimple with fresh troops—Prussians of the 5th Grenadier Guards. One of Kirk's fellow Calgarians, C.K. McDonald, noted that the Germans he saw "were all shined up and shaved and everything." In addition, the Canadians discovered that the German defenders had managed to pull forward twenty-two field guns and twelve heavy artillery to support the defence of the hill. The guns and reinforcements did delay the eventual outcome of the battle.

The 44th Battalion, fresh from its successful attack down the eastern slope of Hill 145 on April 10, took the lead in the push up the Pimple. Despite the poor light, a view of the battalion spread out across the front line reassured most members of the Winnipeg-based battalion. Most inspiring of all, however, was the sight of their Kiplingesque commander, Lt.-Col. Dick Davis, striding forward with his men and armed with only a revolver and his walking stick. The 44th moved up the Pimple at a rate of twenty yards per minute. Ed Russenholt, a sergeant gunner with the Winnipeggers, moved forward in "D" Company, passing over the German front line within minutes. Still tucked in behind the creeping barrage, they continued toward the Germans' support line without opposition. At the dugout line, they battled entrenched troops hand to hand until the Germans surrendered. That yielded fifty prisoners. Russenholt credited the battalion's quick success to the bad light and heavy snow.

Two senior officers then attempted to make contact with troops of the 12th Brigade and disappeared—one was captured, the other killed. That left Tom Goodhall, a sergeant major in command of the company. He moved the troops several hundred yards farther, out beyond the dugout line. He calculated that "the German artillery, knowing their line had fallen, might fire on their own trenches."

That's exactly what happened. The shells began falling on the dugouts behind the Canadians, but without injury. (For the initiative, Goodhall later got a Distinguished Conduct Medal.)

About the same time, Howard Pawley, the lieutenant in a neighbouring platoon, rushed a machine-gun nest that had pinned down members of his 44th Battalion. The citation for his award of the Military Cross said that "during a raid on the enemy's trenches, he led his party with great dash, and personally captured an enemy machine gun." Lt. Pawley received shrapnel wounds in the action and was posthumously awarded the medal. The 44th consolidated the advance in front of those dugouts and then continued up the hill. Meanwhile, Russenholt had called for additional Canadian artillery fire on the final objectives. This action flushed out the remaining German troops.

"Eighty to one hundred of the enemy ran out of the dugouts near the quarries, in the direction of Givenchy," Sgt. Russenholt wrote. "These men were taken by the Lewis guns of 'D' Company so effectively that not a single man reached Givenchy."

The 44th Battalion completed the capture of the Pimple within two hours of the initial barrage. By 7 a.m. the two battalions—the 44th and 50th—were assessing the results of the operation. Atop the hill they had captured four machine guns, three *Minenwerfer* guns, and seventy-seven prisoners of the 5th Prussian Grenadier Guards. The 44th Battalion had suffered the loss of Lt. Pawley and twenty-seven other men, a total of 118 casualties. The Germans attempted a counterattack to reclaim the Pimple, but the Canadians—now digging in—managed to repulse them. Again, the forethought about such potential problems had been considered.

"There was tremendous preparation," Russenholt said. "Immediately behind us, an entire battalion [the 47th British Columbia Battalion] were a carrying and working party . . . who had established great dumps of Lewis-gun pans, Mills grenades . . . everything."

Another of the weapons in the Canadian arsenal that morning on the Pimple was a much less obvious one. Every battalion had them, but few recognized the value of snipers in the Canadian Corps. They didn't have the devastating effect of an artillery barrage or the harassing impact of continuous machine-gun fire. Nor could they overpower a position the way waves of infantry could. But men such as marksman Henry Norwest contributed to the overall victory at Vimy one deadly shot at a time. Born in the early 1880s in Fort Saskatchewan, Alberta, Norwest was Cree. Drawn initially to prairie ranch country, he learned the survival skills of roping, riding, tracking, and hunting. When open-range ranching began to disappear, he found his talents in demand at rodeos and then—when the war broke out—in the army. There was one false start in his army career—a discharge for drunkenness in early 1915. But once re-enlisted, with the 50th (Calgary) Battalion, Norwest's talents as a lone shooter proved extremely valuable.

"Norwest carried out his duty superbly because he believed his special skill gave him no choice but to fulfill his indispensable mission," wrote a comrade at the front. "[He] went about his work with detachment from everything while he was in the line."

As with other snipers, Pte. Norwest worked with a partner. They used the older Ross rifle, not the new Lee Enfields that their battalion comrades used. They tended to conduct their operations at dawn or dusk or when most of the rest of the battalion slept. As a working pair, two snipers would alternate spotting enemy positions and firing on German troops one at a time. But they did so nearly invisibly, often hiding in No Man's Land or beyond it for extended periods of time. They were a psychological menace to the enemy. Another of his 50th Battalion comrades noted that Norwest's eyes were "hypnotic [and] strangely piercing," but in humorous contrast, young Henry earned the moniker "Ducky," he claimed, because on leave in London he said he had to duck the girls pursuing him.

Pte. Henry Norwest recorded no fewer than 115 observed kills during his three years on the Western Front, which some suggest was the highest sniper score in the British or Canadian Expeditionary Forces. Some German prisoners of war even reported that Norwest's reputation was widely known in their army ranks. It was at the Pimple on April 12, however, that he finally earned overdue recognition. As the two western Canadian battalions seized the last of the German-held positions on Vimy Ridge, snipers such as Pte. Norwest ensured that few if any fleeing German troops made good their escape.*

"[Norwest] showed great bravery, skill and initiative in sniping the enemy after the capture of the Pimple," read his Military Medal (MM) citation. "By his activity he saved a great number of [Canadian] lives."

As Sgt. Ed Russenholt of the 44th Battalion caught his breath on the Pimple, he asked another man in the weary 10th Brigade how things had gone during the battle: "If they gave us twenty degrees of frost and a good barrage," he replied, "we'd go right through to Berlin."

### 7 a.m. April 12, 1917—Villers-au-Bois, Vimy

On the day his comrades went over the top in the 4th Division sector to complete the capture of Vimy Ridge, one rifleman with the 73rd Battalion was not with his Black Watch comrades at the front. Harold G. Carter sat somewhere behind the lines—in a military prison—having just composed a letter to his mother to say that he been a "bad boy" and that he was in trouble with military authorities. In fact, Pte. Carter was more than in trouble. A field general court martial had just found him guilty of desertion from the ranks. The charge report, which his mother did not know about, noted that it was his fourth offence of that kind, that Carter had deliberately avoided dangerous duty, and that as a consequence "the sentence of death should be carried out."

Like so many young men in the Canadian Corps, Harold G. Carter had signed up in 1915 underage. Though he had written his birth date on his attestation papers as 1894, it was actually 1897 and he wasn't even eighteen when he enlisted. Following his older brother,

---

* Pte. Henry Norwest served as 50th Battalion sniper through the Battle of Amiens, but during that same campaign—on August 18, 1918—a German marksman shot and killed him; a bar was added posthumously to his MM for "gallantry in the field."

Ernie, into the Canadian Expeditionary Force, Harold got to England and, according to letters home, visited a grandmother and a girlfriend and then failed to return to his barracks on time. Despite the offence, Pte. Carter was posted to the front in the fall of 1916 and saw action at the Somme. He didn't write about the horrors of combat, but in his letters he described sickness and the harshness of front-line conditions. It was there in the trenches of the Western Front, while serving with a work party, that Carter went absent without leave.

At the resulting trial in January 1917, he was found guilty of desertion and sentenced to ten years in prison. With his 73rd Battalion preparing for the Vimy attack, however, authorities suspended Carter's sentence and returned him to duty in the trenches behind Vimy. Two months later, with the Vimy assault just days away, Carter disappeared from yet another work party. It was April 5 when his final court martial handed down his sentence of death by firing squad. The execution was carried out on April 20. Though it was abhorrent to him, Canon Frederick G. Scott had an official role in such military procedures. The long-serving chaplain of the Canadian Corps attended the execution as guards blindfolded and handcuffed the prisoner before entering an ambulance for the drive to the execution site.

"There we got out and the prisoner was led over to a box behind which a post had been driven into the ground," Canon Scott wrote. "The firing party stood at a little distance in front with their backs toward us. It was just daylight.

"The prisoner was seated on the box and his hands were handcuffed behind the post. A round piece of white paper was pinned over his heart by the doctor as a guide for the men's aim. I went over and pronounced the Benediction. . . . The doctor and I . . . blocked our ears, but of course we heard the shots fired. . . . We went back . . . and the doctor felt his pulse and pronounced him dead.

"The body was placed in a coffin and taken in the ambulance to the military cemetery. . . . The usual cross was erected with no mention upon it of the manner of the death. That was now forgotten."

Pte. Harold G. Carter was one of 322 soldiers in the combined services of the British Army and its overseas contingents executed in this fashion during the First World War. Statutory justification for these executions owes to the fact that Canadian troops shipped overseas between 1914 and 1918 were no longer governed by the Militia Act of Canada, but by the legislation in the British Army Act. The law (dating back to 1879) covered a long list of punishable offences: "holding illegal communication with the enemy, failure to keep proper watch when on guard duty, cowardice, mutiny are among the offences which regard for the safety of the whole is held to require such striking punishment as will impress all on duty with their heinousness." In other words, the actual purpose of the executions was to maintain discipline in the ranks.

While not all those condemned to death by firing squad were innocent of the list of indictable offences, often these were men "whose stock of courage and resolution had . . . become exhausted." Bishop George A. Wells, who served with the expeditionary forces, spent a night consoling a Canadian sentenced to death for deserting his unit. The bishop wrote that the young man had struggled with army issue boots that were too small. He had dropped out of his column to bathe his feet in a ditch, but then discovered his swollen feet would no longer fit into the boots. He was later arrested, charged with desertion, court martialled, and executed. In the only case of cowardice involving a Canadian, a private (a recent reinforcement) in the 52nd Battalion refused to accompany his regiment into the front line, saying he'd rather be shot. At his court martial the soldier testified he feared being wounded more than being killed. The military had not yet come to recognize emotional exhaustion or shell shock as a neuro-psychiatric disability.

In addition to the one cowardice case, two Canadians faced the firing squad for murder and twenty-two—including Pte. Harold Carter—were sentenced to death for desertion.

Military protocol demanded that such executions be witnessed by the guilty man's comrades-in-arms. In Pte. Carter's case, members of the Black Watch of Montreal had to watch him shot by firing squad. As well, his brother Ernie Carter, an ambulance driver with the Canadian Expeditionary Force, was contacted, brought to witness

Harold's execution, and then transported with the body to Villers-au-Bois cemetery for the burial. Arthur Pollard was forced to observe the execution of a Canadian soldier. He recalled the entire battalion parading and lining up outside the walls of a farmyard at dawn.

"The silence was intense," he wrote. "When a soldier nervously dropped his rifle to the ground, it could be heard everywhere. We could hear orders being given to the firing squad. Then the shots rang out in the chilly morning. Then we marched back to our quarters. . . . It affected everyone."

A family member later suggested that Harold Carter had been "an overeager teenager" who enlisted in the Canadian Expeditionary Force for "the glory and fame of fighting for one's country, only to discover that he could not handle the horrors of war."

During the Great War, 2,690 soldiers on active service in the British Army and 355 men from overseas contingents were sentenced to death. Of those, 291 British and 31 overseas troops were actually executed.*

## April 13, 1917—Vimy Ridge, France

It was German Gen. von Bacmeister who had written (in captured documents) that "there are no deserters to be found among the Canadians." That's not to say some didn't contemplate it. Fearing he might be a coward during the battle of Vimy Ridge, a young member of the 5th Battalion from Saskatchewan noted in his diary how the experience of the previous three days had affected him. Sgt. John Alvis wrote that "I had always had the impression about desertion in battle that it was the result of cowardice, but I know in my own case it is the result of being lost from good leadership."

The sergeant admitted that leaving the relative safety of a position behind the lines and moving forward to the front created un-

---

* In August 2006, the British government announced it would seek parliamentary approval to pardon all those shot for desertion and cowardice during the First World War.

bearable anxiety and sometimes sparked the urge to run away from it all. As a sergeant with the responsibility for men of lower rank, he sensed that panic became amplified if those in charge exhibited any nervousness or hesitation at crucial times. From the moment he got his initiation at the Somme in the fall of 1916 and right through the war, he feared that his flight reflex might undo him.

"I came very near bringing shame to my unit on April 9, 1917," he wrote. "It was dark, with a low overcast as Zero Hour approached. We all knew the importance of getting across No Man's Land as quickly as possible. . . ."

Crossing a German trench in the 1st Division sector, Sgt. Alvis suddenly heard a cry for help from a Lewis gun crew bogged down in the mud of the trench. In spite of specific orders to keep going, he stopped long enough to help the six-man crew extricate themselves from the mud and move on. When he then discovered that he had been separated from his own battalion comrades, he panicked, searching to the right and to the left. No one. Then returning fire from the Germans drove him into a shell hole, where he wondered "how best to get away from this."

Just in time, the commanding officer of the company appeared at the shell hole. Alvis admitted to the officer that he was lost. He told Alvis to follow him. At the objective—the German trench line—things proved to be just as confused and disorganized. But following the C.O. had given him some direction, an objective to strive for, and, when he finally located his platoon, a renewed sense of what he had to do and the way through the battle.

"The following days I must have shown some courage," Alvis wrote, "as I was singled out for promotion and the Military Medal."

So it was for many Canadian Corps enlisted men like John Alvis. They didn't necessarily feel their "blood was up" the way Royal Flying Corps pilot Billy Bishop did shooting down a German surveillance balloon. Nor did they feel the "lust to kill" that Harvey Crowell's Nova Scotia Highlanders exhibited charging the machine-gun nests atop Hill 145. Rarely in the average soldier's makeup was there the sudden rise of courage exhibited by Pte. Bill Milne, Capt.

Thain MacDowell, L/Sgt. Ellis Sifton, or Pte. John Pattison, who all won the Victoria Cross at Vimy Ridge. The majority of Canadian soldiers on the battlefield those four days in April were more like John Alvis than the V.C. winners, more average than heroic and more satisfied with individual survival than military achievement.

Nevertheless, the victory seemed sweet.

# A FIRST FULL SENSE
# OF NATIONHOOD

T HE PRESS hadn't stalked the Canadian Corps through the
trenches nor over the top to scoop the world on its progress,
but the Canadians' victory at Vimy made front-page news in
Europe. The French press called the victory "Canada's Easter gift" to
their country and commented that "this is a great success, indeed a
splendid victory of which our Allies have the right to be proud and
on which they are to be heartily congratulated." Some newspapers
in Britain offered accounts of the capture of the ridge without even
mentioning the Canadians. Others heralded "the gallant colonials"
and in the case of *The Times*, W. Beach Thomas reported that "Sir
Douglas Haig, by deliberate choice, threw the weight of the British
Army against the strongest force of the enemy ever yet concentrated
in such a fortress." However, the dogged wartime correspondent
Philip Gibbs, reporting to the *Daily Telegraph*, credited the correct
armed force and wrote glowingly that "the Canadians had just fought
their way [to the crest of the ridge] with such high valour." He
summed up the work of expeditionary forces on the Arras front as "the
greatest victory we have yet gained in this war." A Canadian Press
correspondent, Stewart Lyon, wrote from Canadian headquarters
in France that "the Canadian Corps was given the place of honour in

the great event. . . . It was a great occasion and greatly [the Canadians] rose to it."

Across the Hindenburg Line, German reaction to the Canadians' victory at Vimy varied from disbelief to despair. April 9 was Gen. Erich Ludendorff's birthday and the German Chief of Staff wrote in his memoirs, "I had looked forward to the expected offensive with confidence," but he now coped with the realization that "the consequences of a breakthrough . . . are not easy to meet." With the loss of 54 guns, 104 trench mortars, and 124 machine guns and more than 4,000 German soldiers now prisoners of war, German Sixth Army commander Col.-Gen. Ludwig von Falkenhausen had little choice but to pull what was left of his army away from the eastern slope of the ridge. Meanwhile, the commander of the German Army Group, Crown Prince Rupprecht, surmised "that we can not recapture the Vimy Ridge. . . . All this leads to the question: Is there any sense in continuing the war?"

Remarkably, the most effusive praise for the Canadian Corps came from the American press. *The New York Times* said, "April 9th, 1917, will be in Canada's history one of the great days, a day of glory to furnish inspiration to her sons for generations." *The New York Tribune* went further, saying the victory had given Canadians "the opportunity to write the name of Canada on the war map of Europe, and their imprint will be remembered."

It wasn't only the American press that sensed the greater significance of the battle as a statement of Canadian nationalism. Talbot Papineau, a captain in Princess Patricia's Canadian Light Infantry, had long since grasped the way the war and a military brotherhood were forging an independent Canada away from Mother Britain. Not at the front on April 9, Papineau had nevertheless written (in an open letter to his cousin Henri Bourassa, founder and editor of *Le Devoir*) about Canadians fighting on the Western Front. He contended during earlier setbacks in the war in France and Belgium that "Canada was suffering the birth pangs of her national life." He emphasized that on the battlefield even more than at home "her citizens are being knit together into a new existence, because when men stand side by side and endure a soldier's life and face together a soldier's death, they are united in bonds almost as strong as the closest of blood ties." He even described the battlefield as the "foundation of a national construction."*

Others may not have put it quite so eloquently, but they agreed that something extraordinary had occurred to men of the Canadian Corps at Vimy. Capt. Claude Williams had studied medicine before the war and was a skilled Lewis gunner by the end of it. He noted in his letters home that the Canadian Corps had shed its "reputation as a rag-tag army," but instead made him feel "proud to be a Canadian" among other troops on the Western Front.

Alex Jack had gone into battle at Vimy a sergeant major and, because of battlefield losses, had come out the commander of two battalions. The twenty-five-year-old soldier had survived both the March 1 gas attack and the April 9 climb up Hill 145. He had held on to the precious bit of ground gained in the sector and watched German enfilade fire cut down more than 200 of his comrades. But, for their trouble, Jack said, the Canadians "had gained the reputation of being shock troops. The Germans knew if the Canadians . . . appeared on a front, they could expect trouble."

At the end of the first day of fighting at Vimy, Cyril Jones, serving with the 16th (Canadian Scottish) Battalion, made his way back to the original jumping-off point of the attack. For Lt. Jones, the glow of the victory was tarnished by the fact he was carrying back the body of his friend, Mac McGowen, for burial in a village cemetery behind the lines. That night, Jones was the only officer left in his company without a scratch; he had assumed command of the company. Despite his personal loss and the chill of a snowy night, Jones was cheered by the comments of one of his riflemen.

---

* In 1916, Talbot Papineau served in the Canadian War Records Office in France; in May 1917, he became a captain with the PPCLI and was killed in action at Passchendaele on October 30, 1917.

"Well, Mr. Jones," the man said, "they said in Lethbridge that we of the 113th [Battalion] were a bunch of booze-fighters, but we showed them today what we could do."

"Certainly did," Jones responded. "And a gamer bunch never donned the King's uniform."

## 2:40 p.m. April 9, 1917—Farbus wood, 1st Division objective, Vimy

*At 5:30, when the Allied artillery pieces and machine guns initiated their creeping barrage—firing for three minutes on the enemy's foremost trenches and then lifting to a new target farther on, every three minutes—the six leading battalions of the 2nd and 3rd Brigades had reached their first Black Line objectives by 6:15. By just after 7 a.m. Maj.-Gen. Arthur Currie's 1st Division men had arrived at their Red Line objectives, where the 1st Brigade had taken over. Completing its advance to the Blue Line exactly as it had been rehearsed in the practice fields, the 1st Division had captured the Blue Line objectives just after 11 a.m. and then reached the Brown Line by 2:40 p.m. Pte. Bill Milne had won a Victoria Cross (although it was awarded posthumously because he was killed later in the day). And the first of thousands of German prisoners had begun to move westward to pens behind the original Canadian lines.*

Celebration and demonstration were not part of Joe Labelle's victory at Vimy. He had enlisted with the 14th Battalion and immediately joined the rest of the Royal Montreal Regiment (RMR) in September 1914 training at Valcartier, Quebec. At Vimy, final instructions from the acting adjutant, Lt. J.W. Maynard, emphasized "that troops would attack exactly at Zero and not wait for the barrage to lift from the German front trenches at Zero plus three minutes . . . to give the enemy little time to come up from his dugouts and open fire." Labelle absorbed the severity of the order. He was mindful that the French and British had lost more than 100,000 men when they attempted to take the ridge. Nevertheless, Labelle and his comrades stepped into the battlefield directly behind the creeping barrage and watched it mow down the enemy "just like a lawnmower cutting grass." From the jumping-off trench past the Black Line and on to the Red Line, the Royal Montrealers' advance moved like clockwork. Labelle admitted some surprise at the ease of the operation. He said, "The boys felt elated," but once the initial exhilaration of seeing Germans retreating had passed, Labelle recalled his comrades saying, "Well, boys, we're here now. Let's hang on." Taking their piece of the ridge had cost the RMR 274 casualties.

Bill Green didn't take long to celebrate in his part of the 1st Division sector either. In fact, as he and the rest of his 4th Battalion consolidated their victory along the crest of Vimy Ridge above Farbus, Pte. Green took greater notice of the weather than the victory. With the Germans on the run east of Vimy, the scout with the Central Ontario Battalion was now battling the fast-falling snow as he dug into his new position. Some of the snow quickly piled up into drifts, but a lot of it melted and pooled into the mud holes on the ridge. In several spots along the German trench where Pte. Green and a scouting buddy had dug out some funk holes in which to sleep, nearly twelve inches of water suddenly accumulated. They had no clean water with which to cook, wash, or brew tea, so they improvised.

"We took water out of the trench and boiled it," Green wrote. "We made our tea and drank it. Next morning, the water had drained away into the soil and there lay a dead German, right where we had taken the water."

The Canadian Corps had won the right to savour its victory atop Vimy, but like every other engagement of the Great War, the victory came with a price. The "Southern" operation at Vimy Ridge—advancing the front line eastward in the 1st, 2nd, and 3rd Division sectors roughly 4,000 yards—had cost the Corps 7,707 casualties, including 2,967 dead. Overall, the four days of fighting at the geographic centre of the Arras offensive, had inflicted 10,602 casualties on the Canadian side, 3,598 of them fatal. That meant that along with the logistics of processing more than 4,000 prisoners and thousands of wounded from both sides, Canadian troops also had to deal with the corpses of their comrades lost in the victory.

Most troops at the end of the battle were so chilled by the weather and hungry from not eating for most of the day that they hardly recognized the success they had achieved. Signaller Harold Innis wrote in his diary about the aftermath at Vimy. While he commented on the efficiency of his battery mates and recognized that "the whole tension of our district had completely changed and it could be said that Vimy Ridge had been taken," that was the only notice he made of the victory. Then it was back to business as "our task . . . of bringing material to the front line . . . was highly speculative and dependent on the weather and became a complete fiasco because of a heavy snowfall." Innis also noted the "great numbers of dead men whom we saw the next day." Looking at the vast number of dead took the edge off his sense of accomplishment.

It took a week to bury the dead. Burial parties filled up old graveyards and dug new ones. Two brothers from a family of sixteen, in Wyman, Quebec, were among the crews that set to work immediately after the Canadians had taken the ridge. Billy and Lewis Buck had arrived in France a month before Vimy. En route to the front they had spotted wounded aboard trains bound for Etaples and across the Channel to Blighty. They wondered if they might be among the next to be transported out the same way. The Buck brothers—both just over five feet tall—joined the April 9 attack as a stretcher-bearer team in the 4th Battalion. Lewis Buck worried about what he might see going over the top; it turned out to be a "Canadian soldier blown to pieces [and] strung up on the wire." The brothers were told to look for rifles stuck upside down in the ground as markers for wounded soldiers to be picked up. When he looked out into No Man's Land that morning, Lewis Buck said later, "there were rifles stuck in the ground as far as you could see."

Once they had carried all the wounded to dressing stations or clearing stations, the following day the Buck brothers began burying the dead. First they prepared large communal graveyards on top of the ridge. Then they began retrieving the bodies and burying them— twenty or twenty-five per grave. They soon realized the process of erecting crosses would take too much time, so "we got bottles from the village and wrote down the name of each man and put it in the bottle upside down beside the man's head." Part way through the burial procedure, however, the Germans began shelling the area, so Lewis and Billy Buck* never completed the identification. Frank Yates wasn't a stretcher bearer, but as a private in the 3rd (Toronto) Battalion he was assigned such tasks as leading horse teams, running errands on bicycles, and bringing forward the rum rations. Following the Vimy attack, members of his platoon formed a work party building fodder reserves along the Lens-Arras road.

"We saw them burying the German dead nearby," Yates wrote. "They had a steam shovel and dug a deep trench, then lay the bodies covered in blankets side by side, covered them with dirt [and] put on crosses with the inscription: 'so many German dead.'"

As overwhelming as the number of burials—both Canadian and German—might have seemed, what bothered Sgt. R.S. Robertson of the 16th (Canadian Scottish) Battalion even more was the thought of what the Canadian Corps might have faced during those four days on Vimy Ridge.

"If all those [Germans] had been up above ground doing their duty, instead of underground in the dugouts," he said, "fewer of us would be here today."

## 2:40 p.m. April 9, 1917 — Goulot wood, 2nd Division objective, Vimy

*At Zero Hour in the right centre section of the Vimy front, the four leading battalions of the 2nd Division had followed the protective wall of the creeping barrage almost at a running pace, reaching the first Black Line objective forty-five minutes into the attack. Led by the 4th and 5th Brigades, Maj.-Gen. Henry Burstall's 2nd Division had the additional firepower of tanks (although they had eventually become mired in the mud). Opposition had*

---

* In September 1918, two months before the November 11 Armistice, Lewis Buck had to bury his younger brother, Billy, who was killed in action at the Drocourt-Quéant Line.

*stiffened at the Red Line objectives, where the individual initiative of men such as Ellis Sifton (awarded the V.C.) had spurred the eventual takeover of the Red Line objectives by 8 a.m. The 6th Brigade and the 13th Brigade (of the British 5th Division) had moved from there, the halfway mark, and just after 7 a.m. they had captured the Blue Line. Like the units that had leapfrogged through the 1st Division advance, the 6th and 13th Brigades then had reached their final objectives by mid-afternoon. They had captured scores of German machine guns and (combined with the 1st Division) thirty-one German artillery pieces.*

In addition to the captured guns, those troops of the 18th Battalion, given the chance to return to Neuville St. Vaast after the Vimy attack, also brought back the body of one of their own. Ellis Sifton had been killed in the final moments of clearing a machine-gun position in front of Les Tilleuls near the *Turko-Graben* trench system. His initiative at the height of the battle at the Red Line had spared the lives of many in his London, Ontario, regiment. Late that day—April 9— when his comrades buried him behind the original Canadian lines in the Lichfield crater cemetery, the wooden cross they erected showed the field promotion to lance/sergeant for which Sifton had never received his stripes. It also included the V.C. designation, which he would never know had been awarded.

Despite the notorious practice of sending service awards forward with food rations or simply drawing straws for the allocation of Military Medals among enlisted men, sometimes the recognition was refused. Edgar Goldstein, who had enlisted in the Canadian Expeditionary Force in Montreal in 1916, had come overseas to France on a draft with the 66th Battery. For that privilege, he had forfeited his sergeant's stripes. Cpl. Goldstein was then posted to a howitzer battery with the 2nd Division at Vimy, where his service was so notable that he was chosen to receive a Distinguished Service Medal. He refused the award, saying he "was no braver than any of the others." On August 15, 1917, the day he was scheduled to take a well-deserved leave in England and to receive an overdue commission, Edgar Goldstein was killed at the Battle of Loos near Hill 70.

(LEFT) These German troops hold their "potato masher" hand grenades in trenches just 25 metres from their enemy on the Western Front in France. (TOP AND BOTTOM) Reconfigured platoons of the Canadian Corps consisted of an officer, several sergeants, fifteen riflemen, eleven bombers and a equal number of grenadiers, a Lewis machine gun crew of six, a couple of scouts, and stretcher bearers. Each member of the platoon knew how to perform his job and the jobs of nearly every other man in the unit—the key to victory at Vimy.

(LEFT) Using a recent innovation—the 106 fuse—Canadian artillery crews ensured that obstructing German wire was eliminated because the shell's mushroom-shaped head detonated the high explosive on contact with the wire, not above or below it.

(RIGHT AND BELOW) Though instincts might compel assault troops to charge out of the trenches in the attack, they were trained to move at a steady walking pace in column lumps not lines abreast. Lt.-Gen. Julian Byng had told them, "Chaps, you shall go over exactly like a railroad train, on the exact time, or you shall be annihilated." It became known as the Vimy glide.

(LEFT) Youthful bravado and the fact he was fighting at Vimy at the age of sixteen, may have prompted Pte. Roy Henley to pose for this picture in a U.S. doughboy's cap and uniform. (BELOW) Aboriginal troops, including these men from the Files Hills Indian Colony in Saskatchewan, served in every front-line capacity, but excelled as snipers.

Rehearsing the advance helped Canadian troops cope with the idea of "walking into shells that were retreating ahead of you."

(RIGHT) Canadians in the 2nd Division had the psychological lift of marching forward with some of the first tanks used in the war alongside.

(LEFT) Most of the eight tanks on loan from the British Army, however, bogged down in mud and debris and became sitting ducks for German gunners.

(ABOVE AND BELOW) Fire and movement tactics used a portion of a platoon to preoccupy defenders with intense firepower, while the remaining sections manoeuvred to the flanks of an enemy position, such as a gun emplacement or trench, to overwhelm them from the side or behind. (LEFT) After Vimy, Lt. Greg Clark (left) was awarded the Military Cross; he claimed he received it only because he was one of the few Canadian Mounted Rifles officers to survive the battle. His younger brother Joe Clark earned a Distinguished Flying Cross in the Royal Flying Corps in 1918.

(ABOVE) Nearly 19,000 Canadians worked in the medical corps—as physicians, surgeons, nursing sisters, first-aid medics, operating room assistants, field ambulance drivers, and stretcher bearers. (LEFT) Pte. Will Antliff served as a medical clerk and stretcher bearer. He was among the first to document that the Canadians were winning the day; most of his medical cases were German POWs. (BELOW) During three days of battle at Vimy—April 9 to 12—the Royal Canadian Army Medical Corps treated and cleared 7,350 Canadian wounded and 706 German wounded.

(LEFT) Before the battle, the generals had warned medical officers and hospitals behind the lines to expect as many as 25,000 casualties. In fact, they processed 18,000. From field ambulances, wounded were loaded on trains bound for hospitals on the French coast.

(RIGHT) Grace MacPherson drove ambulance in Etaples, France. She had paid her own way to France, defied the generals to serve the Red Cross, and then had to maintain her motor ambulance, dealing with everything from flat tires to oil changes.

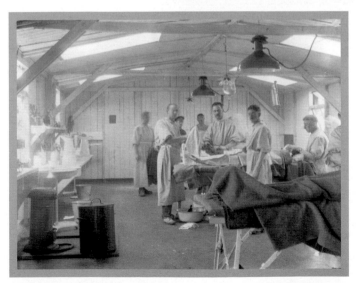

(LEFT) Casualty clearing stations dealt with wounds from machine-gun fire, gas attack, and bayonet lacerations. Seventy per cent of first aid and surgery, however, attended to wounds from artillery shrapnel.

(LEFT) Pte. Harold Carter (right) died near Vimy, but not in battle. Found guilty of desertion and executed in April 1917, he was more likely traumatized by warfare. Carter was photographed here with his cousin Harold Tyers in Toronto before they both left for overseas. (BELOW) Older brother Ernest Carter, a Canadian ambulance driver, was forced to witness the execution and then retrieve Harold's body for burial.

Assisting Canadian stretcher bearers, German prisoners propel push-trucks of Canadian wounded along the tramway. As many as 300 push-trucks carried four stretchers each.

(ABOVE) The number of Germans captured at Vimy varies, but those who processed the POWs say they numbered at least 4,000 men. (BELOW) The victors at Vimy often took full advantage to collect booty from their prisoners. German troops had a saying: "The British fight for glory, the Canadians for souvenirs."

(ABOVE) Seeing the Douai Plain and the village of Vimy for the first time, one Canadian soldier said he thought of "the children of Israel looking at the Promised Land." (BELOW) After two weeks of shelling, the Canadians' objectives, including the village of Farbus in the 2nd Division sector, left little of the spoils of war still standing.

(LEFT) For his rifle grenade attack on the first night of the Vimy assault, Pte. Lyle Pugsley should have won a Military Medal, but the luck of the draw literally prevented it. (BELOW) April 13, 1917, members of the Canadian Corps celebrate their victory aboard trucks bound for rear echelons and a well-deserved rest period.

Off the farm in southwestern Ontario, L/Sgt. Ellis Sifton joined the 18th Battalion, and wrote home hoping "that courage will be mine at the right moment if I am called upon to stare death in the face." When that time came, he rose to the challenge in the Vimy battlefield, but died in action—earning the posthumous Victoria Cross. Four Canadians won VCs at Vimy.

(LEFT) Advancing the front line at Vimy roughly 4,000 yards had cost the Canadian Corps. Four days of fighting inflicted 10,602 casualties, 3,598 fatal. Only rarely was there time for individual burials.

(RIGHT) Arthur Currie presides at the dedication of a temporary memorial to Canadians lost in the artillery battle at Vimy. In 1936 the same spot became permanent home of the Vimy Memorial.

(LEFT) The tribute and burial of hometown hero Lt.-Col. Sam Sharpe was the largest funeral Uxbridge, Ontario, had ever seen. His suicide might well be attributed to shell shock and the wartime loss of so many of his men.

(ABOVE) A veteran of the Great War and member of the entertainment troupe, the Dumbells, Ben Allen (in blackface) led the National Pilgrimage Committee to send 6,000 Canadians to the unveiling of the Vimy Memorial in 1936. The Dumbells depicted: (standing, l to r) Ted Langley, Ross Hamilton, Al Plunkett, Ben Allen, Bill Tennant, Ross McLean, and Jack McLaren (kneeling/ seated l to r) Hall (first name unknown), Allan Murray, Red Newman, Alan Fenwick, and Jack Ayre. (BELOW) Two squadrons of Royal Air Force fighter aircraft and another two squadrons from the French Air Force dipped their wings during their fly-past tribute to the Vimy Memorial.

(ABOVE) King Edward VIII descends the steps at the Vimy Memorial to greet veterans, their families, and the throng of French civilians. The resulting cheers drowned the noise of an artillery salute in the distance. (LEFT) Vimy pilgrim Mrs. C.S. Woods wore the medals of eight sons who had fought and died in the Great War. (BELOW) As the majestic Vimy Memorial is unveiled on July 26, 1936, veteran John Mould can't believe the last time he was there: "It was nothing but a muddy mound of grassless earth, pitted with shell holes filled with water and rotting barbed wire. . ."

Sculptor Walter Allward walks down the steps of his masterpiece on its inaugural day. "I have tried to show in this monument to Canada's fallen," he said, "what we owed them and will forever owe them."

On April 9, a day that had witnessed Canadians achieve the unachievable, not all distinguished service was recognized. When the members of No. 14 gun crew in the 6th Canadian Machine Gun Company reached their objective at Bois-de-la-Ville in front of Farbus, gunner Donald Fraser, and a crew mate named McCormick, rushed into a German gun emplacement. Pte. Fraser came face to face with a German gunner. The man looked pale and had blood running down one cheek. He had been wounded by other members of the Canadian gun crew and had thrown down his dagger in surrender. Fraser ensured that the German was fully disarmed and then reached the enemy gun in time to see other German troops retreating in front of the gun emplacement down the eastern slope of the ridge.

"McCormick and I grabbed the gun, a heavy and clumsy thing it was," Fraser wrote. "Carrying it about fifteen yards [we] turned it around with the intention of shooting the enemy, when we found it was out of action. . . . At this point Sgt. [Ernest] McGirr of our section jumped in between us from the rear and tried to get away a burst, but it was useless . . . the block was removed and thrown away. McGirr had a piece of chalk and when we left him he was writing on the gun 'Captured by the 6th Brigade Machine-Gun Company.' I heard later that this was rubbed out and the capture was claimed by the 27th Battalion."

Fraser noted in his diary that Sgt. McGirr did eventually receive recognition during the war the Military Medal, the French *Croix de-Guerre*, and the DCM—but in his zeal to be part of the attack at Lens, on August 21, was killed in action.

For Elmore Philpott, the reward for service delivered was a pat on the back and his own sense of accomplishment. One of a number of classmates at the University of Toronto to join the Canadian Field Artillery in 1915, Cpl. Philpott had taken his wartime trade seriously. When the opportunity to take additional artillery training in England arose, he jumped at the chance. Lessons in the science of gunnery served him well at Vimy and he consequently was in line for a commission. But almost more important than his lieutenancy, Philpott said, was the sense of pride he and his gunnery mates discovered in

themselves. It hadn't always been there. Philpott remembered recit-
ing the self-deprecating rhyme:

> "We are Sam Hughes's army, twenty thousand men are we.
> We cannot fight. We cannot march. What bloody use are we?
> When we get to Berlin, the Kaiser he will say,
> 'Hoch, hoch, mein gott, what a blinking fine lot, the Canadian
>    infantry.'"

The turning point, Philpott said, occurred during the gas attack
at the Second Battle of Ypres, where Canadians realized it—and
expressed it—that they were as good as any troops anywhere. "Certainly at Vimy, Canadians had convinced themselves. We had convinced ourselves that we were the finest troops on the Western
Front. Vimy was a great sense of triumph," he said. "I saw it as Canadians being tempered into a great nation."

Pte. Andrew McCrindle watched the same transformation of the
Canadian Corps. When members of his 24th Battalion arrived at
Vimy during the winter of 1917, self-esteem was low, morale was
lower, and the opinion of officers the lowest. At their billet in Maisnil
Bouché, his Victoria Rifles of Montreal had received requisite baths,
clean underwear, and pay. Then the brigadier had addressed an assembly of the men. McCrindle wrote that he called them "'a fine lot of
men' and all that baloney and that 'very soon we will be called on to
take part in a most important action'. . . . Then he says 'we must train
as we never have before' and that 'we will be told where to go and
what we have to do.' We could have told him."

After the Vimy operation, Pte. McCrindle* took time to record his
impressions. Along with a scan of the battlefield where he reported

---

* Andrew McCrindle served with the 24th Battalion up to the battle at Hill 70,
where he received bullet wounds severe enough to warrant amputation of his arm;
the surgeon he credits for saving it was Capt. Frederick Banting, later the co-dis-
coverer of insulin in 1921.

"most evident were the bodies of those slain on both sides, although no time was lost in reclaiming ours, but it still made the warm air fetid with the sickly stench of the dead." He documented that Vimy had inflicted 248 casualties on the 24th Battalion. He quoted wartime observers who said "this was the day Canada became a nation," while he lamented that "many of those who took part would never live to enjoy it." Despite his sadness at the loss of fellow Victoria Rifles, in the end, McCrindle found words of pride to applaud his comrades and his country: "On our far right, the French are having difficulty . . . so the British had to rush in some of their troops, but the Canadians stood fast in charge of Vimy Ridge."

## 5 p.m. April 9, 1917—La Folie wood, 3rd Division objective, Vimy

*Because of the pre-attack artillery barrage, like the 1st and 2nd Division, the 3rd Division had encountered only light resistance in the first phase of the assault. Maj.-Gen. Louis Lipsett's 7th and 8th Brigades had also taken full advantage of the saps tunnelled right up to the Germans' second trench lines and had captured hundreds of prisoners immediately. By 6:25, they had seized their Black Line objectives. Reaching the crest of the ridge by 7:30, the leading battalions were then supported by Vickers machine guns to move through La Folie Farm up to their Red Line objectives at La Folie wood. By nine o'clock, however, the 3rd Division men had learned that the 4th Division on the left had not yet seized Hill 145 and, in lieu of a further advance, had moved to protect their exposed left flank from La Folie wood back to the original front trenches. Like the 1st and 2nd Divisions, the 3rd had reached all forward objectives by mid-afternoon.*

John Mason should never had been at Vimy. He joined friends enlisting in Saskatoon and took basic training in the west and then at Valcartier. He rode the train to Halifax, then took a ship to England, and fought with the Canadian Corps as a member of the Black Watch in Belgium and France. It took some time for the system to catch up with him, but his mother's letter with Mason's enclosed birth certificate finally arrived at the front following the Battle at Vimy Ridge. Mason was called before a superior officer the morning after the attack. He feared he had really done something wrong.

"How old are you, Mason?" the officer asked.

"Twenty years old, sir," he replied.

"We have a record here from your mother that you are only sixteen."

Mason gulped. He had joined at age fourteen. He had survived thirteen months in the trenches, initiation at a forward listening post, four gas attacks, and service in the front lines at Ypres, the Somme, and Vimy. They had finally discovered he was still underage. He had just lied by saying he was twenty. He conjured up thoughts of imprisonment, court martial, maybe even firing squad.

"We are going to send you back," the officer said finally, "not back to England, but to Canada."

"That's very nice" was all Mason could think to say. "Thank you, sir."

Embarrassed and for the first time frightened, if only by authority, John Mason made an exit from the war intact. For nearly 4,000, whose remains were gathered up, the aftermath at Vimy meant quick burial and an equally quick ceremony. Then, to the commanding officer, fell the task of composing the obligatory letter to a parent, a sister, or a wife. One such officer in the 58th (Central Ontario) Battalion didn't shrink from his duty of writing such phrases as "cheerful character" or "great friend to comrades" and "you must only be proud." He did, however, agonize about the process of attending solemn burial services in front of inscribed crosses while those present realized there was every likelihood in a subsequent artillery attack that "their bodies [would be] blown across the cemetery, seeded into the soil in a thousand different bits."

Thomas McGill attended one of those funerals a few weeks later when the 3rd Division had erected a cross on one of the highest points on Vimy Ridge. A signaller who had taken a demotion in rank in time to serve at the front on Easter Monday, McGill joined about a hundred other 7th and 8th Brigade troops for the midday service. He later wrote a letter home with a description of the memorial:

> Sharp on the tick of twelve all the big guns in our area fired three volleys at the German lines as a salute, while the men all present presented arms. Then the ceremony began: a hymn, a prayer, a lesson, the Lord's Prayer, God Save The King. I have never seen men stand straighter or with their heads more proudly lifted, for each felt that a little bit of his own heart was buried there too.

McGill finished the letter by noting that as the ceremony concluded the men all filed past a small wooden cross erected at the site. Its inscription read: "Here lies an unknown Canadian who fell in action, 9th April, 1917."

There seemed little or no time for the stretcher bearers to rest. Wherever the advance took the 3rd Division, members of the 9th Canadian Field Ambulance followed immediately. Will Antliff worked in a medical team of half a dozen men, who always rose before 6 a.m. and carried wounded into regimental aid posts until well into the night. If the sheer physical exertion of transporting wounded men weren't stressful enough, there was always rough terrain to cover, as well as sniper bullets and incoming shells to dodge, which Antliff described to his mother in letters as "when the fun started." Soon after the initial Vimy attack, the 9th ambulance crew had moved its dressing stations forward, but still had long distances to cover through areas open to German attack.

"At 1 [a.m.] we were wakened to take a case down," Antliff wrote. "As soon as we got out of the dugout I noticed a peculiar smell in the air and . . . we ran into a heavy cloud of tear and chlorine gas. It was so bad we had to put on our gas helmets and at the same time fix the patient who was suffering from a shell wound in the head. . . . Believe me, it was pretty unbearable. In heavy work like this, one naturally puffs pretty badly. With a helmet on, it is impossible to breathe through the nose. Instead of keeping to the road, we beat it across the fields to get clear and tripped along as best we could around shell holes and across barbed wire. . . .

"By the time we got to the dugout, I for one was nearly smothered and . . . proceeded to take my helmet off. The tear gas fumes were fierce, however, and most of us were coughing like fury. It was also very smarting on the eyes and they burnt pretty bad for half an hour."*

Before the battle, the generals had warned medical officers and hospitals behind the lines there might be as many as 25,000 casualties; in fact, they processed 18,000. In the rush to expedite the traffic after the battle, the clearing areas behind Canadian lines not only proved to be models of efficiency for the wounded, but sometimes careless in their handling of the dead. Alex Gerrard had gone over the top at 5:30 a.m. on April 9 with the first wave of infantry in the 3rd Division sector. He served as the number two Lewis gunner in a 1st Canadian Mounted Rifles gunnery crew. By the end of the day, he had been badly wounded in the face and shoulder and had been carried on a stretcher back to a holding area underground.

"First thing I became conscious of was this officer coming through," Gerrard said. "The whole ward I was in was full of [stretchers] some of them contained the dead, some of them not. So this doctor says, 'Hey, this guy's alive. Get him out of here.'"

Pte. Gerrard was quickly bathed, his wounds were freshly dressed, and he was propped up in a cot in a medical recovery area farther behind the lines. The wound to his shoulder proved so severe, however, that nobody gave him any hope of regaining the use of his arm and hand. Eventually, medical teams moved Gerrard to a hospital on the French coast and then across the Channel to England. By that time doctors had carried out more serious surgery on him, removing

---

* William Antliff served with the 9th Field Ambulance from March 1916 until his return to Canada in March 1919. Though he was awarded the Military Medal in 1918, he noted because his mother had so faithfully sent letters, packages, and newspapers to keep his spirits up throughout his overseas service, that she really deserved the citation and medal.

his eye and repairing his arm so that it was functioning nearly normally again. His return from the dead was completed at the King George Hospital in London.

"I got a very good nurse," Gerrard concluded, "a Scottish nurse who put me on a special diet. I got a bottle of stout, chicken and other foods that helped me regain my strength."

Another member of the Canadian Mounted Rifles (CMR), William Smith, was among the proud 4th CMRs returning from the day's advance in the 3rd Division sector with "hundreds of prisoners, including three officers, one a colonel, passed back through the battalion to the prison cages." But the twenty-three-year-old private, from Barrie, Ontario, and other 4th CMRs brought back vivid impressions of something else they'd experienced during the Vimy attack.

"As they crossed No Man's Land," through snow that had since fallen, the 4th CMR war diary reported, "the men noticed the water in the shell holes was gory. Some of the men were quite positive that the water was red with blood." The regimental diarists go on to speculate, however, that like the blood-red algae "spoerella nivalis," associated with Canadian Arctic snows, the reddish colour of the Vimy snow was more likely "some species of small pigmented protozoan sometimes found in temporary pools and which had been lying in the encysted stage until the snow and rain fell."

For Pte. Smith and any other survivor of those first hectic hours on the Vimy battlefield, spilled blood churned up by driving snow, exploding shells, and thousands of soldiers' boots plodding through the chalky mud seemed the more plausible explanation. One of Smith's comrades in the 4th CMRs saw the mud and blood of the ridge and claimed they had "a mystique." Greg Clark had jumped ship from his job at the *Toronto Daily Star* to join the army and caught up with his regiment on the eve of the Vimy attack. For him the ridge was a symbol. It was a symbol to the Germans as "a sort of bastion of their line of conquest across France." It had become a symbol of death and loss, "a vast cemetery" for the French and British troops who could not win it back. Then, in the winter of 1916–1917, Vimy Ridge had become a symbol of success and independence to Canadians.

"For the first time in our history, the four Canadian divisions lined up along that infernal and stinking front, shoulder to shoulder," Clark wrote, "in order . . . the 1st, 2nd, 3rd and 4th Divisions. There is symbolism . . . Canadians from Atlantic to Pacific, a solid line." And when his Lewis-gun platoon reached the crest of the ridge at 7:05 a.m. on April 9, Clark described the Douai Plain below him, "like the kingdoms of the earth . . . As far as the eye could see, south, north, along the miles of ridge, there were the Canadians. And I experienced my first full sense of nationhood."

## 7 a.m. April 12, 1917—Givenchy and the Pimple, 4th Division objective, Vimy

*The two highest vantage points of the entire ridge had faced the men of the 4th Division. It took four days for Maj.-Gen. David Watson's division to wrest them from the Germans. The 11th Brigade, moving against Hill 145 (on the right), had been initially successful at the first German trenches, but under return fire was then forced to withdraw; only the inspired rush of the 85th Battalion had ensured a Canadian foothold atop Hill 145 by sundown on April 9. On the left, the 12th Brigade had used the advantage of two exploding underground mines to move quickly into the forward enemy trenches toward the Pimple. However, the Germans had then emerged from dugouts to blunt the attack. Here, Capt. Thain MacDowell had used unexpected tactics to capture large numbers of German defenders (and was later awarded the Victoria Cross for his efforts). With only the base of the Pimple in Canadian hands at the end of the first day, at mid-afternoon on April 10, the 10th Brigade had moved to secure the 11th Brigade's Black Line and Red Line objectives. By day's end the 4th Division had linked with the 3rd Division on the right. On April 11 bad weather had postponed the final push against the Pimple to April 12. Following the 5 a.m. barrage on that fourth day, battalions of the 4th Division had moved forward and within an hour were on the objective, securing it two hours later. The action included Pte. John Pattison's solo charge and the award of the fourth V.C. to the Canadians at Vimy.*

In the week leading up to the Easter Monday attack, Allied guns had fired more than a million rounds of heavy and field ammunition. Those 983 artillery pieces had deposited about 50,000 tons of explosive across Vimy Ridge and into the Douai Plain. On the first day of the four-day battle, Allied gunners had pummelled the ground in front of the attacking Canadian infantry with another 200,000 shells, while machine gunners had ripped into that same surface with another five million shells. The bombardment, according to an officer in the 4th Division, "lowered the height of the entire ridge by about three inches." Since the Canadian attack had lasted four days in the 4th Division sector, the resulting lunar landscape of blown mine craters, flooded shell holes, and smouldering gun emplacements, trenches, and dugouts made it next to impossible for anyone to make his way easily across the terrain.

The state of the ridge made movement physically difficult for stretcher bearers such as Harry Bond with the 72nd (Seaforth Highlanders) Battalion. For four days, Bond had struggled to move the hundreds of wounded down the pockmarked slope of the Pimple. It was, however, the psychological barrier of the state of the ridge that seemed even more difficult for newcomers to overcome. Bond and the Seaforths were still stationed on the recently taken northern edge of the 4th Division sector, when a British colonel on horseback rode up, leading a column of troops to relieve the Canadians.

"Where is Givenchy?" the colonel asked.

"It's just beyond the ridge, sir," Bond and the others announced. "Our troops have just taken Givenchy."

"Can't be, can't be," the colonel scowled.

"The enemy's just been driven off the ridge," said the 4th Division men.

"But I've been sent in to take Givenchy," said the man, barely able to contain his disappointment at the news that the Canadians had taken his objective.

If the bombed-out state of the 4th Division sector made the travels of a replacement battalion difficult, it certainly left Art Farmer with an even greater challenge. On April 9, the signaller with the 11th Canadian Machine Gun Company had gone over the top in support of the 102nd Battalion, a battalion in which he had finally caught up with his older brother, rifleman Eddie Farmer. Advancing for the first time in two and a half years side by side, the two brothers fought their way north of Hill 145 until four o'clock in the afternoon, when Eddie was shot and killed. Art Farmer was compelled by orders to keep moving so he left Eddie's body behind, although he vowed to return to the shell hole where his brother had fallen.

"That night I got permission from my officer to go and find my brother and give him a decent burial," Art Farmer said. "I took a buddy with me and went back. I knew every inch of the ridge by now . . . and I knew just where I left him, but we never did find him."

Farmer did find a shell hole recently filled in by a work party from the Canadian Army Medical Corps (CAMC). Atop the makeshift burial ground, the CAMC troops had erected a wooden cross with an inscription indicating the grave contained twenty-four unknown Canadian soldiers. Never having actually seen his brother's body interred, Art Farmer returned to his machine-gun company with a nagging doubt as to Eddie's fate. Had he mistakenly assumed Eddie was dead? Was it possible he'd still show up somewhere, sometime? Those thoughts haunted him for a long time, until he eventually saw a photograph of the Vimy Memorial erected at Hill 145 and showing the inscription of his brother's name, rank, and service number.

"From that day on, I had no doubt," Art Farmer said. "Prior to that time, I'd dream about it at night. I'd sit up in bed thinking that he was sitting at the foot of the bed. I could reach out and touch him."

Other members of the 4th Division created a more substantial memorial to their fallen comrades atop Vimy Ridge. Even as the 44th Battalion prepared to leave Vimy later in 1917, its pioneer troops came up with an impromptu monument by salvaging chunks of concrete from former German gun emplacements along the ridge. Ed Russenholt, a 44th Battalion sergeant who had participated in the costly battles of the 4th Division sector, watched his battalion comrades haul the stones up the slope at the north end of the ridge.

"Cut into the four faces [of the stone monument were] the names of the men of the unit who had fallen in the long series of actions there," Russenholt said. "Willing hands lugged that monument up the ridge and raised it on the lip of a crater on the Pimple."*

The spirit of remembrance moved a former newspaper reporter from Ottawa too. Fred James fought at Vimy as a newly commissioned junior officer, but also as a peacetime member of the Parliamentary Press Gallery in Ottawa. He considered himself fortunate to have come through the four-day battle unscathed, but was quick to point out that Canada should compile an honour roll of former reporters lost at the Western Front. James listed such fallen comrades as John Lewis of the *Montreal Star*, Gordon Southam from the *Hamilton Spectator*, W.M. Scanlon who had reported for both the Montreal *Herald* and the Ottawa *Journal*, and Hal Gordon from the *Toronto Daily Star*.

Lt. James had gone over the top with his 2nd (Eastern Ontario) Battalion soon after 5:30 a.m. on April 9. He had been impressed by the colossal fireworks display of artillery before dawn as well as the speed with which support troops moved railways, roadways, and the machinery of war forward later in the afternoon. And despite the loss of his colleagues, the former journalists, James had come through Vimy inspired by a renewed sense of optimism.

"What of the outlook?" he wrote. "We are satisfied with the way things are going and confident of the result. When will the war end? God alone knows. Personally, I have a hunch it will finish this year. . . ."

Vimy was a confidence builder for Gad Neale too. The nineteen-year-old, originally from Watford, England, had drifted from school to office work, then to Canada, eventually working as a farmer's helper on prairie farmlands near the Saskatchewan–Alberta border. He'd

---

* During the 1920s and 30s when Walter Allward's Vimy Memorial was erected on the highest point of the ridge—Hill 145—Vimy veteran Wesley Runions noted that members of his 44th Battalion dismantled the makeshift memorial atop the Pimple and transported it piece by piece to Vimy Ridge Memorial Park in Winnipeg, the battalion's home base.

always felt "unsettled" and never comfortable with his surroundings. When the war broke out in 1914, he immediately enlisted at Lloydminster. Right away, he fit into the routine of army training and service. Overseas, neither the pomp of British officers nor the discomfort of rats and lice in the trenches ever bothered him. In the army Pte. Neale suddenly found a home.

"The army was a mother and father to me," he said. "For years, and especially for an impressionable boy, all my relations were there. Your battalion was there, your company was there, your platoon was there. You belonged to them. You were an identifiable person."

During the lead-up to the Easter assault, Neal's 46th (Saskatchewan) Battalion rehearsed over the tapes at Chateau de la Haie. On April 9 they would be in reserve with the 10th Brigade in the 4th Division sector. As his training for the main operation continued, Pte. Neale carried out numerous duties—scouting in No Man's Land, working as a "minnie" guard (spotting German *Minenwerfer* shells), and serving with carrying parties. Just weeks before the Easter Monday attack, the 46th became the so-called frightfulness squad, carrying canisters of chlorine and phosgene forward for the gas raid on March 1. He believed the Germans would certainly have known the gas was coming "because of all the noise. . . . We carried the gas cylinders on long bars that would bang on the tank" as they walked.

While the March raid had been a demoralizing debacle, the April attack lifted Neale's spirits like nothing before or after. The 46th Battalion joined the assault on Vimy Ridge on the final day, April 12. Unlike the aborted gas raid, on April 12 the artillery barrage worked perfectly—with high explosives going off like sparks on the ground and shrapnel exploding over the German lines—and they reached their objectives with total precision. Even for a private in the ranks, Neale savoured every part of the Vimy victory.

"It was like being on the other side of a neighbour's fence and you get into his yard," Neale said. "It has always been forbidden ground up till then. And here we are in a place we never thought we'd be. . . .

"As far as Canada was concerned, we became a full-fledged nation [with] an army of our own. Up till then we had always been part of somebody else's army. We had done something of importance. It gave us something we hadn't had before, and that was hope."

"The greatest day in the Canadians' history" was the way medical officer J.N. Gunn summed up the first day of the Vimy attack in his diary. Through the entire military operation Maj. Gunn and his medical staff had worked around the clock—sometimes on just two hours' sleep—trying to keep up with the flood of wounded, both German and Canadian. On the fourth day of the battle, he recorded two memorable events in his diary. First, members of the 58th (Central Ontario) Battalion had captured a dugout and found a rifleman with the Royal Canadian Regiment. The man, named Allison, had been captured by the Germans four days earlier and then abandoned there. Allison had been shot in the leg and went four days without food or medical care. Gunn treated him and arranged for his transport by ambulance. Then he wrote down another indelible observation in the aftermath of this historic battle.

"Roads very bad. Traffic terrific. Water everywhere from melting snow," he wrote. "Counted at least twenty-five dead horses lying all about along the roads. Died from exhaustion and shells. I arranged burial of those that died in our hands."

No statistics totalling the number of equine casualties during the war exist. Two million horses took part and kept every dimension of the war effort moving—artillery shells and guns, food stores, ambulances full of wounded, in addition to the cavalry. Try as they might, each of the four Canadian Mobile Veterinary units found it difficult to cope with the nearly 2,000 animals that required treatment for wounds every month of the war. Insufficient rations, exposure to excessive cold, and parasitic diseases, as well as bullet and shell wounds, accounted for most of the horse casualties. Although, in addition, the haphazard way that nails were discarded from ammunition and supply boxes left countless numbers of horses lame. At Vimy, the Germans planted mats with upturned steel spikes on roads to cripple horse and mule teams. The troops who worked and genuinely cared for the horses at the front called them silent heroes. Bill Hewlett, an artillery engineer with the 14th Battalion, made constant note of the presence of horses in the war effort and in his own wartime service.

"Worked in stables all morning" was among the most frequent entries in his wartime diary during training in Ottawa, at Shorncliffe in England, and behind the lines in Belgium and France. Whether it was because he volunteered or because of his previous farm experience, Pte. Hewlett frequently took on an additional responsibility following major engagements at the front. Because of his "love for the animals," he volunteered to drag away and bury the carcasses of horses killed in artillery attacks or following cavalry charges. He was consequently "sick for twenty-four hours afterward."

## April 12, 1917—Behind German lines, Vimy

Treading on forbidden ground, flexing muscles as an autonomous army, and feeling a sudden Canadian solidarity were not necessarily the prerequisites for nationhood, but many members of the Canadian Corps expressed that sentiment at the time and in the years that followed. The birth-of-a-nation mythology grew out of a post-war urge to restate the rationale for participating in the war. It resulted from a healthy sense that Canada was a British ally by birth, but in the Great War it was also a member of the British family with a voice of its own. The fact remained that the Canadians had achieved a military feat that had eluded other Allied armies for nearly three years on the Western Front. They had captured Vimy Ridge as equal partners with their allies, Britain and France. At the founding of the League of Nations during the Paris Peace Conference in 1919, Canada had an autonomous vote. The Vimy victory also later became a catalyst for groups wishing to memorialize the country's sacrifice and loss both in published print and inscribed stone. The movement for the creation of a war monument at Vimy began as a monument to the valour, heroism, and victories of the Canadian Corps, but also as a memorial to the thousands of Canadian soldiers missing in action and for whom there was no known grave.

Nearly forgotten in any celebrating that might have followed the victory at Vimy was the fate of the Canadian Corps' missing. From the time they had arrived at the Arras front in 1916 until they moved on to the battle at Hill 70 and Passchendaele later in 1917, Canada's four divisions had suffered a substantial number of casualties—those troops killed or wounded, as well as those missing in action. Charlie Venning fell into the last category. Originally from the small farming community of Blackstock, in central Ontario, Venning had joined the 136th Battalion at Port Hope in 1916. Like so many, Pte. Venning had gone to the Western Front as a reinforcement, arriving at Vimy just in time to join the 75th (Mississauga Horse) Battalion and its infamous March 1 gas attack.

Designed to undermine German troops' confidence, gain intelligence, and deplete the enemy's strength along the Vimy front, the surprise raid had done just the opposite. Just after 3 a.m. on March 1, British gas specialists had released the poisonous clouds into the westerly breezes up Hill 145. German alarms brought heavy artillery return fire, which exploded the offensive gas stores amid the Canadian troops in their trenches. Despite the setback, the second release of gas at 5 a.m. signalled the beginning of the infantry attack. About 1,700 men from the 54th (Kootenay) Battalion and the 75th went over the top in a large-scale "reconnaissance in force" raid. Winds had changed direction. Clouds of poison flowed back into the faces of the Canadians. Confusion had reigned. And hundreds of men got caught in their own chlorine and phosgene gas or in the counteroffensive German machine-gun fire. Of the 1,700 men assigned to the raid, 687 had become casualties. The surprise gas attack had shaken 4th Division morale, solidified the Germans' psychological hold in Vimy Ridge, and severely reduced the Canadian 11th and 12th Brigade strength for the coming major Vimy assault. Pte. Venning had become a Vimy casualty on March 1 and therefore missed the successful action five weeks later.

"Charles was shot in the right leg," his wife, Luella Venning, wrote later. A post-war article in the *Toronto Daily Star* picked up Venning's account of the aborted attack by reporting that "he was unable to get away before the Huns captured him. He was twenty-one months [as a POW]. He was in a German hospital for three months [where] the treatment was very cruel and crude."

Following his hospitalization and recovery behind German lines, Venning was assigned work on a prison farm, tending pigs in the camps near Munster and Senelager. As there was little nutritious food in the POW camps, Venning likely survived because of access to farm produce. Though the Great War officially ended on November 11, his German captors refused to release Venning immediately.

"When the armistice was signed," he told reporters later, "I refused to keep on working. I was then on a farm. The other prisoners were given their freedom. When I refused to work, they put me in prison for fourteen more days."

Charlie Venning was repatriated to England in December 1918 and to Canada the following March. For the rest of his life, he suffered chronic asthma (likely a result of the gas attack) and from intestinal ulcers (from lack of nutritious foods during wartime imprisonment). In addition, for many years he was plagued by nightmares of the March 1 attack at Vimy, his wife said. Until an army buddy visited the family farm in Blackstock, Ontario, decades later, Venning never spoke a word about his experiences in the war. He re-enlisted in the Second World War, but was discharged when his back was broken in training. Complications from his First World War wounds and long-term effects of malnutrition during his imprisonment, as well as nightmares of Vimy and the Great War in general, may well have hastened his premature death. He was buried in a small church cemetery, according to his wish, beneath a simple military marker.

For at least 19,000 Canadians serving in the Canadian Expeditionary Force there were no individual gravesites or individual tombstones to commemorate life, service, or final resting place. They were the First World War dead whose remains were never found. Eventually, they would be recognized collectively and by inscription at such monuments as the Menin Gate in Ypres, Belgium, and at the base of the Vimy Memorial atop Hill 145 in France. In total, the Great War took the lives of more than 60,000 Canadians. In number, the loss proved to be an even greater Canadian sacrifice than the Second World War, in which 41,000 Canadians lost their lives. In so many ways, the 10,602 casualties at Vimy, combined with those at Ypres, the Somme, Passchendaele, and the rest, left more than individual families grieving. The effects of a generation lost to warfare between 1914 and 1918 changed homes, neighbourhoods—entire communities.

Harry Loosmore had witnessed the trials of the 4th Division at Vimy Ridge—both during the March 1 gas attack and the full frontal assault on April 9—from the relative safety of the 44th Battery gun pit in front of La Folie wood. Loosmore had enlisted in the artillery in Victoria, B.C., in 1915. At Bramshott, in England, army authorities spotted his abilities as a blacksmith, so they posted the twenty-year-old volunteer to the 44th as a shoeing smith. For Vimy operations, his battery crew was split between the 31st Battery and 32nd Battery. On April 9 during the attack, though he was too busy to assess the 4th Division's progress, at the end of the day Loosmore watched the groups of German prisoners paraded through the Canadian lines en route to POW cages. He also spotted incoming stretcher bearers with Canadian wounded and dead. He lamented in his diary not only about the friends lost that day, but also about the impact their deaths would have on their home community in British Columbia.

"Salt Spring Island paid a high price for her share in the Ridge," Loosmore wrote. "The two Lumley brothers of Fulford were killed by the same shell. Henry Emerson, who operated Mouat's Feed Store, went too—I can still see him practising ball catching with Arthur Drake on Ganges Wharf in the summer of 1915. Donald Craig, aged 20 . . . and Charlie Dean . . . who acted like a big brother to me . . . died of wounds and was buried in Barlin extension cemetery."

Canadians would remember their soldiers had taken Vimy Ridge whether they wished to or not.

# SACRED TRUST

### June 28, 1920—Uxbridge Methodist Church,
### Uxbridge, Ontario, Canada

L ATE IN THE SPRING of 1918, a veteran of the Western Front
arrived back in Canada. The war was now in its final months,
but Lt.-Col. Sam Sharpe had received a leave of absence to
come home. The newspapers speculated that politics had prompted
his early return. The lieutenant-colonel had earlier received Distinguished Service Order honours from the King. And since Sharpe had
also recently won re-election to the House of Commons in Canada,
despite being overseas, the papers also claimed the commander of the
116th Battalion was returning to take a senior cabinet portfolio in
the Conservative government of Robert Borden. Earlier in the winter, however, the forty-five-year-old colonel of the Ontario County
Battalion from Uxbridge had been ordered to the Marlborough
Hospital in Aldershot, England. He'd come down with pleurisy. But
doctors soon discovered he had more than a respiratory ailment. The
colonel had experienced a nervous breakdown.

The fatigue of commanding a fighting regiment on the Western
Front, with its incumbent responsibilities and realities, had caught up
with the man both mentally and physically. With each step the Canadian Corps had made eastward—the night raids across No Man's

Land, the frontal attacks behind creeping barrages—and in response, the repeated counterattacks of German gas, artillery, and infantry, the 116th was faltering. Not in spirit, but in cumulative losses. At Vimy Ridge the battalion had received its baptism of fire. Wiring operations behind the first wave of assault troops, during the four-day battle, had cost the battalion nearly a hundred casualties.* Another hundred had been killed, wounded, or missing at Hill 70 in the Avion sector. The first seven months of service on the Western Front had killed or put out of action nearly a third of the battalion's strength. By 1918, the 116th was reduced to only three fighting companies, each consisting of barely ninety riflemen.

As early as October 1917, when the battalion was ordered into the front to attack the Passchendaele ridge, Lt.-Col. Sharpe was clearly flagging under the strain.

"We have very little protection there and I may not pull through," he wrote his wife. The letter came to Mabel Sharpe back home in Uxbridge as a kind of last will and testament. "If it should be my fate to be among those who fall, I wish to say I have no regrets to offer. I have done my duty as I saw it and have fought in the defence of those principles upon which our great Empire is founded. I die without any fears as to the ultimate destiny of all that is immortal within me."

Following the attack of a ridge at Passchendaele, when the 116th Battalion finally earned a rest behind the lines at Poperinge, it had been reduced by another 158 soldiers—42 killed, 104 wounded in action, and a dozen men gassed. Lyman Nicholls, the young Uxbridge farm boy who had sneaked out a high school window to join the 116th underage in 1915, had lived through the Vimy, Avion, and Passchendaele campaigns, but the Cambrai offensive would be his last.

"Our battalion had lost so many men," he said, "that the signallers

---

* Uxbridge was so impressed by the performance of its homegrown regiment at Vimy Ridge that a year later, on April 22, 1918, a gavel made from the wood salvaged from an oak tree at Vimy was presented to the Zeredatha Lodge of the Masonic Order, in honour of those 116th Battalion men who were also members of the lodge, including Lt.-Col. Sam Sharpe.

and the band had to go over the top with the regular companies. On our advancing, there were seven of us signallers, when we heard this shell coming . . . and all dived into a shell hole. After I regained consciousness my face was warm with blood. . . . The boy on my left was killed and four on my right were wounded. . . . We were just walking wounded."

The battalion that had begun its wartime service numbering 1,100 was eventually reduced to 160 men. By Christmas of 1917, however, Lt.-Col. Sharpe was in hospital in England and then, following his transatlantic trip back to Canada, admitted to Montreal's Royal Victoria Hospital in late May 1918. Just a few days later, Sharpe was wakened in his hospital bed. A nurse left the room while he got dressed for a drive outside the hospital. The newspaper account reported that the nurse said "he showed no signs of mental aberration and talked quite intelligently to her. . . . Col. Sharpe . . . met his death . . . by jumping from a second story window and falling to the concrete pavement below."

After lying in state at the county council chamber in Whitby, Ontario, Sharpe's casket was transported to Uxbridge for interment. The funeral was the largest ever held in the town. The procession stretched for over a mile—in a steady drizzle—and included a gun carriage for transport of his body, military band, and a firing squad of thirty rifles; they fired three volleys over his gravesite. As well as family and friends from the area, the funeral attracted many of Sharpe's political allies and opponents alike and some surviving members of the 116th Battalion. The regiment's former chaplain, Rev. Capt. John Garbutt, delivered the eulogy.

"He accepted your boys as a sacred trust," the reverend said. "And he never spared himself to guard them as such. . . . I was right there and saw your boys led by their colonel go over at Vimy Ridge. . . . He loved his men and wrote of them. I have letters now in which he speaks of their splendid work and enumerates the decorations won."

Whether Sam Sharpe fell from the Royal Victoria Hospital window or jumped was never accurately determined. A short inquiry concluded it was an accidental death. His condition predates identification of post-traumatic stress disorder, but medical and news reports of the day indicated that the lieutenant-colonel suffered from "shell shock and complete physical and mental exhaustion." Many of his friends and family members at home in Uxbridge speculated that the man was heartbroken at the loss of so many of the county's young men, so many of the men in his "sacred trust." Area resident and even then renowned author Lucy Maud Montgomery recalled attending the funeral and noted in her diary that Sharpe had "come home from the front, insane from shell-shock and jumped from a window in the Royal Victoria at Montreal." As the man himself had pointed out in his letter home after Vimy, "Old Ontario County is paying its toll in the great struggle" and Sam Sharpe apparently felt personally and fully responsible.

Two years later—following the 1918 Armistice, the 1919 Paris Peace Conference, the first meeting of the League of Nations in 1920, and the repatriation of the remnants of the 116th Battalion—a commemorative ceremony took place in Lt.-Col. Sam Sharpe's hometown. On that June evening the Uxbridge Methodist Church, filled to capacity, witnessed the inauguration of a "handsome tablet of brass with its background of onyx marble" in honour of the town's wartime "patriot." Following the singing of the national anthem and an address from a flag-draped pulpit by the minister of the church, next the former premier of Ontario, Sir William Hearst, stepped to the platform and delivered the memorial keynote.

"It is an honour and a privilege for me to unveil this tablet to a brave soldier, a devoted statesman, loving husband and faithful friend, Col. Sam Sharpe," Hearst announced to the hushed congregation. He paid tribute to the soldiers of the Great War saying they had saved civilization. He called upon the same men to assist in the reconstruction of civilization. He spoke of his association and admiration for Sam Sharpe. Then he returned to his salute to the fallen, stepped from the platform, and unveiled the commemorative tablet. "In the name of God, these men deserve better monuments than those of wood and stone," he said finally. "No human hands can carve a memorial suitable to the sacrifice our boys have made."

## January 31, 1923—Senate Chamber, Parliament Hill, Ottawa, Ontario, Canada

In truth, after 1918 Canada faced numerous crises that quickly overshadowed the victory over Germany, the November armistice, and those ceremonies organized in tribute to her war dead. The country had to demobilize half a million men into a workplace where employment was limited. It had to cope with an influenza pandemic that quickly spread across the country and killed nearly 50,000 people. Add to that scenario post-war economic inflation and a strong dose of political disunity and very quickly the euphoria of victory and peace seemed to fade. Nevertheless, as Canadian veterans gathered for reunions, read published front-line memoirs, attended theatrical productions about the war, and paid their respects at community cenotaphs each November 11, they began to construct a mythology about the events of 1914 to 1918.

For some the Great War had represented a reflex action among loyal British-born Canadians to rally round the Union Jack and rush off to defend Mother England. Most Canadians who had any sense of events in Europe, however, saw the war coming. They witnessed the threat that German military might posed overseas and when diplomacy failed, they expected to see the inevitable conflagration of large German, French, and British armies clashing on the European continent during a sharp, short war. Young Canadians hurried off in pursuit of a great adventure, wishing to get overseas quickly for fear the war would be over before Christmas. When stories of the trench war of attrition began to emerge in 1915, it became clear the war would last much longer. The war effort then took on the look and sound of a crusade—of defending smaller nations against belligerent larger ones, of freedom over tyranny, of removing the blight of war from the world once and for all. In the years after the Armistice, Vimy

Ridge would eventually emerge—in truth or in myth—as the place where both Canada's nationhood and its crusade against war could be commemorated.*

"Vimy—the achievement—is for the living and always will be," one historian wrote. "The memorial is for the dead."

Pilgrimages to battlefields and military cemeteries were rare in Europe before the Great War. Travel proved cumbersome and time consuming. Seldom had the living marked killing fields with anything more than modest monuments, recording only the names of individual regiments. However, scarcely had the 1918 ceasefire occurred than relatives of British and French soldiers began appearing along the former Western Front, mourning fathers, brothers, and sons. Soon, veterans of various military units began to construct memorials at strategic battle sites in France and Belgium. Calling on the goodwill and memories of their surviving members when they could, those military units generated press and local sentiment just the way the Methodist church had for Sam Sharpe in Uxbridge. Most of the memorials were heartfelt but modest in vision.

Then in July 1919, the government of Belgium offered Canada a large tract of land near Ypres, so that Canada could erect a memorial in honour of the men who had defended that city during the war. The gesture seemed to spark Ottawa's interest in a grander commemorative plan because in September 1920 the federal government established the Canadian Battlefields Memorials Commission. It launched a competition to determine a design for Canada's war memorials and enlisted some military consultants, including former 1st Canadian Infantry Division commander at Vimy Maj.-Gen. Arthur Currie, to assemble a list of eight potential sites on which to recognize the valour and sacrifice of Canadian soldiers in the Great War.

For the commission, the first job lay in deciding which of the 160 submitted designs would be most appropriate for the eight sites. Then it faced the task of clearing the wartorn ground, of planting trees and

---

* Of Canada's 9 million people in 1914, slightly more than 5 million were English speaking and about 4 million were French speaking.

beds of flowers where shells and human remains could still be found, of selecting the designs for the different memorials and then of supervising their construction. In a decade and a half, the commission managed to complete all eight memorials: three in Belgium—at Passchendaele, St. Julien, and Sanctuary Wood—and the remaining five in France—at Dury, Bourlon Wood, Courcelette, Le Quesnel, and at Vimy Ridge. The most ambitious, at Vimy, became the preoccupation of Canadian sculptor Walter Seymour Allward for a decade and a half.

The son of a Newfoundland carpenter, young Walter was expected to follow in his father's footsteps. Instead, he began modelling figures in stone. Even when he became an apprentice at a Toronto architectural firm, Allward spent evenings drawing the famous statues of ancient Greece and the Italian renaissance. When the Ontario government announced plans for a memorial to honour those who had volunteered during the Northwest Rebellion, Allward's design for the figure Peace became a bronze atop the Queen's Park monument in Toronto. A stream of commissioned sculptures, which he called "statues in frock coats," followed, including John Graves Simcoe, Oliver Mowat, William Lyon Mackenzie, Alexander Graham Bell, and Canadian heroes of the South African War. Then came the formation of the Canadian Battlefields Memorials Commission and the design competitions for monuments at the eight battlefield sites of the Great War. The Vimy site suddenly emerged above all the rest on January 31, 1923.

On that day, during the opening session of the Parliament, the Governor General, Lord Byng, rose to speak to a joint assembly of Members of Parliament and senators. Julian Byng, the man who had commanded the Canadian Corps at Vimy, had great news about Canada's largest wheat crop in history. He had words to say about the federal government's budgetary estimates for the coming year. New members were to be introduced, an Oaths of Office bill would be introduced, various standing committees were announced, and an internal commission would be established to assist veterans re-acclimatize themselves to Canadian civilian life. But by far his most important announcement came from outside Canada.

"The Government of France has graciously offered to the Canadian Government a tract of land of 250 acres on Vimy Ridge, at the site selected for the erection by Canada of a monument commemorating the exploits of the Canadian Corps in the Great War," Governor General Byng announced.

The gift and the groundswell for commemoration of the Great War sacrifice suddenly focused attention on Vimy Ridge and galvanized Allward's vision of a sculpted monument there. Some said his first inspiration was recorded on "an envelope out of his pocket and in a few bold pencil strokes indicated the general idea [of] two towering pylons of stone." Allward was forty-four in 1920 when he began working in earnest on his design for Vimy. He generated 150 different drawings to submit to the commission. At the base of his design stood the Wall of Defence, including one sculpture depicting the Breaking of the Sword and another showing the Sympathy of Canadians for the helpless. Above were the mouths of guns covered with olives and laurels. On the principal wall stood the heroic, brooding figure of Canada Mourning Her Dead and behind her, the two pylons symbolizing the two forces—Canadian and French—with the Spirit of Sacrifice throwing the torch to his comrades. Looking up, the soldiers would see the figures of Faith, Charity, Honour, Peace, Justice, Truth, Knowledge, and Sacrifice for which they had fought. Around them were situated the shields of Britain, Canada, and France. Finally, on the Wall of Defence, Allward would have inscribed the names of the missing—the 11,285 Canadians who fell in France and who have no known resting place.* Allward said he had envisioned his concept in a dream.

"I saw a great battlefield," he said. "I saw our men going up in thousands and being mowed down by the sickles of death—regiment after regiment. Suffering beyond endurance, I turned my eyes and found myself looking down an avenue of poplars. Suddenly through this

---

* The names of 7,024 other Canadian war dead missing in Flanders (Belgium) are carved into the arches of the Menin Gate at Ypres; the memorial salutes Commonwealth and Empire troops whose remains were never found.

avenue I saw thousands marching to the aid of our armies. They were the dead. They rose in masses and filed silently by and entered the fight to save the living. So vivid was this impression that when I awoke it stayed with me for months. I have tried to show in this monument to Canada's fallen, what we owed them and will forever owe them."

The commission judges—architects Frank Darling (Toronto), C.H. Reilly (London), and Paul P. Cret (Paris)—unanimously chose Allward's design and awarded him the budget for construction of $1 million. Following a valedictory dinner and send-off at the Arts and Letters Club in Toronto, Allward left for France. He expected to be away from home for about six years. His multi-faceted monument would rest on 11,000 tons of concrete, reinforced with hundreds of tons of steel. The memorial itself—approximately 200 feet square at the base and about 125 feet high—would be cut from 6,000 tons of limestone. His search for the appropriate stone became an obsession and even, as he commented later, "a nightmare." Eventually, he settled on stone retrieved from an abandoned Roman quarry on the Dalmatian coast of Yugoslavia. "We have to contemplate a structure which will endure in an exposed position, for a thousand years—indeed, for all time," Allward said.

In 1930, when Allward had begun to erect the memorial on the site, Vimy veteran Will Bird visited the former battlefield. A wartime member of the 42nd Battalion, the Black Watch, Bird's personal pilgrimage led him across France to Vimy Ridge, where he first realized the magnitude of Allward's project. Clearing the ground of human remains and buried explosives required extraordinary precision and risk. Bird discovered that Allward's labourers—each insured at a cost of 40 percent of wages—had to remove 100,000 yards of earth not with steam shovels, but with picks and shovels, because the top four feet of earth contained leftover stick bombs, dud shells, and grenades. Despite the precautions, two men were killed and many injured during the excavation. The masons had been equally meticulous.

"Mr. Allward has not," so the men at the memorial told Bird, "made a mistake of one-eighth of an inch in all his figures given in five years, a record they say has never been equalled."

Allward himself spent a full fourteen years cutting and installing the stone sculpture at the memorial site.

## July 26, 1936—Vimy Memorial, Vimy Ridge, France

In November of 1928 the Canadian Legion assembled its Dominion Council in Regina, Saskatchewan. The agenda item that attracted most interest that year proved to be the matter of a veterans' pilgrimage to the Vimy monument, to be unveiled by King Edward VIII at some future date. Interest in a pilgrimage suddenly took on tangible form in 1934 when the anticipated unveiling date was announced— July 1936. Dominion president Brig.-Gen. Alex Ross placed an advertisement in *The Legionary*, the magazine of the Canadian Legion, inviting all who had served with the Canadian Corps to join the inauguration of the memorial, an event sponsored by the French, British, and Canadian governments. Members, their wives, and the widows of fallen soldiers across the country began posting their inquiries to the Legion. Their offices were soon dealing with thousands of applications.

"Survivors of the Great War have within them an instinct unpossessed by those who did not share that experience," one veteran wrote. "It is an instinct that stimulates a longing to return to those regions that inspired it."

Because of the resounding response, the Legion formed a pilgrimage committee and hired a small staff of travel agents to work out the details of transportation and accommodation. First World War veteran and now National Pilgrimage Committee organizer Ben Allen spearheaded the massive logistical job. Sensing there was a great "desire to return," Allen sought government, volunteer, and corporate sponsorship. Based in Ottawa, he managed to secure, among other gifts, a one-cent-per-mile return rate on Canadian railway tickets for each pilgrim. The pilgrims would sail from Montreal aboard five ships in mid-July and arrive in Europe in time to reach Vimy Ridge for the unveiling of the monument at the end of the month. Total cost to each pilgrim would be $160.

Among the 6,200 Vimy pilgrims who boarded the passenger liners at Montreal on July 16, 1936, was Florence Murdock, a fine arts graduate from Amherst, Nova Scotia. Florence's older brother Alfred had served as a signaller in Lt.-Col. Andrew McNaughton's 1st Canadian Heavy Artillery Group, while her younger brother Ward had served overseas with the 85th (Nova Scotia Highlanders) Battalion. Since both brothers' units had served with distinction at Vimy, Florence was drawn to the event and joined a group from Nova Scotia and P.E.I. en route to catch up with the tour in Montreal. There she noted the hotels were packed with "a lovely crowd" of Vimy pilgrims. On the morning of July 16 her party boarded the *Antonia*, moored at the Montreal waterfront alongside the other pilgrim ships—*Ascania*, *Montrose*, *Montclaire*, and *Duchess of Bedford*. Florence recalled the excitement of the send-off with flowers, streamers, pipers, and aircraft flying overhead. Each pilgrim received a khaki beret and a haversack containing a Vimy medal, a pilgrim's guidebook, and an envelope for documents. Florence Murdock was one of 1,200 aboard *Antonia*.

"Men with their decorations, women wearing the decorations of their loved ones who were killed, and the mothers with their silver crosses for each son," she noted in her diary. "We had a dear old lady, a Mrs. C.S. Woods from Winnipeg. She had twelve sons in the war. Five were killed at the front and three died of war wounds after."

Four of the pilgrim ships left Montreal within minutes of each other on July 16 (the *Bedford* followed the next day) and were joined at sea by HMCS *Saguenay*, the destroyer that escorted "the peace armada" until the passenger liners docked at Antwerp, Belgium, and Le Havre, France. From there, the pilgrims would wend their way across France to the Vimy unveiling in mid-summer.

The site preparations, logistical arrangements, military and governmental protocol, diplomatic requirements, accommodation of pilgrims' needs, choreography of the events, and, yes, security surrounding the actual unveiling of Walter Allward's million-dollar sculpture had taken two years to complete. As this would be perhaps the most spectacular event of its kind since the war, nearly every department of the administration of France became involved—up to and including President Albert Lebrun. For the first time ever, a British monarch would preside at an event as the King of Canada. The preamble to the memorial's unveiling proved as complicated and delicate as any. Protocol would make it necessary, for example, for King Edward VIII to arrive at Vimy before French officials, so that he could receive the French officially on Canadian soil. On July 19, delegations paid tribute to the five Vimy Ridge communities that had donated the land to Canada for the memorial site. On July 20, a Canadian delegation placed wreaths at the Tomb of the Unknown Soldier in Paris. And on July 25, memorials took place at such former behind-the-lines locations as Mont St. Eloi, commemorating Canadians' lengthy connection to Vimy communities and their citizens during the war.

July 26, 1936, dawned grey and damp. The skies threatened to open up with more of the rain that had followed the Canadians across France most of that week. The night before the unveiling, in fact, most of the nearly 8,000 pilgrims (including 1,500 from Britain) had arrived at their Vimy area billets amid a torrential downpour. However, a substantial breakfast, hints of the sun breaking through the clouds, and anticipation of a historic day seemed to buoy their spirits that Sunday morning. By mid-morning hundreds of buses were moving onto the French roadways all leading to the ridge and its partially cloaked monument. When one of the tour buses passed through the village of Ste Catherine, on the outskirts of Arras, Canadian veteran John Mould couldn't believe his eyes.

"There was a banner across the street which bore the words 'Long live St. Catharines of Canada,'" Mould wrote in his diary. British-born, Mould had emigrated to Canada in 1910 and taken up work as a sign painter in the southwestern Ontario community of St. Catharines. During the lead-up to the Vimy attack in April 1917, Pte. Mould had served in a working party sent to Ste Catherine to repair roads among the few ruined buildings the Arras campaign hadn't levelled. At the time, Mould, deciding to engage in his peacetime trade, painted white letters on a sign recognizing the presence of "the St. Catharines Boys" from Canada. During the war, John Mould had lost his teeth and part of his hearing, but when the Legion invited veterans to return to Vimy, Mould, at forty-five years of age, decided he would take his wife and join the pilgrimage. Almost two decades after the Vimy campaign, the town had not forgotten the Canadians.

By 11 a.m. that Sunday, the bus transporting the Moulds was close to the site. They passed French civilians—men wearing black suits adorned with their own medals, women pushing perambulators with children aboard. They had been gathering since dawn to witness the ceremony from vantage points below the monument. Having arrived three hours ahead of the ceremony, the Moulds took out box lunches provided by their billets. With no chairs or tables on hand, they laid out newspapers on some grass and, dangling their feet over a ledge of ground, sat down to eat ham sandwiches, cheese, boiled eggs, and fruit. It was only then they realized they were seated on the edge of a former shell crater now covered in grass. Then the Moulds began to walk toward the as yet unchristened monument.

"It was during this walk that scenes of the old war days came back to me," John Mould wrote. "Huge craters, shell holes and barbed wire were there the same as they had been on those April days nineteen years ago. . . . Wet weather made the ground rather slippy to walk on. It is the same old clay we used to get during our trips into the trenches. . . . I heard one woman say, 'No wonder they called it No Man's Land.'"

As the groups of French civilians and Canadian pilgrims began to press toward the memorial for the start of the ceremony, three battalions of French infantry and a battalion of engineers took their positions to hold back the crowd—now numbering nearly 100,000. On the main parade ground west of the memorial, the guard of honour included a regiment of mounted Spahis, representing the French Moroccan corps that had fought on the ridge in 1915. Facing the horsemen stood an honour guard of "bluejackets" from HMCS *Saguenay* along with the flag standard bearers, made up of twenty men from each of the five Canadian pilgrim ships. Behind the colour party, the rest of the Vimy veterans assembled in six companies, each identified by a totem pole. Behind them stood 1,500 French veterans and 150

Belgian veterans and the remaining dignitaries not seated at the monument. In front of the memorial to the east, where the ground fell away in a natural amphitheatre (over what had formerly been the German reverse slope of the ridge) stood the rest of the 6,400 Canadian pilgrims and more than 1,500 Canadians who had come from England with the British Legion. Ringing the amphitheatre were 200 nurses and 2,500 "blue berets," the women and children of Canada's war dead. A London news reporter wrote that "they formed a living bank of noble grief." Perhaps most prominent among the sea of pilgrims was a small group of eleven veterans who had been blinded during the Great War.

At 2:15 p.m., King Edward VIII arrived with his entourage and began the formal proceedings. He met Canadian dignitaries such as wartime prime minister Robert Borden, Canadian High Commissioner Vincent Massey, Brig.-Gen. Raymond Brutinel, who had commanded the 1st Canadian Machine Gun Brigade at Vimy, and Gen. John Pershing, wartime leader of the U.S. Army. The King then reviewed the various honour guards and greeted the crowds beyond. He doffed his top hat as the band of the Royal Canadian Horse Artillery played the national anthem. Guns at the base of the ridge north of the Pimple began firing a royal salute and the band then played "O Canada," thus setting a precedent—the first time the Dominion's national hymn was used as an anthem. Following a review of the bandsmen, the King and his RCMP escort in scarlet tunics strode to the eastern rampart of the memorial, where the masses of pilgrims below spotted him and cheered wildly. He waved back and descended the steps to meet them.

The Canadian dignitaries with the King introduced him to some of the veterans, including silver-cross mother Mrs. C.S. Woods, who wore the medals of eight sons who'd fought and died during the war. He met a quadruple amputee named Curly Christian and several of the nursing sisters and stopped in front of the small group of veterans positioned in front of the rest.

"The King began to shake hands with the small group of blind men," John Mould wrote. "Tremendous cheering broke out, which thoroughly drowned the noise of the distant guns. It was a touching scene to see the faces of those blind veterans light up as he passed along the line and they heard the sound of his voice."

As the crowds pressed the line of guards to get a better look at the King, suddenly the gendarmes withdrew and the throng of Canadian pilgrims and French citizens surged closer. In spite of the mass of people closing in around him, King Edward continued to move through the crowd to loud shouts from French schoolchildren of "*Vive le roi!*" and strains of "For He's a Jolly Good Fellow." After nearly half an hour in the midst of the pilgrims, one of the King's aides approached Duncan Macintyre of the Canadian delegation. Lt.-Col. Macintyre had served as a major with the 4th Infantry Brigade at Vimy, but throughout the pilgrimage he had coordinated the pilgrims' transportation and accommodation needs and also represented Canada at numerous ceremonies in Vimy-area communities. The British aide to King Edward wanted to know if things were on schedule for the arrival of the French president.

"How much time have we got?" the aide asked Macintyre.

"About six minutes," Macintyre told him.

"Well, there is time for a little chat," he said and quickly mounted the steps to prepare for the next segment of the ceremony.

As the King completed his walkabout in the next minutes and returned up the monument stairs, the crowd heard the bandsmen of the 3rd Regiment of (French) Engineers offer a fanfare and the opening strains of the "Marseillaise." King Edward arrived back at the parade ground just in time to meet President Albert Lebrun. As they shook hands on the platform at the base of the monument, two squadrons of Royal Air Force fighter aircraft and another two of the French Air Force roared overhead and dipped their wings in salute. At the podium clergymen were first to speak, including Rev. C.C. Owen of Vancouver, who had lost a son in the war, and former padre Rev. George Fallis of Toronto, who spoke of the soldiers of all ranks and how the monument represented from all people "a fresh pledge that we shall not break faith." Monsignor A.E. Deschamps of Montreal pleaded for a permanent peace "until the word 'enemies' has passed from the lexicon of mankind." There followed addresses from both the French and Canadian governments. Delivering a message on behalf of the Canadian people, Ian A. Mackenzie said, "We claim no monopoly of sacrifice, for valiant ally and gallant foe alike knew its anguish and its terror."

Moments before King Edward spoke, the sun finally pierced through the clouds. Canadian veteran John Mould was struck by the monument's "snowy white" colour against the otherwise darkened sky to the west. But the sudden burst of sunshine drew his attention to an even more spectacular sight eastward. The view was reminiscent of the moment of victory on April 9, 1917, when the sun emerged in time to show members of the Canadian Corps the vastness of the Douai Valley ahead of them and the significance of their achievement.

"The sun shone with unexpected brilliance on the assembled pilgrims and wreaths of remembrance and the huge throng of French people gathered on the grassy slopes around," Mould wrote. "As I looked across this wide sunny plain, with its yellow cornfields and villages, it seemed almost impossible that nineteen years ago, it was nothing but a muddy mound of grassless earth, pitted with shell holes filled with water and rotting barbed wire. . . .

"It was a place of horror in those days and must have brought back terrible memories to those blind veterans who had journeyed from Canada in darkness to again visit the spot where they had lost their sight."

First in French and then in English, King Edward expressed gratitude to the French for their hospitality and respect paid to Canada's war dead and the pilgrim survivors who had travelled across the ocean to see the memorial unveiled. He offered a rationale for locating so powerful a symbol of Canadian sacrifice in France. "We raise this memorial to Canadian warriors," he said. "It is an inspired expression in stone, chiselled by a skillful Canadian hand, of Canada's salute to her fallen sons. It marks the scene of feats of arms which history will long remember, and Canada will never forget. And the ground it covers is the gift of France to Canada." Moments later he released the folds of a Union Jack that had shrouded the figure of Canada Mourning Her Dead. The Last Post was sounded and two minutes' silence observed in memory of the fallen.

"The King, the President, ministers, nurses and pilgrims—every one around were like statues," John Mould wrote in his diary. "Nothing stirred, only the wind rustling leaves of the trees nearby." The two minutes' silence was followed by the crisp notes of the Reveille and then by the speech from the French president. Then the King and president placed wreaths on the memorial, as the band played "Land of Hope and Glory." The two men walked to their waiting cars and as they departed cheer upon cheer went up from the thronging pilgrims. The entire ceremony had been broadcast back to Canada on radio; a Canadian Radio Broadcasting Commission reporter had climbed a ladder inside one of the hollow pylons and was able to describe the entire event from the highest vantage point.

Said Florence Murdock, one of six pilgrims from Amherst, Nova Scotia, "The whole picture will always remain with us as of one gorgeous painting."

With the dignitaries disappearing in the distance, the crowd respectfully swarmed the monument. Legion groups and various regimental representatives placed more than 400 wreaths at the base of the Vimy pylons. Those veterans who knew him simply as "Canon Scott" invited Archdeacon Frederick Scott to recite a prayer as ashes of the dead from Flanders Fields were scattered beside the Canada Mourning Her Dead sculpture. Meanwhile, pilgrims searched for and touched the names of relatives and friends among the 11,285 names carved into its limestone walls. They read the memorial's dedication:

To the valour of their countrymen in the Great War
and in memory of their sixty thousand dead,
this monument is raised by the people of Canada.

There was still time for the veterans and their families to take final walks across the grounds and through the preserved tunnels and trenches. New growth had taken over the pockmarked surface of the ridge—Canadian maple and Hungarian pine trees encircling some of the former shell holes and lush grasses nearly filling some of the zigzag trenches that had been the Germans' forward positions during the battle. In contrast, underground little or nothing had been allowed to change. The twenty-two miles of passageways, trenches, subways, galleries, and storage spaces remained like the rabbit's warren they had been. *Ottawa Citizen* reporter Bruce Hutchison noted that rusty rifles, revolvers, tin hats, mess tins, and the remains of cot beds still lay where their owners had left them during the war.

"Everywhere Canadian soldiers wrote their names into the soft chalk walls and each name has been carefully preserved," he wrote. "In one hospital room you can see a crucifix cut into the chalk by a wounded man and in another the head of a soldier with his tin hat. They will remain as long as the chalk lasts, a better memorial perhaps than the monument above, because they were made by the hands of the men who lived and died here."

In some of the conversations that emerged that afternoon, one Canadian noted that the French were impressed by two things—that so many Canadians had come to France to fight when they were not obliged to and that the Canadians had accomplished something their own regular troops had failed to do. During the spring and summer of 1915, the French Army had attempted to take the ridge with the loss of 40,000 men killed. Following them, native Moroccan troops had successfully taken and briefly held the north end of the ridge in 1915. The British too had paid dearly—with another 100,000 casualties—for their attempts to seize the ridge from the Germans. Then, during the four-day Vimy assault of 1917, the Canadians had added 10,000 casualties to the total. Beneath the length and breadth of Vimy Ridge—from Souchez to Arras—a distance of roughly ten miles, lay the bones of 200,000 men—French, British, Canadian, and German. Appropriately, the French called this region "the Graveyard of France." If the military ratio of three wounded to every man killed can be considered accurate, then Vimy had inflicted no fewer than 800,000 casualties during the Great War. And since the hilltop battlefield constituted but one small part of the 300-mile-long Western

Front, many of the Vimy pilgrims, if they needed to, came to recognize the cost of war in human lives.

Andrew McCrindle, whose Sun Life employers had paid for his pilgrimage to Vimy, had very specific memories of his wartime experience in April 1917. Then a private in the 24th Battalion, McCrindle had spent a lot of time with a former McGill theology student, a man named Jarvis, whom he nicknamed "The Rev." Shortly before the main assault on April 9, Cpl. Jarvis and Pte. McCrindle were hunkered down in a shell hole in the middle of a German artillery barrage.

"Say, Mac, are you scared?" Jarvis asked McCrindle.

"No, Rev.," McCrindle snapped. "Of course not."

"Neither am I," said Jarvis, not wanting to appear any less the man. Then after a short pause, he continued, "Geez, aren't we a couple of bloody liars!"

Not long after the strenuous, four-day battle, members of McCrindle's Victoria Rifles of Montreal reassembled to take stock of things. Someone in charge rattled off the names of those in the platoon in a kind of roll call. Cpl. Jarvis could not be accounted for. McCrindle concluded respectfully that his friend "had answered a higher call," but made a special effort to remember him during the Vimy pilgrimage in 1936.

Veteran Duncan Macintyre managed to generate another act of remembrance during the pilgrimage. A few days before the July 26 ceremony, Lt.-Col. Macintyre had approached the five communities that had donated land to Canada for the Vimy Memorial. He had suggested that each village send fifty schoolchildren with their teachers to the historic event. Macintyre had then ensured that each of the 250 children was given a Canadian flag to be placed among the wreaths and other tributes to the 11,285 names inscribed in the plinth.

"My thought was that long after the Canadians had gone home," he wrote, "these children would be living in the shadow of the memorial for the rest of their lives and would never forget the occasion. . . . I hoped that they would thenceforth feel responsible for decorating the memorial on the anniversary of the battle."

By four o'clock on that Sunday afternoon of the pilgrimage to Vimy, the crowds began to thin as the buses filled with Canadians preparing to leave the monument. Volunteers served the last of the refreshments to weary pilgrims. The portable post office affixed stamps to the hundreds of postcards the veterans wanted mailed home to family and friends overseas. Lingering pilgrims placed the remaining wreaths at strategic spots near the base of the memorial. Some veterans, including John Mould and his wife from St. Catharines, Ontario, had been on the site for six hours, but he recorded in his diary finally: "The most memorable day of our lives." A few last snapshots captured images of those who'd made the memorable pilgrimage to Vimy Ridge for the unveiling. Among those last photographs taken was that of a lone figure in a fedora and carrying a walking stick, descending the stairs past one of the memorial's stone figures. The camera had captured an image of the monument's creator, Walter Allward, stepping past the stone Mourner sculpture at the base of the Wall of Defence.

"We carved the figures of stone instead of casting them in bronze," Allward said later. "Bronze might be melted down for munitions . . . if war came again."

In spite of the Canadians' sacrifice at Vimy, war did come again. Despite the pleas during the Vimy Memorial unveiling—entreating the world not to resort to killing—the world did resort to it, just three years after the pilgrimage. Another war in 1939 consumed Europe, Asia, and parts of Africa. And though the Vimy Memorial miraculously survived six years of war all around it unscathed, other predators—weather and soot in the air—took their toll on Allward's priceless work. By the turn of the second millennium, as many as a quarter of the 4,449 Vimy Memorial's stones needed replacement and leaking lime had begun to obscure many of the names carved into its foundation wall. Then, nearly seventy years after the stone structure atop Vimy Ridge was unveiled by King Edward VIII to thousands of Great War pilgrims in France, it finally received life-saving repair—in time for the ninetieth anniversary of the Battle at Vimy Ridge and a rededication of the memorial in April 2007.

Every Canadian who served in the Great War overseas had begun his days in the Canadian Expeditionary Force at a recruiting depot somewhere in the country. He had signed his attestation papers and health records. Then, with any number of other enlistees or an officer as witnesses, he had been told to raise his right hand and swear: "I do make Oath that I will be faithful and bear true Allegiance to His Majesty King George the Fifth, His Heirs and Successors . . . against all enemies, and will observe and obey all orders . . . of all the Generals and officers set over me. So help me God." Most described their commitment "to King and country."

At the top of Vimy Ridge, many of those same CEF soldiers considered that oath in a new context. For the first time they had tasted significant victory. Their counter-batteries had nearly annihilated the opposition. Fellow infantrymen had rehearsed their fire and movement over the tapes and replicated it on the battlefield. With every man in the Canadian Corps fully aware of the precise battle plan, they had followed a creeping barrage across No Man's Land and, in near perfection, rooted out their enemy and pushed him off the most strategic heights in northern France. For the first time, they had witnessed their enemy in full retreat. And they had succeeded in all this as a national army. Their service to their King was never in question, but their allegiance suddenly seemed directed to those other than royalty—to their comrades from Cape Breton, Quebec, the regiments of Ontario, the prairies, the Kootenays, and the big cities of Toronto, Montreal, and Vancouver. The actions of Canadian troops at Vimy had been the equivalent of an oath to Canada—an expression of ultimate allegiance to their country, and then to their King.

Neither the Canadians' powerful sentiment nor their tragic sacrifice ended at Vimy. During the remaining months of the war, the CEF would experience other setbacks and victories at Passchendaele, Amiens, Canal du Nord, and Cambrai. For the surviving veterans, however, that revelation at Vimy had to be preserved. More than 600,000 among a nation of only eight million had chosen to serve in the Great War. Nearly two decades after the Armistice, more than 6,000 Canadians had returned as pilgrims to memorialize the 61,326 who had died in the war to end all war. The sentiment in 1936 clearly entreated those who followed not to forget the loss or the sacrifice. As with John McCrae's poetic gesture "from failing hands" passing the torch in Flanders or Rev. Garbutt's "sacred trust" eulogy in Uxbridge, those who had experienced Vimy in 1917 or in 1936 were making a statement. Sons and daughters of the maple leaf needed to acknowledge what had happened there. They needed to mark the pivotal victory and the awakening of that full sense of nationhood. Succeeding generations needed to remember that gift from Canadians to Canadians.

# Notes

CHAPTER ONE — SNIP A FEW EPAULETTES

*page*

4  "closest of blood ties": Talbot Papineau quoted in "Canadian Nationalism and the War" (pamphlet), 1916.

4  "blood brothers, friends": Greg Clark, CBC Radio interviews, "In Flanders Fields" broadcasts, Nov. 1964 to March 1965, Library and Archives Canada, RG 41-B-III-1, Vol. 7-22.

4  "lions led by donkeys": phrase used by British First World War historians Alan Clark and P. A. Thompson, but coined during the Crimean War, when *The Times of London* reported, "The Russians say we are lions led on by asses."

5  had to be buried: Arthur Bonner, CBC Radio interviews, "In Flanders Fields" broadcast, Nov. 1964 to March 1965, Library and Archives Canada, RG 41-B-III-1 Vol. 7-22.

5  holding three canisters: Gad Neale, Pierre Berton papers, William Ready Division of Archives and Research Collections, McMaster University.

6  secured with earth-filled sandbags: Tim Cook, *No Place to Run: The Canadian Corps and Gas Warfare in the First World War*, p. 95.

7  "bottle of white wine": Eric Grisdale, Pierre Berton papers, McMaster.

8  kill most of the enemy troops: Alex Jack, CBC Radio interviews.

8  "snip a few epaulettes": Alex Jack, CBC Radio interviews.

8  a bill of goods: John Quinnell, letter to Pierre Berton, Feb. 16, 1985, McMaster.

9  "worthy of recognition": Eedson Burns, Oct. 23–25, 1979, Reg Roy Military Oral History Collections, University of Victoria Libraries, Special Collections.

10  "command 'Gas'": Alvin Kines, Canadian War Museum, George Metcalf Archival Collection, 58A1 118.10.

11  breathe safely through his mouth: Cook, *No Place to Run*, p. 88.

12  "best-built communication trench": Harvey Crowell, CBC Radio interviews.

13  "orders as laid down": Maj. J.B. Bailey, Cinquante-Quatre Regimental History.

14  "nightmare of a raid": Alex Jack, CBC Radio interviews.

14  "Meade, and my colonel": John Quinnell, Pierre Berton interview, Toronto, 1985.

17  "like a dream": David Thompson, *Letters from the Front*, Canadian Bank of Commerce letters, Vol. 1, pp. 184–85.

## CHAPTER TWO — THE SIX-FOOT BURY

*page*

22  thriving military centre: Alan McGillivray, p. 61.

23  departed for France: "How the County Battalion Crossed Channel for France," *Uxbridge Times*, March 1, 1917.

24  "an ardent desire": The Adjutant, *The 116th Battalion in France*, p. 17.

24  first casualty of the war: "First Casualty 116th Battalion," *Uxbridge Times*, June 7, 1917.

26  feature of the battlefield: A. Fortescue Duguid, "Canada on Vimy Ridge," *The Legionary*, April 1938.

28  "in a rowboat": George Hancox, CBC Radio interviews.

28  "having some experience": Sharpe Correspondence, Uxbridge Scott Museum, April 20, 1917.

29  "be the pioneers": Gordon Thomas, interview Aug. 28, 1980, Reg Roy Collections, UVIC.

29  "I'm damned": D.E. Macintyre, *Canada at Vimy*, p. 112.

30  downtown Vancouver: Pierre Berton, *Vimy*, p. 139.

34  chalk into the craters: George Hambley, diaries, Manitoba Archives, MG7 H11.

35  "blow up the ridge first": Wilfred Darknell, letter to Pierre Berton c. 1985, McMaster.

35  pump in fresher air: Alexander McKee, *Vimy Ridge*, p. 21.

36  "blew it up completely": Alfred Pearson, CBC Radio interviews.

37  "guarding the dead from rats": Percy Twidale, interview June and August 1983, Elizabeth Hazlitte Oral History Collection, University of Victoria Libraries, Special Collections.

37  "the six-foot bury": John Keegan, *The Face of Battle*, p. 264.

38 "any loose conversation": Bill Laurie, interview April 1986, Reg Roy Collections, UVIC.

40 the Yuletide exchange: Charles Keeler, CBC Radio interviews.

41 acquainted with the battlefield: Brereton Greenhaus and Stephen Harris, *Canada and the Battle of Vimy Ridge, 9–12 April, 1917*, p 54.

43 shells, dust, and smoke: Andrew McNaughton quoted in Swettenham, *McNaughton*, p. 77.

43 "all ranks would give": Macintyre, *Canada at Vimy*, p. 85.

44 boxing and soccer: Charles Keeler, CBC Radio interviews.

44 "there's a wig": Jack McLaren quoted by John McLaren in *J.W.: The Life Story of John Wilson McLaren*, p. 19.

45 dumbells insignia: Herbert Whittaker, "Dumbells' Rag: from Vimy to Broadway," *The Globe and Mail*, June 27, 1977.

45 "held the mirror up": Herman Goodden, "Jack McLaren, A One Man Show," *Village Squire*, McLean Bros. Publishing, July 1980.

CHAPTER THREE — WEEK OF SUFFERING

*page*

47 "Fritzy [German] aeroplane overhead": Will Antliff letter to mother, March 21, 1917, Canadian War Museum.

48 "Red Devil": Will Antliff letter to mother, Canadian War Museum, April 8, 1917.

48 "to my room": von Richthofen quoted in Ralph Barker, *A Brief History of the Royal Flying Corps in World War I*, p. 209.

49 loss of 119 planes: Barker, *A Brief History of the Royal Flying Corps in World War I*, p. 278.

49 at the Somme: Dan McCaffery, *Air Aces: The Lives and Times of Twelve Canadian Fighter Pilots*, p. 99.

49 "adventure of my life": Bishop letter to mother, March 25, 1917, courtesy Fred MacKay.

50 "offensive work": Billy Bishop, *Winged Warfare*, p. 42.

50 "Hun to my credit": Billy Bishop letter to father, March 29, 1917, courtesy Fred MacKay.

51 "great satisfaction": Billy Bishop letter to mother, April 21, 1917, courtesy Fred MacKay.

52 "to their deaths": Clarence Goode, interview June–July 1987. Reg Roy Collections, UVIC.

53   contemplated parachuting: Berton, *Vimy*, p. 167.

53   the threatening gun: G.W.L. Nicholson, *The Gunners of Canada*, p. 315.

53   "whiz-bangs": McKee, *Vimy Ridge*, p. 20.

54   Germans' 400 guns: H.C.B. Rogers, *A History of Artillery*, p. 162.

55   "shooting too": Andrew McNaughton, CBC Radio interviews.

55   "methodical progression": McNaughton quoted in Swettenham, p. 58.

55   "not on Berlin": Gordon Beatty, "Reminiscences of an Old Soldier," unpublished.

56   "fandoodle": McNaughton quoted in Swettenham, p. 51.

57   "oil and water": Elmore Philpott, CBC Radio interviews.

59   "water from a hose": *Far From Home*, documentary, Norflicks Productions.

59   eleven straight days: J.A. MacDonald, *Gunfire: An Historical Narrative of the 4th Brigade*, Canadian Field Artillery, Ch. 1.

60   "babe in a crib": L.D. Giffin, letter, McMaster.

61   *"rupture"*: John Keegan, *The First World War*, p. 322.

61   "the results obtained": Raymond Brutinel, CBC Radio interviews.

62   "in offensive war": Raymond Brutinel CBC Radio interviews.

62   an eight-day course: C.S. Grafton, *The Canadian Emma Gees*, p. 60.

62   harassing fire: Raymond Brutinel memo, March 3, 1917, courtesy Fred Tripp, Canadian Society of Military Medals and Insignia.

62   80 percent: Richard Hocken Joyce papers, courtesy Fred Tripp.

64   "hellish concert": excerpt, Battles of the World War—The Easter Battle at Arras 1917, Part I, Between Lens and Scarpe, Dept. of National Defence, Directorate of History.

64   two million horses: Mary Thomas, *David's War*, p. 111.

65   "It was butchered": John Holderness, unpublished memoir, May 1985, McMaster.

65   four shells into each pack: C.C. Allen letter to Pierre Berton, Jan. 10, 1985, McMaster.

66   1,400 horses at a time: Mary Thomas, p. 112.

66   "nothing to say about it": James Robert Johnston, *Riding Into War*, p. 39.

67   "polishing harness and grooming horses": Harold Innis autobiography, UofT Archives, courtesy John Watson, Ottawa.

67   "a horse than a cow": Harold Innis quoted in Sandra Gwyn, *Tapestry of War*, p. 366.

68   "our worst enemies": Harold Innis autobiography.

68   sense of nationalism: Alexander John Watson, *Marginal Man*, p. 84.

68  "Canada alone": Innis quoted in Gwyn, *Tapestry of War* p. 367.

69  first major offensive: Keegan, *The First World War*, p. 325.


CHAPTER FOUR — COUNTDOWN TO ZERO HOUR

*page*

71  "guns could be plainly heard": Leslie Frost quoted by R.B. Fleming, *The Wartime Letters of Leslie M. Frost and Cecil G. Frost 1915–1920*, with permission, to be published Wilfrid Laurier University Press, p. 126.

72  "as a colonel": Leslie Frost quoted by Thomas H.B. Symons in *The Wartime Letters*, p. 5.

72  Umpty-Umps: The Adjutant, *116th Battalion in France*, p. 28.

72  "discontented army": Cecil Frost, letter, Dec. 23, 1916, in Fleming, *The Wartime Letters of Leslie M. Frost and Cecil G. Frost 1915–1920*.

73  "lit by candles": Canon Frederick George Scott, *The Great War as I Saw It*, p. 166.

73  447 Canadian clergymen: Duff Crerar, *Padres in No Man's Land*, p. 5.

74  "reading their shirts": Claude Williams, interview, Dec. 19, 1983, McMaster.

74  in an emergency: Crerar, *Padres in No Man's Land*, p. 121.

75  "in such a cause": Scott, *The Great War as I Saw It*, p. 166.

75  a hundred thousand bags: Fleming, *The Wartime Letters*, p. 14.

75  "I am well": Dodge Rankine, Pierre Berton interview, McMaster.

76  Jack Johnsons and Coal-Boxes: McKee, *Vimy Ridge*, p. 20.

76  "explosion and concussion": Sid Smith, CBC Radio interviews.

76  "third place in our company": Ellis Sifton letter, Dec. 12, 1914, courtesy Blair Ferguson and the Elgin Military Museum.

77  "how serious it is": Ellis Sifton letter, May 2, 1915.

77  "from the maple leaf": Ellis Sifton letter, June 21, 1915.

77  "must expect that": Ellis Sifton letter, Oct. 17, 1915.

77  "bomb proof jobs": Ellis Sifton letter, Dec. 19, 1916.

77  "stare death in the face": Ellis Sifton letter, Aug. 10, 1916.

77  "so many changes": Ellis Sifton letter, Jan. 7, 1917.

78  "promoted me to sergeant": Ellis Sifton letter, April 5, 1917.

78  "ever experienced": Jay Moyer letter, April 6, 1917, courtesy The Memory Project, Dominion Institute.

78  support and reserve trenches: Bishop, *Winged Warfare*, p. 79.

79  "O. Pips": D.C. MacArthur, *The History of the Fifty-Fifth Battery*, p. 20.

79  "bricks without straw": F.J. Godfrey, "A Vimy Memory," *The Legionary*, April 1937.

80  "no deserters": Gen. Von Bacmeister quoted in F.A. McKenzie, *Canada's Day of Glory*, p. 70.

81  "the heights of Vimy": Crown Prince Rupprecht, excerpts from *My War Diary*, March 26, 1917, Library and Archives Canada.

81  "captured Canadian": Crown Prince Rupprecht, *My War Diary*, April 1, 1917.

82  "escaped destruction": Alfred Dieterich, "The German 79th Reserve Infantry Division in the Battle of Vimy Ridge," *Canadian Military History*, p. 74.

82  "soldiers buried alive": Michael Volkheimer, quoted in McKee, *Vimy Ridge*, p. 61.

83  "into the trenches": Ray Crowe, CBC Radio interviews.

83  "I'm not coming back": Art Castle, Pierre Berton interview, 1985, McMaster.

84  "Frost & Wood binder": Ed Russenholt, "Vimy Ridge Memorial Park," *Metro One*, Winnipeg, May 1977.

85  "troops on earth": Ed Russenholt, CBC Radio interviews.

87  "sentence of prayer": George Kilpatrick, CBC Radio interviews.

87  "Henry V at Agincourt": Harry Clyne, CBC Radio interviews.

87  "recite Shakespeare": F.C. Bagshaw, Pierre Berton papers, McMaster.

87  "tell by their faces": Alfred Thomson, Pierre Berton papers, McMaster.

88  "that split second": David Moir, "At What Price?" *Legion* magazine, April 1977.

89  "Zero Hour": Robert Clements, "Merry Hell, the way I saw it," Dept. of National Defence, Directorate of History, 84/69 unpublished manuscript.

89  "a thousand bees": Frank MacGregor, CBC Radio interviews.

89  Four seconds before Zero Hour: Nicholson, *The Gunners of Canada*, p. 283.

CHAPTER FIVE — OUT OF THE HANDS OF GENERALS

*page*

91  "shall be annihilated": Gus Sivertz quoting Byng, CBC Radio interviews, tape 299.

92  "cough or whoosh": Sgt. W.G. Smith quoted in McKee, *Vimy Ridge*, p. 90.

92  "a mighty furnace": William Breckenridge, "From Vimy to Mons," unpublished memoirs, McMaster, p 25.

92  "a thousand unmuffled motors": George F. Murray, "Covering the Battle of Vimy Ridge," memoir, Feb. 1985, McMaster.

92   "rent by screaming shells": Sgt. Layton, 15th Warwicks, quoted by McKee, *Vimy Ridge*, p. 90.

92   "smote the senses": Lewis Duncan, April 17, 1917, Ontario Archives, MU 4693.

92   use of greatcoats: R.C. Fetherstonhaugh, *The 24th Battalion C.E.F.*, p. 130.

93   "teeth of the enemy": Ralph Hodder-Williams, *Princess Patricia's Canadian Light Infantry 1914–1919*, p. 215.

93   "reds and yellows and greens": Alex Gerrard, interview June 1977, Reg Roy Collections, UVIC.

94   "bayonets fixed": Cyril Jones letter, April 15, 1917, in Charles Lyon Foster, *Letters from the Front*, p. 202.

96   "Hell itself has been uncorked": Fred James, "A Letter from the Past," *The Legionary*, August 1938.

96   two-thirds the way: Macintyre, *Canada at Vimy*, p. 88.

96   "ten thousand thunders": George Alliston quoted in McKee, *Vimy Ridge*, p. 100.

96   "Dante's Inferno": Arthur Pollard, McMaster.

97   "guts to give him any water": George Alliston, Pierre Berton interview, 1985.

97   "someone that had fallen": Percy Twidale, interview June and August 1983, Elizabeth Hazlitte Collections, UVIC.

98   "a rich harvest": Alfred Dieterich, "The German 79th Reserve Infantry Division in the Battle of Vimy Ridge," p. 77.

98   rushed the survivors: W.W. Murray, "Vimy V.C.s Another chapter from the record of the Canadians who were awarded the Victoria Cross during the Great War," *Maclean's* magazine, Feb. 15, 1929.

99   "devotion to duty": H.M. Urquhart, *History of the 16th Battalion*.

100  "extraordinary experience": Macintyre, *Canada at Vimy*, p. 107.

100  "gentleman's agreement": Royden Barbour, CBC Radio interviews.

101  "I got lucky": Charles Dale, Pierre Berton correspondence, McMaster.

102  "to keep going": Claude Williams, interview Dec. 19, 1983, McMaster.

103  "five or six boys": Greg Clark, CBC Radio interviews.

104  "come up and surrender": Jules De Cruyenaere, letter to Pierre Berton, March 8, 1985, McMaster.

104  "two thousand rounds": Harry Loosmore quoting 31st Battery diary in "Recollections of Vimy" unpublished memoirs.

105  "heavy drum-fire": Otto Schroeder (262nd Reserve Reg't) quoted in Dept. of National Defence, Directorate of History, SGRII 202.

105  30 to 50 percent: Cy Peck diaries, British Columbia Archives.

105  "on the road west:" Gus Sivertz, CBC Radio interviews. LAC sound archives.

107  "khaki-yellow corpses": McKee, *Vimy Ridge*, p. 143.

108  "dripping onto his new tunic": John Quinnell, letter to Pierre Berton, Feb. 16, 1985, McMaster.

109  "undestroyed machine guns": Dieterich, "The German 79th Reserve Infantry Division in the Battle of Vimy Ridge," p. 79.

110  "supply of Perrier water": Thain MacDowell quoted in Canadian War Records Office, *Thirty Canadian VCs*, p. 23.

110  "bumpy as Satan": Charles Smart quoted in Barker, *A Brief History of the Royal Flying Corps in World War I*, p. 262.

111  "incandescent light": Bishop, *Winged Warfare*, p. 84.

111  friendly fire: Maj. H. Smithson quoted in McKee, *Vimy Ridge*, p. 93.

111  "a great bore to them": Bishop, *Winged Warfare*, p. 85.

112  sound a klaxon horn: McKee, *Vimy Ridge*, p. 113.

112  "job was to kill them": Leonard Youell, Pierre Berton interview, Guelph, Ont.

112  "start of the show": Leonard Youell, diary, McMaster.

## CHAPTER SIX — ARTILLERY CONQUERS, INFANTRY OCCUPIES

*page*

115  "retreating ahead of us": A.J. Watson quoting Harold Innis, correspondence with Barris, March 2006.

116  dismantled one church tower: Nicholson, *The Gunners of Canada*, p. 282.

116  Female tanks: McKee, *Vimy Ridge*, p. 106.

116  "masses of tanks": Dieterich, "The German 79th Reserve Infantry Division in the Battle of Vimy Ridge," p. 77.

117  "lumbering, growling machine": Claude Williams, CBC Radio interviews.

117  "tanks were mired": L.R. Fennel, CBC Radio interviews.

117  finished them off with shellfire: McKee, *Vimy Ridge*, p. 106.

118  "a gadget": Andrew McCrindle, "From private to private in 36 months," McMaster.

120  "last two machine guns": Der Weltkrieg: 1914 bis 1918, Vol. 12. 1939.

120  "bomb-proof jobs": Ellis Sifton letter, Dec. 19, 1916.

120  "never see the end": Ellis Sifton letter, Feb. 14, 1916.

120  215 casualties: McKee, *Vimy Ridge*, p. 109.

121  McLean, was killed: War Diary, 18th (Western Ontario) Battalion, April 9, 1917.

121 shoot Sifton dead: Canadian War Records Office, *Thirty Canadian VCs*, pp. 30–31.

121 "success of the operation": Ibid.

122 "shake hands with this Frenchie": Fred Claydon, interviews July–August 1982, Roy Collections, UVIC.

123 "whole German army": Harold Carter, letter to Pierre Berton, Jan. 31, 1985, McMaster.

124 "He *was* batty": Hal Wallis, interview, McMaster.

125 15,000 rounds: Grafton, *Emma Gees*, p. 66.

125 "tumpline is a simple contrivance": F.R. Phelan, field communiqué, 11th Canadian Infantry Brigade, Aug. 27, 1917, Richard Hocken Joyce papers, courtesy Fred Tripp.

126 "built like a bull": Norman Evans, interview, McMaster.

127 "The English are coming": Michael Volkheimer quoted in McKee, *Vimy Ridge*, p. 102.

128 "pieces of men": Jack Pinson, CBC Radio interviews.

128 "sons of bitches": F.C. Bagshaw, Pierre Berton papers, McMaster.

130 "get there fast enough": Cyril Jones letter, April 15, 1917, in Foster, *Letters from the Front*, p. 202.

130 "It's Ray": Ray Crowe, CBC Radio interviews.

131 "terribly confused": Stewart Scott, CBC Radio interviews.

131 in a shell hole: McKee, *Vimy Ridge*, p. 149.

132 "totally blinded": Gordon Mitchell, "A Close Shave," *The Legionary*, June 1955.

133 "Distinguished Conduct Medals": Ernest Morison letter, March 30, 1917, McMaster.

133 "a great big needle": E. Douglas Emery, Pierre Berton papers, McMaster.

134 "worse than the wound": Cyril Smith, Pierre Berton interview, McMaster.

134 19,000 members of CAMC: Cook, *No Place to Run*, p. 144.

134 edged weapons: Keegan, *The Face of Battle*, p. 269.

135 "scarcely distinguishable": Andrew Macphail, diary, McMaster.

135 "debridement": Keegan, *The Face of Battle*, p. 271.

136 "300 cases lying on stretchers": J.N. Gunn diary, April 9, 1917, McMaster.

136 "in a British subject": Fred Hodges, letter to Pierre Berton, Feb. 6, 1985, McMaster.

137 "the last I saw of him": Gavin McDonald, WWI unpublished memoirs, courtesy Jean Gordon and Judy Wood.

CHAPTER SEVEN − "CHASING HUNS TOWARDS THE FATHERLAND"

*page*

140 "as if we were rabbits": Eedson Burns, interview Oct. 23–25, 1979, Reginald Roy Collections, UVIC.

140 "as warlike as rabbits" Eedson Burns, *General Mud.*

141 "fellow of twenty-five": Alex Jack, CBC Radio interviews.

142 "dropped into a shell hole": Art Farmer, CBC Radio interviews.

144 "wore privates' uniforms": Eric Finley, CBC Radio interviews.

145 "blind being pulled down": George Kilpatrick, CBC Radio interviews.

145 "clean it up": Gus Sivertz, CBC Radio interviews.

147 "they were hare-hunting": Otto Schroeder (262nd Reserve Reg't) quoted in Dept. of National Defence, Directorate of History, SGRII 202.

149 "playing possum": Byron Morrison, LAC interviews.

149 "more prisoners than our men": Andrew Macphail, *Official History of the Canadian Forces During the Great War 1914–19. The Medical Services*, p. 282.

149 "over the [rehearsal] tapes at Bruay": Harold Barker, Pierre Berton interview, McMaster.

150 "4,000 of them": W.D. Willis, ed. *Saga of the Cyclists*, p. 57.

150 "2,050 prisoners": Macphail, *Official History of the Canadian Forces*, p. 284.

150 "souvenirs the Boche has": Evan Ryrie, letter to Pierre Berton, Oakville, Ont., Oct. 10, 1985.

151 two men in every company: Lt.-Col R. Hayter, General Staff 3rd Cdn Infantry Bde. secret correspondence, Aug. 30, 1916, Canadian War Museum archives.

151 "ninety-five per cent of messages": W.H. Osman, *Pigeons in the Great War*, p. 57.

152 "Signature: R. McCalmont": Osman, *Pigeons in the Great War*, p. 27.

152 "Germans needed reinforcements": Charles Lindsey quoting note in Royal Canadian Military Institute files, Toronto.

153 "tourist on the battlefield": Gordon Shrum, Pierre Berton interview, McMaster.

155 "1898 instead of 1901": Roy Henley, interview Aug. 2, 1982, Reginald Roy Collections, UVIC.

156 "One of our shells": Bill Green, "An Autobiography of World War I," McMaster.

157 "cavalry or motorized units": Michael Volkheimer quoted in McKee, *Vimy Ridge*, pp. 169–70.

157 "victory over the enemy": George H. Hambley diary, Manitoba Archives, MG7 H11.

158 "picking horse's guts": Steve Keay quoted in McKee, *Vimy Ridge*, p. 175.

159 "in reserve that morning": J.C. Uhlman, interview June–August 1979. Reginald Roy Collections, UVIC.

161 "those were our orders": Harvey Crowell, CBC Radio interviews.

161 "while we were advancing": Harvey Crowell in letter to Col. J.L. Ralston, Oct. 4, 1939. McMaster.

162 "saved many lives": Ibid.

164 "written down now": J.L. Ralston, quoted in *Far From Home* DVD, Norflicks Prod.

CHAPTER EIGHT — THE PROMISED LAND

*page*

165 *"c'est possible"*: Nicholson quoting Maj W.J.H. Ellwood, Jan. 19, 1965, *The Gunners of Canada*, p. 287.

166 "Promised Land": Elmore Philpott, CBC Radio interviews.

167 "broke and scattered": Lewis Duncan, letter in the field, April 17, 1917, MU 4693, Ontario Archives.

168 eighteen horses and a hundred men: McKee quotes W.G. Smith, 2nd Division field artillery.

168 "a chance like this": L.R. Fennel quoting FOO, CBC Radio interviews.

168 "a piece of cake": Ibid.

169 "Canadian eye-witness": Heather Robertson, *A Terrible Beauty*, p. 14.

169 heavy camera gear: Herbert Fairlie Wood, *Vimy!* p. 144. "a little drawing": Reuben Jucksch diary, April 6, 1917, courtesy Gary Roncetti. "to be out of the war": Ibid.

170 "To look at the map": Fred James, *The Legionary*, August 1938.

171 "The Byng Boys": McKenzie, *Canada's Day of Glory*, p. 89.

172 "I got a lot of credit": Conn Smythe, quoted in *If You Can't Beat 'Em in the Alley*, p. 57.

172 "wiring schemes": The Adjutant, The 116th Battalion in France, p. 23.

173 "the great struggle": Lt.-Col. Sharpe, letter to sister, April 20, 1917.

174 "turned a blind eye": Arthur Bonner, CBC Radio interviews.

174 "cement and chilled steel": McKenzie, *Canada's Day of Glory*, p. 86.

175 "empty bottles everywhere": Fred Hodges, letter to Pierre Berton, Feb. 6, 1985, McMaster.

176 "safely by daylight": Macintyre, *Canada at Vimy*, pp. 119–120.

177 "east side of the ridge": H.W. Lovell, letter to Pierre Berton, May 21, 1985, McMaster.

178 "officer and forty men": Will Antliff letter to mother, April 13, 1917, Canadian War Museum.

178 "the horse ambulance": Ibid.

179 "room for initiative": Macphail, *Official History of the Canadian Forces*, , p. 93.

179 "going back fifteen kilometres": Royden Barbour, CBC Radio interviews.

180 "mind the hard work": Grace MacPherson interview March 9, 1963, Library and Archives Canada, RG41, Vol. 22.

183 "How I hate the moon": Rubie Duffus quoted in E.A. Landells, *The Military Nurses of Canada*, p. 32.

183 "the most wonderful sight": George Hancox, CBC Radio interviews.

183 "a little white mare": Alan Brown, Pierre Berton papers, McMaster.

184 "dead bodies everywhere": George Walker, "Account of Events at Vimy Ridge, World War I," unpublished memoir, McMaster.

184 "victim of hallucination": Hal Kirkland, "A Memorable Easter Monday, A Private Soldier's Story," *The Legionary* magazine, April 1967.

186 "All they could do was go": Arthur Goodmurphy, CBC Radio interviews.

186 prayer or counsel: Crerar, *Padres in No Man's Land*, p. 123.

187 "quiet hamlet in England": Scott, *The Great War as I Saw It*, p. 170.

187 "blessing on our arms": Scott, *The Great War as I Saw It*, p. 172.

CHAPTER NINE – "DISHING OUT SOME MORE HELL"

*page*

190 "not had time to bury": F.W. Noyes, *Stretcher Bearers at the Double*, p. 157.

190 "picking up the German dead": Lyle Pugsley quoted by Dave Beatty, "Seventy Summers Ago, World War I with Lyle Pugsley," *The Citizen*, Cumberland, N.S., Sept. 29, 1984.

191 muster any concentrated fire: Dieterich, "The German 79th Reserve Infantry Division in the Battle of Vimy Ridge," p. 82.

191 in their bare feet: Greenhous and Harris, *Canada and the Battle of Vimy Ridge, 9–12 April, 1917*, p. 121.

192 "never returned to tell the tale": George Murray, "Personal Account of Service in the Canadian Army During the Great War, Covering the Battle of Vimy Ridge," unpublished memoir, Feb. 1985, McMaster Archives.

194 "They were playing cards": Lewis Robertson, interviewed by Pierre Berton, Toronto, 1985.

195 "last need is a thing to heed": David Moir, letter to Pierre Berton, Jan. 28, 1985, McMaster.

197 "forward toward their objective": Ed Russenholt, "Vimy Ridge Memorial Park," *Metro One*, Winnipeg, May 1977.

198 "bullet through the chest": John Spears, Pierre Berton interview, McMaster.

199 "just like in the book": D.M. Marshall, CBC interviews.

199 available shell holes: Michael Benedict, *On the Battlefields*, p. 110.

199 "caught him up": 50th Battalion war diary quoted in Greenhous and Harris, *Canada and the Battle of Vimy Ridge*, p. 122.

202 "different and unexpected times": Norman Howard Pawley letter, Feb. 21, 1917.

203 "hell from there down": Sam Kirk quoted in notes by Pierre Berton, McMaster.

204 "all shined up and shaved": C.K. McDonald, CBC Radio interviews.

204 walking stick: Wesley Runions, letter to Pierre Berton, Nov. 21, 1984, McMaster.

205 awarded the medal: Norman Howard Pawley textual records 58A 1 79.7, Canadian War Museum.

205 "tremendous preparation": Ed Russenholt, CBC Radio interviews.

206 "in the line": Victor Wheeler, *The 50th Battalion in No Man's Land*, p. 320.

206 "hypnotic [and] strangely piercing": James Dempsey, "Persistence of a Warrior Ethic among the Plains Indians," *Alberta History*, Vol. 36, No. 21, Winter 1988.

207 "great bravery, skill and initiative": Military Medal citation quoted in Janice Summerby, *Native Soldiers, Foreign Battlefields*, p. 12.

207 "bad boy": Harold G. Carter letter of April 5, 1917, quoted in Shawn McCarthy, "Casualties of Shame," *The Globe and Mail*, Toronto, Dec. 22, 2001.

207 "sentence of death": Charge report, quoted in Ibid.

208 "prisoner was led over to a box": Scott, *The Great War as I Saw It*, p. 214.

209 Statutory justification: Desmond Morton, "The Supreme Penalty: Canadian Deaths by Firing Squad in the First World War," *Queen's Quarterly*, Autumn 1972, Vol. LXXIV, No. 3. p. 345.

209 "holding illegal communication": "Executions in War," *Montreal Gazette*, April 3, 1925, MG26H v.268 pt. 2. Library and Archives Canada.

209 "become exhausted": Morton quoting Lord Moran, p. 347.

209 struggled with army issue boots: Bishop Wells, *The Fighting Bishop*, reference in *Globe and Mail* Letters to the Editor, Aug. 19, 2006.

209 court-martialled, and executed: Jon Blair, Letters to the Editor, *Globe and Mail*, Aug. 19, 2006.

210 "silence was intense": Arthur Pollard, "Memoirs of a Soldier/Airman in World War I, 1914-1919, unpublished memoir, p. 5.

210 "the horrors of war": Glen Carter (nephew), *The Globe and Mail*, Dec. 22, 2001.

210 "no deserters": Gen. Von Bacmeister quoted in McKenzie, *Canada's Day of Glory*, p. 70.

210 "lost from good leadership": John Alvis diary, April 1917, quoted by Gordon Reid, *Poor Bloody Murder*.

CHAPTER TEN — A FIRST FULL SENSE OF NATIONHOOD

*page*

213 "heartily congratulated": "French Praise: Vimy Ridge Key to Lens and Douai," *Petit Parisien*, April 10, 1917.

213 "in such a fortress": W. Beach Thomas, "Flower of German Army Beaten," *The Times of London*, April 9, 1917.

213 "the greatest victory": Philip Gibbs, *Source Records of the Great War*, Vol. v. ed. Charles F. Horne, National Alumni, 1923.

214 "[the Canadians] rose to it": Stewart Lyon, "Canadians Put in Front to Capture Vimy Ridge," *Canadian Press* report, April 9, 1917.

214 "offensive with confidence": Erich Ludendorff, *My War Memories 1914–1918* (1920), p. 421.

214 prisoners of war: Nicholson, *Canadian Expeditionary Force*, p. 265.

214 "continuing the war": Crown Prince Rupprecht, *My War Diary*.

214 "her sons for generations": *New York Times* quoted by M.B. Clint, *Our Bit: Memories of War Service by a Canadian Nursing Sister*, p. 95.

214 "imprint will be remembered": *New York Tribune* quoted by Clint, *Our Bit*, p. 94.

215 "closest of blood ties": Talbot Papineau quoted in "Canadian Nationalism and the War" (pamphlet) 1916.

215 "proud to be a Canadian": Claude Williams, Pierre Berton interview, Dec. 19, 1983, McMaster.

215 "shock troops": Alex Jack, CBC Radio interviews.

216 "gamer bunch": Cyril Jones, letter April 15, 1917, Foster, *Letters from the Front*, p. 203.

216 "Zero plus three minutes": R.C. Fetherstonhaugh, *The Royal Montreal Regiment*, p. 144.

217 "lawnmower cutting grass": Joe Labelle, CBC Radio interviews.

217  "lay a dead German": Bill Green, "An Autobiography of World War I," p. 5.

217  3,598 of them fatal: Nicholson, *Canadian Expeditionary Force*, p. 265.

218  "Vimy Ridge had been taken": Harold Innis autobiography, courtesy John Watson, pp. 63–64.

218  "soldier blown to pieces": Lewis Buck, Pierre Berton interview, McMaster.

219  "so many German dead": Frank Yates, "Recollections," John Francis Yates (unpublished manuscript).

219  "fewer of us would be here": R.S. Robertson, CBC Radio interviews.

220  "no braver than any of the others": Edgar Goldstein quoted in Arthur Daniel Hart, *The Jew in Canada*, p. 508.

221  "claimed by the 27th Battalion": Donald Fraser, quoted by Reginald H. Roy, *The Journal of Private Fraser*, p. 266.

222  "We are Sam Hughes's army": Elmore Philpott, CBC Radio interviews.

222  "a fine lot of men": Andrew McCrindle, unpublished manuscript, McMaster Archives.

224  "you are only sixteen": John B. Mason, *Veterans' Review*, pp. 83–84.

224  "a thousand different bits": W.A.P. Durie, quoted by Veronica Cusac, *The Invisible Soldier: Captain W.A.P. Durie, His Life and Afterlife*, p. 96.

225  "sharp on the tick of twelve": Thomas McGill, letter July 6, 1917, in Foster, *Letters from the Front*, p. 227.

225  "at 1 [a.m.] we were wakened": Will Antliff, letter to mother May 1, 1917, File 58A1 182.5, Canadian War Museum.

226  processed 18,000: Stanley Baker, CBC Radio interviews.

226  "get him out of here": Alex Gerrard, interview June 1977, Reginald Roy Collections, UVIC.

227  "red with blood": S.G. Bennett, *The 4th Canadian Mounted Rifles*, p. 55.

228  "first full sense of nationhood" Greg Clark, "The Symbol," *Toronto Telegram*, April 4, 1967.

229  50,000 tons: Nicholson, *Canadian Expeditionary Force*, p. 251.

229  "about three inches": Harvey Crowell, CBC Radio interviews.

229  "Where is Givenchy": Harry Bond, CBC Radio interviews.

230  "we never did find him": Art Farmer, CBC Radio interviews.

231  "who had fallen": Ed Russenholt, "Vimy Ridge Memorial Park," *Metro One*, Winnipeg, May 11, 1977.

231  an honour roll: Fred James, "A Letter From The Past," *The Legionary*, August 1938.

231  "it will finish this year": Fred James, ibid.

232  "mother and father to me": Gad Neal, Pierre Berton papers, McMaster.

233  "in the Canadians' history": J.N. Gunn diary, April 9, 1917, McMaster.

234 "love for the animals": Bill Hewlett, quoted by Harold Sutherland, "An Ontario Farmer Carried on in Wartime," *Saturday Night*, August 2, 1941, pp. 4–5.

234 "in stables all morning": Bill Hewlett, diary, Feb. 1915, courtesy Barbara Pratt.

235 "shot in the right leg": Luella Venning, "Grandma Remembers," personal memoirs with permission, April 1995.

236 "very cruel and crude": Charles Venning quoted in "Two Weeks' Jail After Singing of Armistice," *Toronto Daily Star*, March 1919.

237 "Salt Spring Island paid": Harry Loosmore, "My Recollections of Vimy, April 9, 1917," unpublished manuscript, McMaster.


CHAPTER ELEVEN — SACRED TRUST

*page*

240 "immortal within me": Sam Sharpe in letter to Mabel Sharpe, Oct. 21, 1917.

240 a dozen men gassed: The Adjutant, The 116th Battalion in France, p. 52.

241 "just walking wounded ": Lyman Nicholls interview, July 2, 1981, courtesy Uxbridge Township Museum.

241 to 160 men: "Return of the 116th," *Uxbridge Journal*, April 3, 1919.

241 "concrete pavement below": "Lieut.-Col. Sharpe Dies Before Reaching Home," *Toronto Daily Star*, May 30, 1918.

241 "the decorations won": Rev. Capt. John Garbutt, quoted by K.K.S. in "How Col. Sharpe Came Home," *Toronto Telegram*, May 30, 1918.

242 "physical and mental exhaustion": "Ontario Town Honors Its Heroic Dead," *Toronto Telegram*, June 28, 1920.

242 "the Royal Victoria at Montreal": Lucy Maud Montgomery diary, May 29, 1918, p. 247.

242 "handsome tablet": "Ontario Town Honors Heroic Dead," *Toronto Telegram*, June 28, 1920.

243 50,000 people: Eileen Pettigrew, *The Silent Enemy*, p. xv.

243 political disunity: Terry Copp, speech delivered to Arts and Letters Club, Toronto, Nov. 19, 1997.

244 "memorial is for the dead": Wood, *Vimy!* p. 170.

244 fathers, brothers, and sons: John Hundevad quoted in W.W. Murray, *The Epic of Vimy*, p. 6.

245 at Vimy Ridge: "Parliament's Tribute," *The Legionary*, July 1938.

245 "statues in frock coats": Allward quoted by Donald Jones in "Walter Allward's great work is monument to Canadian dead," *Toronto Daily Star*.

246 "Canadian Corps in the Great War": *Hansard*, Jan. 31, 1923.

246 "towering pylons of stone": D.E. Macintyre, "The Vimy Pilgrimage," *The Legionary*, July 1961.

246 no known resting place: Macintyre, *Canada at Vimy*, p. 157.

247 "will forever owe them": Allward quoted in biographical papers, Arts and Letters Club, Toronto, M.L. 5/55.

247 "a nightmare": Allward quoted by Margaret McBurney in *Looking Back*, Arts and Letters Club newsletter, Feb. 2003.

247 "indeed, for all time": Allward quoted in Will R. Bird, *Thirteen Years After*, p. 75.

247 "never been equalled": Ibid., p. 77.

248 "regions that inspired it": W.W. Murray, "The Vimy Pilgrimage," *Canadian Geographical Journal*.

248 "desire to return": Ben Allen quoted in Murray, *The Epic of Vimy*, p. 8.

249 "three died of war wounds after": Florence Murdock quoted in Beatty, *The Vimy Pilgrimage*, p. 19.

249 "the peace armada": W.K. Walker, "Pilgrimage Recollections," *The Legionary*, January 1937.

250 "Long live St. Catharines of Canada": John Mould diary, donation by Audrey Ball to Ontario Archives, p. 41.

252 "noble grief": Murray, "The Vimy Pilgrimage," p. 421.

252 used as an anthem: Murray, Ibid.

253 "the sound of his voice": John Mould diary, p. 60.

253 "we shall not break faith": Rev. George Fallis, pp. 146–147.

254 "lexicon of mankind": Monsignor E.A. Deschamps quoted in Beatty, p. 31.

254 "its anguish and its terror": Ian A. Mackenzie quoted in Macintyre, *Canada at Vimy*, p. 191.

254 "the gift of France to Canada": King Edward quoted in Murray, *The Epic of Vimy*, p. 96.

255 "one gorgeous painting": Florence Murdock quoted in Beatty, *The Vimy Pilgrimage*, p. 13.

256 "lived and died here": Bruce Hutchison, "A Visit to Vimy," *The Legionary*, October 1937.

257 "answered a higher call": Andrew McCrindle letter to Pierre Berton, Oct. 18, 1984.

257 "anniversary of the battle": Macintyre, *Canada at Vimy*, p. 180.

258 "memorable day of our lives": John Mould diary, p. 69.

258 "if war came again": Allward quoted in "Vimy Designer W.S. Allward Dies," *Toronto Daily Star*, April 25, 1955.

258 leaking lime: Brian Bethune, "Monumental Obsession," *Maclean's*, April 16, 2001.

# Bibliography

Allen, Ralph. *Ordeal by Fire*. Toronto: Doubleday, 1961.

Adjutant, The. *The 116th Battalion in France*. Ottawa: CEF Books, 2003.

Barker, Ralph. *A Brief History of the Royal Flying Corps in World War I*. London: Robinson, 2002.

Beatty, David. "Seventy Summers Ago, World War I with Lyle Pugsley," *The Citizen*, Cumberland, N.S., Sept. 29, 1984.

Beatty, David Pierce. *The Vimy Pilgrimage, July 1936: From the Diary of Florence Murdock*. Amherst, Nova Scotia: Acadian Printing, 1986.

Benedict, Michael, ed. *On the Battlefields: Two World Wars That Shaped a Nation, Canada at War*, Vol. II. Toronto: Penguin, 2002.

Bennett, S.G. *The 4th Canadian Mounted Rifles, 1914–1919*. Toronto: Murray Printing, 1926.

Berton, Pierre. *Vimy*. Toronto: McClelland & Stewart, 1986.

——. *Marching as to War: Canada's Turbulent Years 1899–1953*. Toronto: Doubleday Canada, 2001.

Bird, Will R. *And We Go On*. Toronto: Hunter-Rose, 1930.

——. *Ghosts Have Warm Hands*. Ottawa: CEF Books, 1997.

——. *Thirteen Years After: The Story of the Old Front Revisited*. Toronto: Maclean Publishing, 1932.

Bishop, William A. *Winged Warfare*. Folkstone: Bailey Brothers & Swinfen, 1975.

Bongard, Ella Mae. *Nobody Ever Wins a War: The World War 1 Diaries of Ella Mae Bongard*. Ottawa: Janeric, 1997.

Boyden, Joseph. *Three Day Road*. Toronto: Viking, 2005.

Breckenridge, William. "From Vimy to Mons." Unpublished memoirs, William Ready Division of Archives and Research Collections, McMaster University.

Burns, E.L.M. *General Mud: Memoirs of Two World Wars*. Toronto: Clarke Irwin, 1970.

Callaghan, Barry, and Bruce Meyer. *We Wasn't Pals: The Canadian Poetry and Prose of the First World War*. Toronto: Exile Editions, 2001.

Canadian War Records Office. *Thirty Canadian VCs, 23rd April 1915 to 30th March, 1918.* London: Skeffington & Son, 1920.

Carroll, Jock. *The Life and Times of Greg Clark, Canada's Favorite Storyteller.* Toronto: Doubleday, 1981.

Christie, N.M. *Winning the Ridge: The Canadians at Vimy Ridge, 1917.* Nepean, Ont.: CEF Books, 1998.

——. *For King & Empire: The Canadians at Vimy April 1917.* Ottawa: CEF Books, 2002.

Clark, Greg. "The Symbol." *Weekend Magazine, Toronto Telegram.* Toronto, April 4, 1967.

Climo, Percy L. *Let Us Remember: Lively Letters from World War One.* Cobourg, Ontario: Haynes, 1990.

Clint, M.B. *Our Bit: Memories of War Service by a Canadian Nursing Sister.* Montreal: Alumnae Association, Royal Victoria Hospital, 1934.

Cook, Tim. *No Place to Run: The Canadian Corps and Gas Warfare in the First World War.* Vancouver: UBC Press, 1999.

Crerar, Duff. *Padres in No Man's Land: Canadian Chaplains and the Great War.* Montreal & Kingston: McGill-Queen's University Press, 1995.

Cusac, Veronica. *The Invisible Soldier: Captain W.A.P. Durie, His Life and Afterlife.* Toronto: McClelland & Stewart, 2004.

De Cruyenaere, Jules. "The Battle of Vimy Ridge and Hill 70," unpublished memoir, William Ready Division of Archives and Research Collections, McMaster University.

Dempsey, James. "Persistence of a Warrior Ethic among the Plains Indians." *Alberta History*, 36, 1, Winter 1988.

Dieterich, Alfred. "The German 79th Reserve Infantry Division in the Battle of Vimy Ridge," *Canadian Military History*. Waterloo: Wilfrid Laurier University, Winter 2006.

Duguid, A. Fortescue. "Canada on Vimy Ridge." Ottawa: Dominion Bureau of Statistics, 1936.

——. "Canada on Vimy Ridge: A Proud Memory." *The Legionary*, Vol. XIII, No. 9, April 1938.

Fallis, George O. *A Padre's Pilgrimage.* Toronto: Ryerson Press, 1953.

Fetherstonhaugh, R.C., ed. *The Royal Montreal Regiment, 14th Battalion, C.E.F., 1914–1925.* Montreal: The Gazette, 1927.

——. *The 24th Battalion C.E.F., Victoria Rifles of Canada, 1914–1919.* Montreal: Gazette Printing, 1930.

Findley, Timothy. *The Wars.* Toronto: Viking, 1977.

Foster, Charles Lyons, ed. *Letters From the Front, Being a Record of the Part Played by Officers of the Bank in the Great War 1914–1919*, Vol. I and II. Toronto: Canadian Bank of Commerce, 1920.

Frost, Leslie. *Fighting Men.* Toronto: Clark Irwin, 1967.

Gaffin, Fred. *Forgotten Soldiers.* Penticton, B.C.: Theytus Books, 1985.

Goodspeed, D.J. *The Road Past Vimy, The Canadian Corps 1914–1918.* Toronto: Macmillan, 1969.

Grafton, C.S. *The Canadian Emma Gees: A History of the Canadian Machine Gun Corps.* London: Canadian Machine Gun Corps Association, 1938.

Granatstein, J.L., and Desmond Morton. *Canada and the Two World Wars.* Toronto: Key Porter, 2003.

—— and Desmond Morton. *Marching to Armageddon: Canadians and the Great War 1914–1919.* Toronto: Lester & Orpen Dennys, 1989.

—— and Norman Hillmer. *First Drafts: Eyewitness Accounts from Canada's Past.* Toronto: Thomas Allen, 2002.

Green, Bill. "An Autobiography of World War I." Unpublished memoir, William Ready Division of Archives and Research Collections, McMaster University.

Greenhous, Ben, and Stephen J. Harris. *Canada and the Battle of Vimy Ridge, 9–12 April, 1917.* Ottawa: Canada Communication Group, 1992.

Grescoe, Audrey and Paul. *The Book of War Letters.* Toronto: McClelland & Stewart, 2003.

Gunn, J.N. *Historical Records of No. 8 Canadian Field Ambulance.* Toronto: Ryerson Press, 1920.

Gwyn, Sandra. *Tapestry of War: A Private View of Canadians in the Great War.* Toronto: Harper Collins, 1992.

Hart, Arthur Daniel, ed. *The Jew in Canada.* Toronto: Jewish Publications, 1926.

Hodder-Williams, Ralph. *Princess Patricia's Canadian Light Infantry 1914–1919.* Toronto: Hodder and Stoughton, 1923.

Hopkins, J. Castell. *Canada at War: A Record of Heroism and Achievement 1914–1918.* Toronto: The Canadian Annual Review, 1919.

Horne, Charles F., ed. *Source Records of the Great War*, Vol. V. London: National Alumni, 1923.

Hundevad, John, ed. *Guide Book of the Pilgrimage to Vimy and the Battlefields, July–August 1936.* Montreal: Perrault Printing, 1936.

Johnston, James Robert. *Riding Into War: The Memoir of a Horse Transport Driver, 1916–1919.* Fredericton, N.B.: Goose Lane Editions, 2004.

James, Fred. "A Letter From The Past," *The Legionary*. Ottawa: August 1938.

Keegan, John. *The Face of Battle.* London: Jonathan Cape, 1976.

——. *The First World War.* New York: Alfred A. Knopf, 1999.

Keene, Louis. *Crumps: The Plain Story of a Canadian Who Went.* Boston: Houghton Mifflin, 1917.

Kerr, Wilfred Brenton. *Shrieks and Crashes: Being Memories of Canada's Corps 1917.* Toronto: Hunter Rose, 1929.

Kirkland, Hal. "A Memorable Easter Monday, A Private Soldier's Story," *The Legionary*. April 1967.

Knightly, Philip. *The First Casualty.* New York: Harcourt, Brace Jovanovich, 1975.

Landells, E.A., ed. *The Military Nurses of Canada: Recollections of Canadian Military Nurses*, Vol. II. White Rock, B.C.: Addison Graphics, n.d.

Loosmore, Harry. "My Recollections of Vimy, April 9, 1917." Unpublished memoir.

MacArthur, D.C. *The History of the Fifty-Fifth Battery, CFA*. Hamilton: Robert Duncan, 1919.

Macintyre, D.E. *Canada at Vimy*. Toronto: Peter Martin, 1967.

Macphail, Andrew. *Official History of the Canadian Forces During the Great War 1914–19. The Medical Services*. Ottawa: Department of National Defence, 1925.

——. Unpublished papers, Library & Archives Canada, MG30 D150.

Matheson, William D. *My Grandfather's War: Canadians Remember the First World War, 1914–1918*. Toronto: Macmillan, 1981.

Mattfeld, Julius. *Variety Music Cavalcade: Musical-Historical Review 1620–1969*. Englewood Cliffs, New Jersey: Prentice-Hall, 1952.

McCaffery, Dan. *Air Aces: The Lives and Times of Twelve Canadian Fighter Pilots*. Toronto: James Lorimer, 1990.

McCrindle, Andrew. "From private to private in 36 months or a worm's eye view of World War One." Unpublished manuscript, William Ready Division of Archives and Research Collections, McMaster University.

McDougall, Phyllis. "Henley of the Black Watch," *The Islander*, Victoria: November 1984.

McGillivray, Allan. *Tales from the Uxbridge Valley*. Uxbridge: Uxbridge Millennium Committee, 2000.

McKee, Alexander. *Vimy Ridge*. London: Souvenir Press, 1966.

McKenzie, F.A. *Canada's Day of Glory*. Toronto: William Briggs, 1918.

McLaren, John. *J.W., The Life Story of John Wilson McLaren, 1895–1988*. Toronto: McLaren Press, 2006.

Moir, David Alexander. "At What Price?" *Legion* magazine, April, 1977.

Murray, George F. "Personal Account of Service in the Canadian Army During the Great War, Covering the Battle of Vimy Ridge." Memoir, February 1985, William Ready Division of Archives and Research Collections, McMaster University.

Murray, W.W. *The Epic of Vimy*. Ottawa: Legionary, 1936.

——. *The History of the 2nd Canadian Battalion (East. Ontario Regiment) Canadian Expeditionary Force in the Great War*. Ottawa: Mortimer, 1947.

——. "The Vimy Pilgrimage," *Canadian Geographical Journal*. Vol. 13, No. 8, 1936.

Nasmith, George G. *On the Fringe of the Great Fight*. Toronto: McClelland, Goodchild & Stewart, 1917.

*Native Studies Review*. Vol. 5, No. 2. Saskatoon: University of Saskatchewan, 1989.

Newman, Stephen K. *With the Patricia's: Capturing the Ridge*. Saanichton, B.C.: Bellewaerde House, 2005.

Nicholson, G.W.L. *Canadian Expeditionary Force 1914–1919*. Ottawa: Queen's Printer, 1962.

——. *The Gunners of Canada: The History of the Royal Regiment of Canadian Artillery*, Vol. 1, 1534–1919. Toronto: McClelland & Stewart, 1967.

Noyes, F.W. *Stretcher Bearers at the Double*. Toronto: Hunter-Rose, 1936.

Osman, A.H. *Pigeons in the Great War: A Complete History of the Carrier-Pigeon Service during the Great War, 1914–1918*. London, U.K.: Racing Pigeon Publishing Co., 1929.

Pettigrew, Eileen. *The Silent Enemy: Canada and the Deadly Flu of 1918*. Saskatoon, Sask.: Prairie Books, 1983.

Ray, Anna Chapin, ed. *Letters of a Canadian Stretcher Bearer*. Boston: Little, Brown, 1918.

Reid, Gordon. *Poor Bloody Murder*. Oakville: Mosaic Press, 1980.

Remarque, Erich Maria. *All Quiet on the Western Front*. New York: Little, Brown and Co. 1929.

Robertson, Heather. *A Terrible Beauty: The Art of Canada at War*. Toronto: James Lorimer, 1977.

Robbins, Keith. *The First World War*. Oxford: Oxford University Press, 1984.

Rogers, J.C.B. *A History of Artillery*. Secaucus, New Jersey: Citadel Press, 1975.

Roy, Reginald H., ed. *The Journal of Private Fraser, 1914–1918 Canadian Expeditionary Force*. Victoria, B.C.: Sono Nis Press, 1985.

Rubio, Mary, and Elizabeth Waterston, eds. *The Selected Journals of L. M. Montgomery*, Vol. II 1910–1921. Toronto: Oxford University Press, 1985.

Ruck, Calvin W. *The Black Battalion, 1916–1920: Canada's Best Kept Military Secret*. Halifax, N.S.: Nimbus, 1987.

Russenholt, E.S. *Six Thousand Canadian Men, Being the History of the 44th Battalion Canadian Infantry 1914–1919*. Winnipeg: 44th Battalion Association, 1932.

—— "Vimy Ridge Memorial Park," *Metro One*. Eight-part series, April/May 1977.

Scott, Frederick George. *The Great War as I Saw It*. Toronto: F.D. Goodchild, 1922.

Senior Scribes. *Uxbridge 200, Through the Years, An Anthology of Memoirs, Poems and Short Stories*. Uxbridge: 2005.

Shackleton, Kevin R. *Second to None, The Fighting 58th Battalion of the Canadian Expeditionary Force*. Toronto: Dundurn, 2002.

Smythe, Conn, with Scott Young. *If You Can't Beat 'Em in the Alley*. Toronto: McClelland & Stewart, 1981.

Stephens, W. Ray. *The Canadian Entertainers*. Oakville, Ont.: Mosaic Press, 1993.

Summerby, Janice. *Native Soldiers, Foreign Battlefields*. Ottawa: Veterans Affairs Canada, 1993.

Sutherland, Harold. "An Ontario Farmer Carries on in Wartime," *Saturday Night*. August 2, 1941, pp. 4–5.

Swettenham, John. *McNaughton*. Toronto: Ryerson Press, 1968.

Thomas, Mary. *David's War: The Boys of Gananoque in WWI*. Belleville: Epic Press, 2003.

Thompson, Harvie, ed. *Veterans' Review*. Toronto: Sunnybrook Medical Centre, 1983.

Vance, Jonathan F. *High Flight, Aviation and the Canadian Imagination*. Toronto: Penguin, 2002.

Vansittart, Peter. *Voices from the Great War*. London: Jonathan Cape, 2003.

Walker, George. "Account of Events at Vimy Ridge, World War I." Unpublished memoir, William Ready Division of Archives and Research Collections, McMaster University.

Ward, G. Kingsley, and Edwin Gibson. *Courage Remembered*. Toronto: McClelland & Stewart, 1989.

Watson, Alexander John. *Marginal Man: The Dark Vision of Harold Innis*. Toronto: University of Toronto Press, 2006.

Wells, Bishop George Anderson. *The Fighting Bishop*. Toronto: Cardwell, 1971.

*Der Weltkrieg: 1914 bis 1918*, Official German WWI history, Vol. 12, 1939.

Wheeler, Victor. *The 50th Battalion in No Man's Land*. Calgary: The Alberta Historical Resources Foundation, 1980.

Willis, W.D., ed. *Saga of the Cyclists in the Great War 1914–1918*. Canadian Corps of Cyclist Battalion Association, n.d.

Wood, Herbert Fairlie. *Vimy!* Toronto: Macmillan Canada, 1967.

Yates, Frank. "Recollections." Unpublished manuscript, Scarborough, Ontario, 1984.

# *Photograph Credits*

FIRST SECTION

*page*

1 Masked soldier and horse, Library and Archives Canada PA-005001; Charlie Venning, courtesy Venning family; German gas attack, courtesy Whitcombe collection

2 Elgin Park, Uxbridge send-off, Uxbridge Scott Museum; Lyman Nicholls, courtesy Marjorie Cole; Sam Sharpe, Uxbridge Scott Museum

3 Over the tape, Library and Archives Canada PA-3666; Comedy Company, courtesy John McLaren

4 Pumping air, Library and Archives Canada PA-306; Gavin McDonald, courtesy Judy Wood, Jean Gordon; Crenellated trench, Library and Archives Canada c-14151

5 Road grading, Library and Archives Canada PA-686; Railway, Library and Archives Canada PA-1215; Corduroy road, Library and Archives Canada PA-1226

6 King, Currie, Horn, Library and Archives Canada PA-1502; Sleeping in trenches, Library and Archives Canada; Lunch and duck boards, Library and Archives Canada PA-166; Funk hole, Dept. of National Defence DHist-6

7 All photos courtesy Whitcombe collection

8 Canned meat, Library and Archives Canada PA-255; Sand-bagging, Library and Archives Canada PA-95; Ablutions, Canadian War Museum AN-19920085-180

9 All photos courtesy Whitcombe collection

10 British balloon, Canadian War Museum AN-19920085-257; British balloon basket, Library and Archives Canada PA-2057; Billy Bishop, Library and Archives Canada PA-1651

11 All photos courtesy Whitcombe collection

12 Blacksmiths, Library and Archives Canada PA-1563; Horse and mule, Canadian War Museum AN-19920085-591; Dead horses, Library and Archives Canada PA-207908; Bill Hewlett, courtesy Barbara Pratt

13 Railway ammunition, Library and Archives Canada PA-1757; Pack horses, Library and Archives Canada PA-001229; Empty shell cases, Library and Archives Canada PA-1349

14 9-inch gun by day, Library and Archives Canada PA-1182; Shell carriages, Canadian War Museum AN-19920085-323; Anti-aircraft guns, Library and Archives Canada PA-974

15 9-inch gun by night, Library and Archives Canada PA-1178; Harold Innis, University of Toronto Archives B-1972-0003/034(08); Vickers machine gun, Library and Archives Canada PA-1017

16 Fraternizing, Library and Archives Canada PA-3683; Cyclist, Canadian War Museum AN-19920085-623; Carrier Pigeon, Canadian War Museum AN-19920085-303

### SECOND SECTION

*page*

1 Battle ready, Canadian War Museum AN-19920085-669; Germans with grenades, courtesy Whitcombe collection; To the front, Library and Archives Canada PA-832

2 Shell burst, Canadian War Museum AN-19920085-335; Over the top, Library and Archives Canada PA-648; Vimy glide, Library and Archives Canada PA-1086

3 Roy Henley, courtesy Henley family; Native group, Library and Archives Canada PA-66815

4 Creeping barrage, Library and Archives Canada PA1087; Tank and troops, Canadian War Museum AN-19920085-479; Tank on trench, Library and Archives Canada PA-2253

5 Gun position, Library and Archives Canada PA-1101; Greg and Joe Clark, courtesy Clark family; Trench, Library and Archives Canada PA-1085

6 Ambulances, Library and Archives Canada PA-852; Will Antliff, Canadian War Museum AN-20020130-003 #1; Wounded, Library and Archives Canada PA-813

7 Loading wounded, Canadian War Museum AN-19920085-705; Grace MacPherson, Canadian War Museum AN-19920085-357; Casualty Clearing Station, Library and Archives Canada PA-104

8 Harold and Ernest Carter, courtesy Glen and John Carter; Tram wounded, Library and Archives Canada PA-1024

9 POW pens, Library and Archives Canada PA-3035; POWs march, Library and Archives Canada PA-1142

10 Douai view, Canadian War Museum AN-19920085-244; Farbus, Library and Archives Canada PA-1084

11 Lyle Pugsley, courtesy Paul Pugsley; Victory truck, Library and Archives Canada PA-1267

12 Ellis Sifton, Elgin Military Museum, Blair Ferguson; Ellis Sifton gravesite, Elgin Military Museum, Blair Ferguson

13 Burial, Library and Archives Canada PA-652; Artillery Memorial, Library and Archives Canada PA-2390; Sharpe funeral, Uxbridge Scott Museum

14 Dumbells, courtesy John McLaren; Vimy fly past, Library and Archives Canada PA-148872

15 Vimy dignitaries, Library and Archives Canada PA-18131; Mrs. C.S. Woods, Library and Archives Canada PA-148875; Vimy pilgrims, Library and Archives Canada PA-148874

16 Vimy aerial, Library and Archives Canada PA-148873; Walter Allward, Library and Archives Canada PA-148871

# Index of Formations, Units, and Corps

# General Index